THE Adobe®

PageMill™

2.0 HANDBOOK

THE Adobe®
PageMill™
2.0
HANDBOOK

Hayden
Books

Rita Lewis

The Adobe PageMill 2.0 Handbook

Library of Congress Catalog Number: 96-77656
ISBN: 1-56830-313-0

Copyright © 1997 Hayden Books

Printed in the United States of America 3 4 5 6 7 8 9 0

Warning and Disclaimer

PUBLISHER	Lyn Blake
PUBLISHING MANAGER	Laurie Petrycki
MANAGING EDITOR	Lisa Wilson
MARKETING MANAGER	Kelli Spencer
ACQUISITIONS EDITOR	Michelle Reed
DEVELOPMENT EDITOR	Kezia Endsley
COPY/PRODUCTION EDITOR	Kevin Laseau
TECHNICAL EDITOR	Brad Miser
PUBLISHING COORDINATOR	Karen Flowers
COVER DESIGNER	Aren Howell
BOOK DESIGNER	Gary Adair
MANUFACTURING COORDINATOR	Brook Farling
PRODUCTION TEAM SUPERVISORS	Laurie Casey and Joe Millay
PRODUCTION TEAM	Kim Cofer, Cynthia Fields, Tricia Flodder, William Huys Jr., Linda Knose, Daniela Raderstorf
INDEXER	Cheryl Dietsch

About the Author

Rita Lewis is a freelance writer with nine years of formal training in fine arts and design. She applied her MA in cultural anthropology to the participant observation of computer companies during her 10 years working as a proposal manager for various networking and mainframe organizations. In 1984, Rita fell in love with her first lowly Mac 512K and hasn't looked back. Rita is a collaborative author of the hardware section of Hayden Books' *Maclopedia* as well as the author of nine other Macintosh titles, including *Show Me The Mac* from Alpha Books and the *WordPerfect 3.5 Visual QuickStart Guide* from PeachPit Press.

Trademark Acknowledgments

All terms mentioned in this book that are known to be trademarks or service marks have been appropriately capitalized. Hayden Books cannot attest to the accuracy of this information. Use of a term in this book should not be regarded as affecting the validity of any trademark or service mark. PageMill is a trademark of Adobe Inc.

Dedication

Dedicated to my best friend and husband, Doug, without whom I would be lost.

Acknowledgments

I wish to gratefully acknowledge the following people without whom this book would not have been published.

To Michelle Reed, whose professionalism and good nature in the hard task of managing all of the myriad permissions and legal issues of this book kept this very fast ball rolling.

To Kezia Endsley, whose sober appraisal of my technical abilities enhanced the content of the book one hundred-fold. Kezia is the most pleasant and sane Development Editor I ever had the luck to work with. Thank You.

To Brad Miser, whose cogent analysis of what should be included in a book on PageMill made me grow and extend my abilities, and thus enriched the depth of the book. Brad was more than a technical editor and I am forever grateful.

To Kevin Laseau, who jumped in the middle of the fire and kept on stoking throughout the process of developing outlines and copyediting the book. Thank you for your dedication and kindness.

To Steve Mulder, who taught me about CGIs when all was confusion and set me on the proper path. Thanks.

To the production staff and rest of the team at Hayden Books who produce such wonderful books on such crazy deadlines. What a talented, dedicated bunch. I salute you.

To David Siegel, whose *Creating Killer Web Sites* Web page and book was an inspiration and great help.

To all of the kind people throughout the Web who lent me their Web pages for examples and shared their knowledge so openly.

Lastly, to my girls and husband who patiently put up with my late nights and strange dinners so that I could complete my work. As always, I can't do this without you, thanks.

Hayden Books

The staff of Hayden Books is committed to bringing you the best computer books. What our readers think of Hayden is important to our ability to serve our customers. If you have any comments, no matter how great or how small, we'd appreciate your taking the time to send us a note.

You can reach Hayden Books at the following:

Hayden Books
201 West 103rd Street
Indianapolis, IN 46290
317-581-3833

Email addresses:

America Online: Hayden Bks
Internet: hayden@hayden.com

Visit the Hayden Books Web site at: http://www.hayden.com

Contents at a Glance

Introduction   1

Chapter 1: Welcome to WYSIWYG
    Web Publishing   11

Chapter 2: A Tour of PageMill 2.0   23

Chapter 3: Getting Started   43

Chapter 4: Text and Graphics Basics   69

Chapter 5: Working with Links   121

Chapter 6: Creating Active Images and
    Imagemaps   137

Chapter 7: Tables and Frames   165

Chapter 8: Working with Forms   197

Chapter 9: Working with HTML   257

Chapter 10: Common Gateway Interfaces   285

Chapter 11: Putting It All Together   311

Chapter 12: Getting Online   329

Chapter 13: Future Trends   351

Appendix A: Toolbar Summary   355

Appendix B: Glossary   375

Index   413

Contents

Introduction   **1**

    Objectives of this Book 2

        What You Need to Know Before You Start 2

    What's New in PageMill 2.0? 3

    Using this Book 5

        Command Summaries 6

    What's In Each Chapter? 6

        Chapter 1: Welcome to WYSIWYG Web Publishing 7

        Chapter 2: A Tour of PageMill 2.0 7

        Chapter 3: Getting Started 7

        Chapter 4: Text and Graphics Basics 7

        Chapter 5: Working with Links 7

        Chapter 6: Creating Active Images and Imagemaps 8

        Chapter 7: Frames and Tables 8

        Chapter 8: Working with Forms 8

        Chapter 9: Working with HTML Directly 8

        Chapter 10: Common Gateway Interfaces 8

        Chapter 11: Putting It All Together 9

        Chapter 12: Getting On-Line 9

        Chapter 13: SiteMill and Server Management 9

        Chapter 14: Future Trends 9

Chapter 1   **11**

    Welcome to WYSIWYG Web Publishing 11

    About the Internet vs. the World Wide Web 12

        What is the Internet? 12

            The Origins of HTML 13

            The Birth of the WWW 13

            The Web goes Commercial 14

    Network Publishing Grows Up 14

    Webmasters vs. Web Publishers 15

    What You Can Do with PageMill 16

Getting Your Document on The Web: Working with HTML 17

PageMill and HTML—A Symbiotic Relationship 19

Publishing without HTML 22

Summary 22

Chapter 2   **23**

A Tour of PageMill 2.0 23

The Edit and Preview Window Modes 24

The PageMill Edit Window 25

The Toolbar 27

The Content Area 29

The Link Location Bar 29

PageMill's Menu Bar 30

PageMill's Other Controls 32

The Inspector 33

The Inspector's Page Screen 33

The Inspector's Object Screen 35

The Inspector's Forms Screen 36

The Inspector's Frames Screen 36

The Pasteboard 38

The Out-of-Place Editor 39

The Color Panel 41

Summary 41

Chapter 3   **43**

Getting Started 43

Content Design: Determining What to Say 44

Intended Purpose of Your Site 45

The Audience 47

The Structure of Your Site 48

For More Information 51

Appearance Design 51

Collecting Your Data 53

Determining How the Site Will Work 53

Determining Your Links 54

Collect Your Materials 57

Select the Right File Format 57

More Tips for Speeding Up Download Times 59

For More Information 60

Construct Your Site 60

The Home Page 60

Support Pages 61

Design Your Graphics for Navigation 62

Testing Your Site 64

Setting Up Your Resources 65

Organizing Your Files 65

Summary 68

Chapter 4   **69**

Text and Graphics Basics 69

A PageMill Practicum 70

Page Formatting 73

Naming Your Files 74

Using the Inspector to Format the Page 75

Manipulating Body Text Color 76

Manipulating Background Color 78

Manipulating Background Images 79

Manipulating Hypertext Link Colors 82

Adjusting Hypertext Link Colors 83

Applying Existing Colors Using the Color Panel 83

Customizing Colors with the Color Wheel 83

Paragraph Formatting 84

Applying Heading Styles 85

Applying Alignments 85

Adding Indentations 86

Character Styles 88

Creating Lists 90

Making Bulleted Lists 91

Making Directory and Menu Lists 93

Making Numbered Lists 94

Making Definition and Term Lists 95

Using Rules 97

Adding Graphics 99

   Adding Images Using Drag-and-Drop 99

   Adding Images Using the Pasteboard 103

   Adding Graphics Using the Place Object Button 104

   Aligning Text 106

Manipulating Images 107

   Creating a Placeholder for Your Image 108

   Resizing Graphics 109

   Changing Image Borders 112

Controlling the Behavior of Your Image 113

Using Find and Replace 116

Using the Spelling Checker 117

Saving Your Work 118

Summary 119

Chapter 5   **121**

Working with Links 121

   Understanding Links 122

      URLs 124

      Relative vs. Absolute Pathnames 126

   Working with Hypertext Links 127

      Adding Links Using the Page Icon 127

      Adding Links Using Anchors 129

      More About Links 131

   Linking to the Outside World 133

   Deleting a Link 134

   Testing Your Links 134

   Summary 135

Chapter 6   **137**

Creating Active Images and Image Maps 137

A Short History of Active Images 138

How Client-Side and Server-Side Mapping Works 139

What Is an Active Image? 141

   How Do Active Images Work? 142

Preparing Your Site To Use Active Images 144

   Understanding Hot Spots 146

Creating the Hotspot 148

    More about Defining Clickable Regions 152

    Editing Defined Regions 153

Understanding the Map File 153

How the Map File Works 154

More Information About the Out-of-Place Editor 157

    Using the Out-of-Place Editor to Create Links 157

    Dragging and Dropping Images Using the GIF Icon 158

    Interlacing Images 160

    Transparent Images 160

    Zoom Tools 162

Summary 163

Chapter 7   165

Tables and Frames 165

Creating Tables 166

Selecting and Moving Cells 170

Formatting Cells Using the Toolbar 171

Formatting Cells Using the Inspector 174

    Adjusting the Width of Cells 174

    Aligning the Contents of Cells to the Cells 176

    Adding Background Color to Cells 176

Formatting Tables Using the Inspector 177

    Changing the Size of a Table on a Page 179

    Adding or Deleting Borders from a Table 180

    Changing the Spacing of Rows and Columns in a Table 181

Using the Table Toolbar 182

    Adding or Deleting Cells 182

    Joining and Splitting Cells 183

Using Objects with Tables 185

Creating Links with Tables 185

Using Frames 187

    Making a Simple Frame 188

        Formatting a Frame 189

Completing the Frame 191

Adding Targets to Frames 192

Summary 195

Chapter 8   197

Working with Forms 197

Creating a Fill-In Form 198

Form Elements 199

Fields 200

Pop-Up Menus 200

Buttons 201

Working with Radio Buttons and Checkboxes 203

Working with Pop-Up Menus 206

Setting Up the Form for the CGI 207

Declaring Variables 208

Naming Text, Password Fields, and Text Areas 209

Multiple Options Lists 211

Offering Multiple Selections in a Pop-Up Menu 213

Offering Multiple Options Using Radio Buttons 215

Providing Multiple Options Using Checkboxes 217

Setting Password Fields Using the Inspector 219

Submit and Reset Buttons 220

Using the Form Mode of the Inspector 221

Retrieving Form Data 222

Summary 223

Chapter 9   225

Working with HTML 225

How HTML Works 228

Applying Tag Pairs to Format Items 229

Using Attributes and Values to Modify Tags 229

Creating Hypertext Links 230

Placing Objects into a Page 230

Working with Paragraph and Line Spacing 232

Basic HTML 232

   The Head Area 233

   The Body Area 234

    Adding Special Characters 238

   HTML Version 3.2 and PageMill 2.0 241

   What HTML PageMill Doesn't Support 241

   What PageMill Doesn't Understand 243

The Source Code View 244

Using HTML "Placeholders" 247

Using Cascading Style Sheets with PageMill 2.0 250

Working with Unrecognized HTML 251

Adding Comments 252

Using Java Applets and JavaScript Macros 254

   Placing Java Applets on a Page 254

Summary 256

Chapter 10   257

Common Gateway
Interfaces 257

What Is a CGI? 258

How CGIs Work 259

What Do You Need to Know to Use CGI Scripts on Your Server? 261

Writing CGIs 261

Setting Up PageMill to Run a CGI Script 263

   What About Windows and Mac Servers? 264

   Running a Form Processing CGI: A Setup Example 265

   Configuring CGI Scripts 266

Document- and Form-Based Queries 269

Form-Based CGI Scripts 270

Examples of CGIs 273

Forms and Guestbooks 273

   Scripts in C 274

   Scripts Written in AppleScript/Frontier 275

Counters 276

Active Images 277

Animations 278

    Client-Pull Animations 279

    Server-Push Animation 279

    Animated GIFs 280

    For More Information 280

Online Stores 280

Database Processing 281

For More Information 283

Summary 284

Chapter 11   285

Putting It all Together 285

Human Interface Design 286

Web Publishing for the Masses 290

The Evolution of Web Site Design 292

    First-Generation Web Site Design 292

    Second-Generation Web Site Design 293

    Third-Generation Web Site Design 295

A Scientific Approach to Web Site Design 296

    For More Information 298

So, What Does This Mean for Me? 299

    Using Active Images 302

    Using Links Wisely 302

    Grouping Links 303

    Generating Themes and Web Design 304

    Signing Your Name 305

Creating a Clean, Concise, and Consistent Design 307

Web Site Interaction 308

Summary 310

Chapter 12   311

Getting Online 311

Gaining Access to the Web 312

    Commercial Online Services 313

    Internet Service Providers 315

    Corporate Servers 315

Uploading Your Page 316

    Uploading Your Site Using PageMill 2.0 for Windows 319

Managing Your Site 322

    SiteMill 323

Summary 328

Chapter 13   329

Future Trends 329

    Component Software and the Web 330

        Java and JavaScript 332

        ActiveX 334

        OpenDoc 336

    Multimedia Tools 337

        Databases for Multimedia 338

        Audio Broadcasting 340

        Digital Video 343

        Animation 345

        3-D Images and Virtual Reality 346

    Helper Applications 347

    Electronic Publishing 349

    Summary 350

Toolbar Summary 351

Appendix A   351

Appendix B   355

Index   375

Introduction

Welcome to the exciting world of publishing on the Web with Adobe PageMill. With PageMill you don't need to learn the cumbersome HyperText Markup Language (HTML) to get your information Web-ready. PageMill provides a WYSIWYG (What-You-See-Is-What-You-Get) interface enabling you to focus on the content and style of your Web page instead of on learning a computer language. PageMill provides a simple, integrated environment for editing and previewing your HTML documents in one program.

Objectives of this Book

This book teaches you how to create pages that can be published on the World Wide Web, including:

■ How to format text

■ How to implement lists, frames, tables, and graphics

■ How to create clickable active images and links to other Web sites

■ How to use Java, MacPerl or Perl, AppleScript, and CGIs to energize your Web site

■ How to create and use forms

■ How to integrate new technologies, such as Shockwave, VRML, and RealAudio into your site

■ How to use SiteMill to manage directories and files as Webmaster of your site

Each chapter teaches you practical skills to create visually interesting pages. The chapters build upon each other so that by the end of the book you will have both a mastery of the PageMill program and an understanding of Web publishing techniques.

What You Need to Know Before You Start

■ **About the Computer**—Before creating Web pages with PageMill, you need a working knowledge of the computer. You should understand how to use the mouse and be familiar with menus, windows, and standard commands such as opening, saving, and closing files.

■ **Everyone!**—In addition, you should have a working knowledge of the Internet's parts (the difference between email and ftp protocols, for example), as well as some experience

Web surfing with a browser. You should also understand common Web page terms, such as **imagemap** (a file containing the coordinates of clickable areas on an image); a **button** (a graphic that initiates an action, such as submitting data to the server); an **object** (a file, such as a graphic image, sound, video, or animation); **GIF**, **JPEG**, and **MPEG** (image and video formats supported by the Web); and **hypertext link** (an object or selected text that, when clicked, moves you to another location on a page or another site).

What's New in PageMill 2.0?

PageMill 2.0 is a second generation product. The first iteration of PageMill provided basic desktop publishing tools to overlay the HTML it was generating. This capability to show you the results of your tags while you were programming provided the "gee whiz" factor that few other HTML editors could accomplish. But, there were parts of HTML that PageMill 1.0 couldn't support, such as tables and frames. In addition, tools such as a spell checker and find/replace capability were missing, making the program slightly awkward to use. All the while, HTML standards were revised twice (they now stand at Version 3.2) to support new common gateway interfaces (CGIs) for animation, realtime movies, sounds, online PDFs readers, and so forth. (It has been said that one week on the Web is equal to a year of real time.) Adobe had to revise PageMill to take advantage of this swift development of Web's features and functionality. The result is PageMill 2.0. The revised program is not revolutionary, but evolutionary—building on the desktop publishing metaphor to provide a richer environment for Web page design.

The following features have been added or enhanced in Version 2.0.

- ■ **WYSIWYG Tables.** PageMill 2.0 lets you build tables supporting wrap-around text, easy resizing, and full drag-and-drop features. You can now dispense with the Preformated Text command and design flexible tables to hold text, graphics, other tables, and so forth. Microsoft Excel spreadsheets can be imported directly into PageMill and converted to tables.

■ **WYSIWYG Frames.** You can place multiple URL addressable areas on a single page by using fully navigable frames.

■ **Multimedia plug-ins and advanced browser specifications supported.** You can directly use ActiveX Controls (Microsoft Internet Explorer) and Netscape's plug-ins and associated helpers, such as Adobe PDF reader, MacZilla, Shockwave, Real Audio, QuickTime VRML Readers, and so forth within your PageMill page by dragging and dropping the associated file into your page as you would any other object. Animated GIFs that follow Netscape specifications will appear animated in PageMill 2.0's Preview window without requiring your readers to have special plug-ins. (Note that you must build the animations in another program and import the GIF89 images into PageMill as you would any other object.) You can directly embed PDFs in your document that are readable on screen using the appropriate plug-in. PageMill directly plays or converts sound files, such as AIFF, WAV, SND, and AU formats.

■ **Better control over desktop publishing features.** You get true desktop publishing power because text will flow in multiple lines around a graphic. You can scale and color characters individually, instead of by the page or paragraph. You can create more typographic effects, such as leaded capital letters.

■ **Better word processing features, such as spellchecking.** A user-definable dictionary and Internet-specific dictionary lets you check your spelling within PageMill (including within forms and tables). You can search for and replace any selection with another selection, including within forms and tables). You can search for and replace all forms of media, including sounds, images, text, video, and so forth.

■ **HTML advanced coding supported.** You can instantly toggle between the PageMill Edit mode and the source code that underlies it. More tags and attributes are preserved, and the HTML tags are easier to edit, because they are presented more clearly. Both <P> and <BR> tags are supported for added flexibility. You can use hidden HTML tools, such as anchors, hidden fields, comment fields, and HTML placeholders to add scripts, database queries, and links within pages. The HTML placeholder lets you add third-party products, such as database frontend tools, snippet libraries, and automatic HTML generators, by dragging and dropping the object into PageMill. You can also link to remote objects and Java applets across the network from within PageMill.

The basic difference between PageMill 1.0 and PageMill 2.0 is that you are able to do more directly on the screen. Toolbars are available via the click of a mouse. You can manipulate a richer array of information tools, for example, rather than just graphics. All objects (such as a Java applets, sound files, animated GIF files, PDF, and so forth) are treated like an image—they can be placed, linked to, manipulated, and formatted. This increase in the breadth of HTML support as well as the more desktop friendly interface has changed some of the terminology used with PageMill. For example:

■ "Images" are now "Objects" and encompass many more formats of things that can be embedded in or linked to on a page.

■ The former "Attributes Inspector" has become simply the "Inspector" since most of its text and layout functions have been placed directly on the PageMill Edit mode's toolbar.

■ The "Image View" has become the "Out-of-Place editor" since you can create client-side imagemaps directly on the PageMill desktop without having to open a separate window (except to perform editing required for better server performance, such as interlacing and transparencies).

Using this Book

The Adobe PageMill 2.0 Handbook provides information for Web publishers of all skill levels. To help you use the book more effectively, we provide the following special features.

Tips and Notes

Each chapter takes you from beginning, introductory concepts through advanced techniques. Tips and notes provide helpful information to Web publishers of all skill levels.

Command Summaries

FYI

Occasionally, we've added additional background information that might be of interest to you.

Throughout the book we provide easy-to-reference Command Summaries. These summaries provide steps to using PageMill's many features and tools. An example of a Command Summary follows:

 Aligning Text

1   Type the following text into your new PageMill document:

Greetings from Asbury Park, N.J.

The Wild, The Innocent and the E Street Shuffle

Born to Run

Darkness on the Edge of Town

2   Highlight the text and select the Center Align Text button from the toolbar.

 A CD icon indicates a file that can be found on the CD-ROM.

What's In Each Chapter?

The following paragraphs provide a thumbnail sketch of what is covered in each chapter of the book.

Chapter 1: Welcome to WYSIWYG Web Publishing

This chapter provides a short history of the Internet and orients you to PageMill's role in World Wide Web (WWW) publishing. Chapter 1 includes a discussion of what PageMill can and cannot do and introduces you to issues of Web page design.

Chapter 2: A Tour of PageMill 2.0

This chapter introduces the various components of PageMill 2.0, including the Edit and Preview modes, the menu bar, toolbar, link location bar, Color Palette, Inspector, Out-of-Place editor, and the Pasteboard.

Chapter 3: Getting Started

This chapter discusses how to plan the design of a Web page. Included are descriptions of how to create schematic diagrams of the Web site, how to storyboard a site, and how to set up your resources and image folders.

Chapter 4: Text and Graphics Basics

This chapter is broken down in to three sections: formatting a page, formatting paragraphs, and character-level formatting. In addition, you are shown how to insert and manipulate images on your page. Find and Replace and the spelling checker are described.

Chapter 5: Working with Links

This chapter introduces the concept of hypertext and linking pages together—the backbone of the Web. You are shown how to create links to text by dragging and dropping page icons and anchors and by using the toolbar and dialog boxes to create connections within and between page elements.

Chapter 6: Creating Active Images and Imagemaps

This chapter takes the concept of hypertext links one step further by showing you how to break up your graphics into "hot spots" (called imagemaps) linking that portion of the image to another element on the page or to another site. Client-side versus server-side imagemaps are explained.

Chapter 7: Tables and Frames

This chapter shows you how to create tables on the page using the toolbar. The concept of multiple URLs on a page (frames) are described and you learn how to create and manipulate frames.

Chapter 8: Working with Forms

This chapter describes how to create fill-in forms in the PageMill Edit mode window using the toolbar. The different components available for forms (text fields, text areas, password fields, radio buttons, check boxes, pop-up menus, and the submit/reset buttons) are described. The concept of a common gateway interface (CGI) to process form information on the server is introduced.

Chapter 9: Working with HTML

This chapter presents a discussion of how to insert HTML tags not currently supported by PageMill and how to use the HTML placeholder to insert Java applets and other plug-ins into your document. The Source Code view is also described.

Chapter 10: Common Gateway Interfaces

In this chapter CGIs are described as they pertain to imagemaps, interactive Web pages, new technologies, Netscape Navigator helpers, and forms processing.

Chapter 11: Putting It All Together

This chapter presents a deeper discussion of human interface design and usability testing and how it is applied to Web site design. You are introduced to the evolution of Web site design from both an artistic and scientific point of view and given tools to design effective Web sites.

Chapter 12: Getting Online

This chapter discusses the ins and outs of transferring your files on to the server using either AppleShare (if you are using a Mac-based server) or an FTP program if you are transferring your site to a Windows NT or Unix-based server. This chapter also discusses how to manage links, file management and naming conventions, and other maintenance issues from the client-side. Various site managemnt programs are described, such as NetObjects Fusion and Adobe SiteMill.

Chapter 13: Future Trends

This final chapter discusses some future developments in Web site design and introduces some of the more spectacular effects you can create today using newly developed CGIs and helpers. Shockwave, Real Audio, VRML, and NetPhone are described.

Chapter 1

Welcome to WYSIWYG Web Publishing

About the Internet vs. the World Wide Web

Before we start learning how to build documents to be distributed through Web servers and the Internet, it is important to understand how the different elements of Web publishing work.

What is the Internet?

"Internet" and "intranet" are bandied about a lot these days. The Internet is a conglomeration of computers linked by a myriad of networks into a baffling, decentralized global network. An "intranet" is a corporation's version of the Internet—an internal Internet for that firm. The Internet is the invention of the Defense Department and its affiliated labs and universities. It is old and complicated; the network is based on 1960's software technology, namely Unix. In 1991, The National Science Foundation lifted its restrictions on commercial use of the Net, and "Net surfing" tools proliferated. That same year, for example, Gopher, a search engine for Usenets, was published by Paul Lindner and Mark McCahill of the University of Minnesota. Tim Berners-Lee at the University of Illinois' National Center for Supercomputing Applications developed the graphical entry-way to Internet information—the World Wide Web (WWW). By 1992, there were one million host computers connected to the Internet. The public's interest in using these networks to communicate was astounding.

The Internet really consists of computers that manage data and networks, called servers. These servers consist of software that receives requests for information, goes out and finds it in its databases, and returns the proper "pages" of data to the requesting computer. These servers are all different. They speak different languages (variations on Unix, such as SCO, Xenix, AIX, Windows NT, Macintosh, and so forth) and all work differently. The wonder of early efforts to share information was simply the ability to find it and retrieve it over telephone lines.

The Origins of HTML

The secret of the Internet and later the World Wide Web is the separation of the act of transmission of data from the display of data. By separating the processes, transmission could be faster because the server did not have to worry about how the data looked at the other end because display was left to the local receiving computer. The problem to be solved was how to get different computer platforms to translate data into something that could be displayed on a monitor. The solution was to send information along side the data (called tags) that tells the receiving computer how to display different types of information.

Several methods of tagging data were developed to assist in the display of data (ways to tell your computer that a stream of data is a paragraph, a list, or a citation, for example). These coding methods, called "markup languages" travel with the data and are interpreted by the retrieving software. Hypertext (such as Apple's Hypercard) supplied ways to connect disparate pieces of data. Code telling the computer how to interpret hypertext documents is called HyperText Markup Language (HTML). HTML became the standard way to tag pages of information traveling over the Internet.

The Birth of the WWW

So there are two parts of using the Internet: managing the data (the data creator's and later the server's job) and retrieving and displaying it on your computer (the computer user's job). Early users had to be Unix gurus to understand Unix communications protocols because they were still dealing with the server software to query and receive information. Data coming across the Internet was in textual form because nothing stood between you and the server except Unix. Then a revolution quietly occurred. Computer science students began to write programs, called Web browsers, that served as intermediaries, interpreting the HTML tags and speaking the multitudinous server languages. Browsers assisted users in finding information on the Web and properly displaying it on your computer screen. At first, only text was supported. As browsers became more sophisticated at interpreting HTML codes, graphics, sounds, movies, realtime animations, and so forth have started to appear as ways to present information.

The Web goes Commercial

By 1994, commercial online services also made the WWW available to their subscribers by building gateways and browsers from their proprietary sites. America Online, CompuServe, and Prodigy all have gateways to the Web. With commercial access providers becoming more ubiquitous and prices for access becoming cheaper, millions of regular folks are exploring what used to be the sole providence of scientists and students. Meanwhile, the growth in users and resulting marketing possibilities of the Internet made commercial tools for browsing the Web a possibility. Today, 90 percent of all Internet users use Netscape Navigator 3.0 and Microsoft Internet Explorer 2.0 as browsers. These browsers are growing in capabilities of what they can interpret and display. The problem of displaying retrieved information was solved.

Meanwhile, more and more businesses and organizations saw the possibilities inherent in a network of millions of connected computers. The ease of use of the publishing and serving side of the Internet equation began to be addressed. Inevitably, individuals and companies wanted to use the Web for commercial purposes, transferring what had been published on paper and broadcast on television and radio on to this new medium. The fact that users could be led between pieces of information via hypertext links created the concept of Web sites (collections of documents, called pages, interconnected via hypertext links). People who developed these Web sites were not computer wizards, but commercial artists and marketing folks. They needed tools to match the ease of use of the browsers used to display the results of their endeavors.

Network Publishing Grows Up

In the past, scientists and their students did not care about the aesthetics of how information was presented on the Web. Commercial enterprises and non-technical computer users needed easier ways to publish and access information. Yet, until recently, the only way to publish a page was by dealing with the data's underlying structure. You had to add HTML tags to your

---

FYI

The Web community debates whether it's better to create pages utilizing Netscape extensions or to design pages for the HTML 2.0 standard. Many Web pages state: "This page looks best when viewed with Netscape 2.0" or "Best when viewed with Microsoft Internet Explorer," and often provide a link for the Net surfer to download that browser. Some people in the Web community want to open the description of how pages are tagged so that one company can't dictate de-facto standards. In fact, Microsoft has turned over ActiveX standards to a third-party and Sun Microsystems has turned over Java to a third-party to preclude the accusation of proprietary standards. Some say that waiting for standards slows innovation, and the market should decide whether extensions such as Real Audio, QuickTime, and Acrobat are accepted as the standard. Ultimately, the market will decide, although the debate

---

documents that could be read and interpreted by browsers so that they could properly interpret and display information broadcast by the Web. A few adventurous vendors began to write desktop publishing (dtp)-based layout tools to overlay the HTML spoken by the Web. So was PageMill and its related cousins born. We are now in the second generation of Web generation tools offering more than just an overlay to HTML, but also providing tools to build upon this code to create highly professional graphic pages.

But, as with the desktop publishing revolution, Sturgeon's Law ("99 percent of everything is junk") began to happen on the Web—bad design proliferated because the tools advanced faster than the knowledge needed to use them. As the Web became more public, researchers in businesses and universities began to apply the same human interface design theories used to upgrade print and broadcast journalism to network journalism. They developed usability engineering guidelines for Web sites. (Usability engineering studies show how computer users search and use information on computers.) This book shares the results of these studies on how to create great Web sites with you and applies this information to using PageMill 2.0's powerful features so that you can publish the most informative and useful pages possible without having to be a HTML programmer.

Webmasters vs. Web Publishers

You have probably heard the terms "Webmaster" and "Web publishing" in the wave of press concerning the Internet. You can design and publish pages on the Web without having to know how they are managed once they are "out there." Web publishing is the process of putting information into a Web-presentable form. A Web publisher can be anyone who has something to say or has information that he or she wants to make available. Business people, for example, might want to use the Web to publish their product catalogs or collect information about potential buyers via interactive forms. The point is, the with PageMill you can be the designer without having to be the techie Web guru.

A Webmaster, on the other hand, is someone with a wider range of Web skills. A Webmaster is responsible for managing and configuring the Web server. He usually addresses networking issues associated with a Web server and creates or employs special applications extending its functionality.

Most Webmasters are Web publishers. Not all Web publishers, however, are Webmasters. The PageMill 2.0 Handbook focuses on Web publishing without requiring any knowledge of networking, server management, or computer programming. (Although Chapter 12 does provide a short overview of Web management through the use of SiteMill, PageMill's companion Web server management software.) With applications such as Adobe PageMill (and other more personal Web-building programs, such as Claris' Home Page), Web publishers can create Web documents and transfer them to Webmasters for inclusion on Web servers without having to know how to create scripts in hypertext markup language (HTML)—the language of the Web. In addition, experienced HTML coders can still use PageMill to create the page and then augment PageMill's WYSIWYG approach with HTML tags for more fancy effects not yet supported by PageMill. You can have your cake and eat it too by using the PageMill HTML placeholder tools.

What You Can Do with PageMill

PageMill is a graphical tool for creating Web pages on a Macintosh. These pages can be served via an HTTP (HyperText Transfer Protocol) server, also called a Web server, to other people connected to the Web. Here are some other features provided by PageMill.

■ Provides a single environment for creating pages, viewing the pages, and testing hypertext links to other pages.

■ Provides a functionality for creating so-called client-side clickable active images and their associated imagemap files.

■ Support of drag-and-drop architecture facilitates easy page generation. You can readily drag and drop icons to connect your page to others via hypertext links, and add images and portable digital files (PDFs) to your page, all with the click and drag of your mouse. Drag and drop objects on to and off the Pasteboard to manage libraries of commonly used Web-page elements.

Getting Your Document on The Web: Working with HTML

As mentioned earlier, at first, the only way to place information on a Web server was to place tags in your document defining the **structure** of text (whether it would be a paragraph, list, heading, or other), but not the appearance of a document. These structural markup tags are called HyperText Markup Language (HTML). HTML is useful because it is portable; anyone with a browser can access the tagged information and have it presented on-screen in a comprehensible fashion. You can feed tagged text into databases, indices, and other mechanized data repositories, where it can be searched and presented in customized ways for each searcher, based on the criteria of their search. HTML tags are arcane.

HTML uses a syntax where you turn on and off effects by using pre-defined codes called tags. Here's an example of HTML:

```
<H1>Welcome to the EmmaZone</H1>
```

The text Welcome to the EmmaZone is enclosed by the tags <H1> and </H1>. The first tag, <H1>, tells the browser that the following text is to be formatted as a first-level heading (you'll understand what a first-level heading is later) until the browser encounters the end tag, </H1>. Figures 1.1 and 1.2 show the difference between what the browser displays and what is hidden behind the Web page. This gives you a good feeling for the difference between the appearance and reality of creating Web pages prior to the advent of WYSIWYG Web page publishing software, such as PageMill.

Note

HTML comes in several versions. The current version is 3.2. Only certain browsers, namely Netscape Navigator and Microsoft Internet Explorer, support the client-side mapped graphics, rotated text, multi-layered text and images, frames, tables, animated GIFs, movies, and so forth supported in HTML 3.2. Although PageMill 2.0 also supports HTML 3.0, keep in mind that some readers may be using older browsers that cannot see pictures and fancy stuff. Design your pages for both image-poor and image-rich browsers.

Figure 1.1
A beautifully designed Web page...

Figure 1.2

...and the HTML tags that define how the page appears.

PageMill and HTML—A Symbiotic Relationship

The benefit of HTML is that it presents a structure for presenting text, images, live animation, sound, and so forth in a standardized manner for browsers running on all computer platforms. The procedure goes something like this: browsers know how to read HTML; PageMill knows how to generate HTML (it hides the complexities by providing an intuitive interface); therefore, when browsers read pages generated with PageMill, they are reading HTML.

The corollary here is that you are bound by the same constraints and issues as someone constructing a Web page with HTML. So, even though you'll be publishing without actively encountering HTML, there are a few things about HTML and browsers that you need to know:

■ **HTML is displayed differently on different browsers.** You don't have any control over this. These inconsistencies are a part of the Web. Even though HTML is a standard, various browser manufacturers implement the standard differently. Though these are usually subtle differences, they are differences nonetheless, and a good Web publisher will have several browsers available to test what the output will look like. Because 90 percent of the world is using Netscape Navigator or Microsoft Internet Explorer in different versions with different levels of capabilities, you can concentrate on the capabilities of the most up-to-date browsers (Version 3.0 of Navigator and 3.x of Explorer). This is what PageMill's Preview mode displays.

Because HTML is such a rudimentary markup language, page proportions and line breaks will vary depending on the size of the monitor your reader is using to view your page. Try, as a default, to design pages that are 640 x 480 pixels (a standard monitor screen).

Because images are treated as text by HTML, you cannot precisely place a graphic on a page. The graphic will be resized and move should your reader resize his/her browser's window. So, don't plan on using precise layouts of text and graphics unless you place them as images from a page layout program.

HTML does not support typographical precision. You cannot, for example, set the leading or kern text using HTML because line breaks, letter spacing, and word spacing are determined by the size of the browser's window and the specific font settings of the browser being used. The following type characteristics are not supported by the WWW browsers, or cannot be specified with PageMill or imported as text into a page:

- Font, type size, and leading

- Font width

- Font tracking

- Font special effects, such as strikethroughs, outlines, shadows, reverse type, and super- and subscript styles

- Tab positions

- Spacing before and after paragraphs

- **Plug-ins, Helpers, and Extensions.** Microsoft and Netscape Communications are two of the main commercial organizations fueling Web page design. Netscape created the immensely popular Netscape Navigator browser and Microsoft is coming in a close second with its Internet Explorer browser. Between Netscape Navigator's estimated 80 percent of the market and Microsoft Internet Explorer's 10 to 15 percent of the browser population, these companies find themselves in the enviable position of being able to introduce their own extensions to HTML without waiting for the standards organization's approval. PageMill implements some but not all of these extensions. It does, for example, support JavaScript, frames, and tables but it does not support cascading style sheets ar the <FONT> tag. It does provide space holders so that you can write the HTML tags to support new extensions into your PageMill document. Although you will not be able to view these within PageMill, HTML written in PageMill is usable.

- **You are in control.** It's important to understand the control you have in designing your Web page, such as:

  - Inclusion of graphics that serve as links directing your readers to different areas of your site or to other sites

  - Inclusion of layed out documents as downloadable files (portable document files (PDFs)) that can be read either on- or offline exactly as they were designed

  - Inclusion of three-dimensional graphics that serve as guides taking your readers to where you want them to go

  - Other tools enabling you to manage the information on your pages

  Yet, you do give up a type of control, depending on the user's browser (because not all browser versions can see everything that you have built into your site). In addition, a user can set his browser's preferences to determine what fonts are used, the size of the text, and the colors used for fonts, hypertext links, and backgrounds. You cannot override these controls, and you need to be aware of these issues to make design decisions.

Publishing without HTML

The PageMill Handbook helps you understand what you do and don't have control over when designing your pages with PageMill and the choices you need to make about designing for various browsers.

Fortunately, you don't have to learn the cryptic HTML because PageMill generates the commands for you. Do you still need HTML? Eventually, you might want to learn some HTML to do some of the more advanced tricks or take advantage of browser-specific features. PageMill gives you a rich set of tools that enable you to get your information Web-able in the simplest manner possible. If your goal is to publish information on the Web, PageMill is all you'll ever need.

Summary

The PageMill 2.0 Handbook teaches you how to use PageMill 2.0 to create great Web sites. It covers the basics of PageMill on the Mac and Windows 95 platforms and introduces usability engineering concepts to enhance how you use the program to publish Web sites. The book is structured with chapters on conceptualization of your Web site to chapters on publication on the Web (or working with Web servers). Other chapters discuss formatting with PageMill, using CGIs, and tricks and tips for great designs.

Chapter 2

A Tour of PageMill 2.0

PageMill 2.0 provides a familiar environment to help you intuitively build Web pages. The program provides a true WYSIWYG feel. Think of PageMill as a word processor with delusions of page layout glory, and you get the correct mind-set to work with the program. The following pages provide you with a tour of its features.

The Edit and Preview Window Modes

The PageMill interface looks like a Web browser but acts like a funky page layout program with two interchangable windows: Edit and Preview. Switching between these windows is accomplished by clicking the Edit or Preview button to change the mode.

The Edit mode button (shown in Figure 2.1) toggles the screen between the Edit and Preview windows. The Edit window is used to build a Web page or a collection of pages, called a *Web site*. Text layout and formatting, the placement of images and objects, and the creation of hypertext links take place within the Edit window.

Figure 2.1
Toggle the Edit mode button to display the PageMill Edit window.

The Preview mode button (shown in Figure 2.2) lets you switch to the mock browser window to see what your page will look like on a Web browser and to test the links to other pages on your Web site. Although PageMill has the appearance of a Web browser, it is not a functioning Internet browser; it is a preview browser. You cannot "surf" the Net using PageMill, nor can you use it to read newsgroups, send email, create bookmarks to other Web sites, or perform any of the other tasks associated with Web browsers. PageMill is a Web-page creation program. It is designed to look like a browser so that you, the Web-page author, can preview how your pages will appear on a fully functional browser.

Figure 2.2
Toggle the Preview mode button to display the PageMill Browser or Preview screen.

Tip

You can select which window is the default window that appears each time you open PageMill. Choose the Preference command from the Edit menu, in the General screen select Preview or Edit from the pull-down menu (see Figure 2.3).

Mac

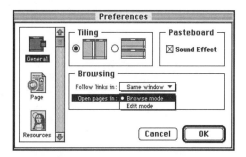

Windows

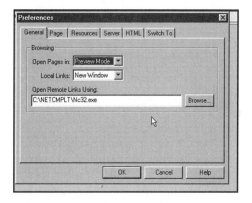

Figure 2.3
Select how you want PageMill to open from the Browse section's pull-down menu.

The PageMill Edit Window

The PageMill Edit window displayed in Figure 2.4 consists of the following elements:

- The toolbar
- The content area
- The link location bar

On the Mac when you open PageMill in the Edit mode window, you are presented with an untitled HTML document displaying the toolbar, content area, and link location bar. Most of your Web page creation is done using these three areas. We'll look at PageMill's assistance palettes a little later in this chapter. The PC version works slightly differently. Each page has its own tool bar, title bar, and content area. The Window menu controls how pages are displayed on the screen.

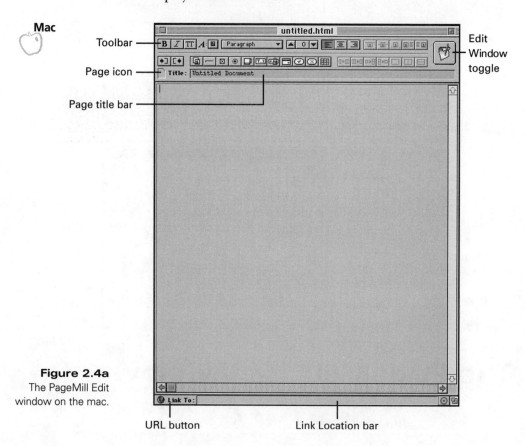

Mac

Toolbar

Page icon

Page title bar

Edit Window toggle

Figure 2.4a
The PageMill Edit window on the mac.

URL button   Link Location bar

Windows

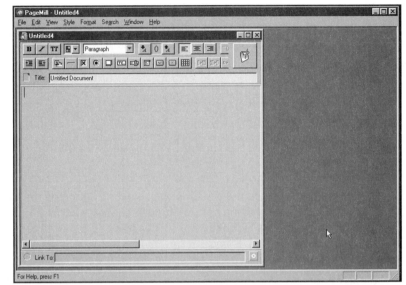

Figure 2.4b
The PageMill Edit in
Windows.

The Toolbar

The toolbar in PageMill's Edit window (see Figure 2.5) contains a
collection of buttons enabling you to do the following to your
Web page:

- Insert objects such as graphics, Java applets, movies, sound
  files, and so forth

- Insert horizontal rules

- Assign paragraph and character styles to text

- Align text and objects on your Web page

- Enter a page title that appears when someone loads your
  Web page

- Create forms and add form-functional areas such as check
  boxes, pop-up windows, and fields

- Access the Page icon for creating links

- Toggle between Edit and Preview mode windows

- Set how text will flow around an object

- Create and manipulate table cells

Font format   Font Color   Font size increment
elements   menu   selectors

Right and left
indent buttons

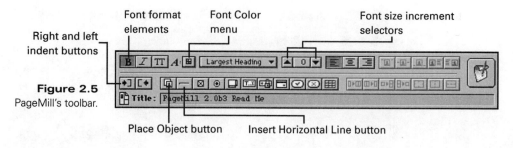

Figure 2.5
PageMill's toolbar.

Place Object button   Insert Horizontal Line button

 Tip

When the cursor is placed over a button on the toolbar, a description of the button's function appears to the right of the toolbar (see Figure 2.6).

Figure 2.6
Pointing at an icon
on the toolbar
displays its
description in the
right-hand area.

 PageMill 2.0 Jargon Explained...

In PageMill 1.0 you could only place graphics or text on to your page. PageMill 2.0 supports all of the features of HTML version 3.2, including the inclusion of Java applets, videos, animated GIF files, sounds, and so forth on to a page. To indicate this extended support, Adobe changed the name of the toolbar button from "Insert Image" to "Place Object," since that is what you are doing.You can now manipulate and link to and from every item on a page, including table cells, applets, graphics, text, PDFs, imagemaps, and so forth; all of these items are termed *objects*.

A large icon, located in the upper-right corner of the PageMill window, enables you to switch between PageMill's Edit and Preview modes (see Figures 2.1 and 2.2). The graphic on the icon changes depending on the mode. You'll also find the Page icon, the heart of PageMill's powerful drag-and-drop capabilities for creating hypertext links, on the left end of the toolbar. You can create hypertext links in PageMill by dragging the Page icon to an object on the page that you want to specify as a link.

Note

Documents need to be saved in order for a link to be created. Otherwise, the Page icon is displayed as a gray outline of a page.

The Content Area

Like the text area of a word processor or page layout program, the content area is where you layout and manipulate the pieces of your Web page (see Figure 2.7).

To enter text click the content area. An insertion point appears and you can begin typing. Alignment and formatting commands can be applied from menu commands or with the toolbar. Page elements such as horizontal rules, objects such as graphics, applets, PDFs, movies, and so forth, and form elements, can also be added using the toolbar. In addition, you can drag and drop text and other objects into the content area.

Windows

Tip

You can change the size of the content area by clicking the bottom right corner of the area and dragging the window to a new size. You can close a window by clicking the close box on the content area.

The Link Location Bar

The link location bar, located at the bottom of the PageMill window, is where you enter URL (Uniform Resource Locator) addresses for hypertext links to other Web pages both on your Web site and on the Internet (see Figure 2.8). URLs are standardized addresses for Internet sites. In Preview mode, URL addresses appear in the link location bar as the arrow pointer passes over objects that serve as hypertext links. You need to select the linked object in order to view and edit the link from the location bar.

Insertion point ———

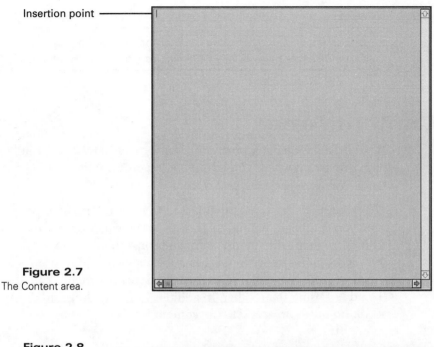

Figure 2.7
The Content area.

Figure 2.8
The Link Location bar.

PageMill's Menu Bar

PageMill uses the standard placement of the File and Edit menus (see Figures 2.9a and 2.9b). These menus contain the usual commands for opening a new document, opening an existing document, saving a new or existing document, and printing, as well as the editing commands of Cut, Copy, and Paste.

PageMill provides keyboard shortcuts for many commands for those of you who like to keep your fingers on the keyboard. These equivalent keystroke combinations are displayed to the right of the command in the menu.

PageMill provides four other menus with special commands dealing with formatting quirks of HTML and commands to augment those of the toolbar. Figures 2.9c through 2.9f display the various menus and their contents.

Note the new frame saving commands on the File menu. These new commands let you set up more than one URL on your page and manipulate these designated areas as if they were separate pages nested within your page. We discuss how to use Frames in Chapter 7.

Mac

 Windows

Figure 2.9a
The File menu.

Mac

 Windows

Figure 2.9b
The Edit menu.

Mac

Style	Format	Search	Wi
Plain			⌘P
✓**Bold**			⌘B
Italic			⌘I
Teletype			⌘T
Strong			⌘S
Emphasis			⌘E
Citation			⌘C
Sample			⌘A
Keyboard			⌘K
Code			⌘O
Variable			⌘U
Increase Font Size			⌘.
Decrease Font Size			⌘,

Windows

Style	
Plain	Ctrl+Shift+P
Bold	Ctrl+B
Italic	Ctrl+I
Teletype	Ctrl+Shift+T
Strong	
Emphasis	
Citation	
Sample	
Keyboard	
Code	Ctrl+Shift+C
Variable	
Increase Font Size	Ctrl+Shift+>
Decrease font size	Ctrl+Shift+<

Figure 2.9c
The Style menu.

Mac

Format	Search	Wind
Indent Right		⌘]
Indent Left		⌘[
Paragraph		⌥⌘P
Heading		▶
Preformatted		⌥⌘F
Address		⌥⌘A
List		▶

Windows

Format	
Indent Left	Ctrl+[
Indent Right	Ctrl+]
✓ Paragraph	Ctrl+Shift+0
Heading	▶
Preformatted	
Address	
List	▶

Figure 2.9d
The Format menu.

Mac

Search	Window	
Find...		⌘F
Find Next		⌘G
Replace		⌘L
Replace & Find Again		⌘=
Replace All		
Check Spelling...		⌘`

Windows

Search	
Find...	Ctrl+F
Find Next	Ctrl+G
Replace	Ctrl+L
Replace & Find Again	Ctrl+=
Replace All	
Check Spelling...	F7

Figure 2.9e
The Search menu.

Mac

Window	
Show Pasteboard	⌘/
Hide Inspector	⌘;
Show Color Panel	⌘'
Stack	
Tile	
Close All	
untitled.html	⌘1

Windows

View	
Show Inspector	F8
Show Color Panel	F6
Show Pasteboard	F5
✓ Status Bar	
Switch To	▶

Figure 2.9f
The Window menu.

PageMill's Other Controls

In addition to the commands available via the toolbar and menu bar, four other palettes and windows are used to manipulate your Web pages:

■ Inspector

■ Color Panel

■ Out-of-Place editor

■ Pasteboard

Although you learn a bit about them here, the Inspector and Out-of-Place editor are discussed in greater detail in Chapters 4 and 6, respectively.

The Inspector

The Inspector palette is used to view and set page appearance attributes, such as the color or pattern of your background, active and inactive links, and to set up variables and names for objects placed on your Web page. It is PageMill's command center; you can position it anywhere on-screen.

Activate the Inspector palette on the Mac by choosing Show Inspector from the Window menu or pressing [cm]+; (see Figure 2.10). Activate the Inspector on the PC by selecting Show Inspector from the View menu (F8). You can move through the four screens of the Inspector palette by clicking the icons on the four tabs at the top of the window: Frames, Page, Forms, and Object. You will find that you use the Object screen the most. Each object type produces its own object screen to provide information about that object. For example, selecting a table cell opens the Table object screen where you can add captions, designate the width and height of cells, and add borders and padding between cells. We'll discuss the various uses of the Inspector's Object, Frame, and Form screens in Chapters 5, 6, 7, and 8, respectively.

The Inspector's Page Screen

The Inspector's Page screen (see Figure 2.11) lets you set the color of the foreground, background, and the hypertext links. You can also set the default font type for the page by HTML base font number (because the browser controls which actual font will be displayed, HTML offers seven font types, whose number you can select on this screen). The Page screen is also where you apply those cool background patterns that have become so popular on the Web.

The Frame tab —— The Object tab

The Page tab —— The Form tab

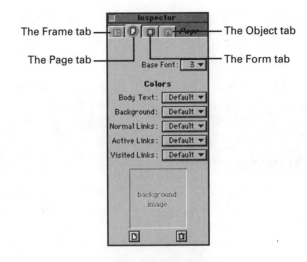

Figure 2.10
PageMill's Inspector palette.

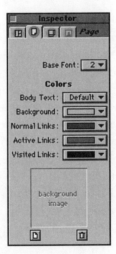

Figure 2.11
Use the Page Window of the Inspector palette to set colors for different link options, fonts, and background images for your Web page.

 Mac

 Tip

If you are using PageMill for Macintosh, you can use the Apple Desktop Patterns Control Panel to create a background.

1 Open the Desktop control panel and click through the various desktop images until you find one that suits your purposes.

2 Drag the image on to the desktop where it becomes a PICT clippings file.

3 Drag the file onto the Background square in the Page
Window of the Inspector (or select the clipping from the
Open dialog box by clicking the Document icon under
the Background square).

You can use any PICT, GIF, or JPEG image or photograph as a
background.

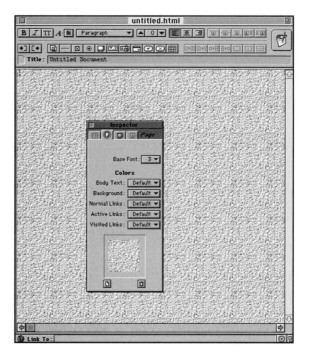

Figure 2.12
Dragging Desktop
clipping 34 from the
Desktop control
panel to the
Background box
causes the page's
background to
change to that
pattern.

The Inspector's Object Screen

The Object screen was formerly called the "Image window" in
PageMill 1.0. In honor of PageMill's increased support of other
types of file formats, the screen was renamed and its functions
slightly enhanced. The Object window of the Inspector palette
(see Figure 2.13) is very versatile. As mentioned earlier, any item
you create or insert into your page is considered an object that
can be linked to, sized, or modified.When you select an item on
your page, such as an image or table cell, the Object screen is
displayed for that specific object. With this screen you can:

- Scale and resize objects

- Define borders

- Identify an image as an inline or static picture, a series of hot spots on an image (called an imagemap) that links to other areas on your page or to other Web pages, or an image used as a button (a single link)

Mac   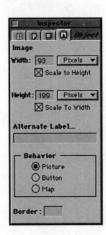  **Windows**

Figure 2.13
Select an object
with the Inspector
open to switch to
the Object window
(or click its tab with
an object selected).
Use the Object
window to set up
specifications.

The Inspector's Forms Screen

With PageMill, you can create input forms to collect information from your page's visitors. The Forms window of the Inspector (see Figure 2.14) enables you to name your form elements, assign their default values, and in the case of text fields and text areas, specify their size.

 Note

See Chapter 8, "Working with Forms," for more information.

The Inspector's Frames Screen

 Frames are independent areas within your page that contain the contents of separate URLs. Think of them as nested pages. Frames can have independent scroll bars, contain links to other frames, and generally behave like separate entities. The Microsoft Site Builder Network site (http://www.microsoft.com/sitebuilder/

site06.htm) makes extensive use of frames to lead you through various articles and other subjects of their workshop (see Figure 2.15).

Figure 2.14
The Forms window of the Inspector.

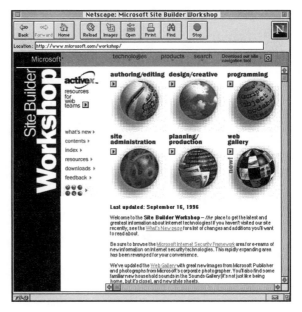

Figure 2.15
The Microsoft Site Builder Network uses frames to lead readers through the site's workshops.

Use the Frame window of the Inspector (illustrated in Figure 2.16) to set up your page's frames. Create a frame by dragging the edge of the content area horizontally or vertically. Select that area with the Inspector open and the Frames window is displayed. See Chapter 7 for more information about working with Frames.

Mac Windows

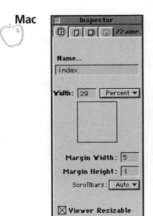

Figure 2.16
The Frames
window of the
Inspector.

The Pasteboard

The Pasteboard (see Figure 2.17), activated by selecting Show Pasteboard from the Window menu ([cm]+/), is your library or repository for objects you may want to use multiple times on your site. Select show Pasteboard from the View menu (F5) in Windows.

Logos, copyright notices, and icon bars are examples of elements you might want to keep on your Pasteboard. The Pasteboard provides you with five pages for easy organization of frequently used items. Each page can include multiple items, and the Pasteboard can be sized using the size box in the lower-right corner. As with much of PageMill, the Pasteboard supports drag-and-drop technology to simplify transferring text and images. When you place text containing hypertext links into the Pasteboard and then drop that text into another page, the links are maintained. See Chapter 4 for more details on how to use the Pasteboard.

Figure 2.17
Use the Pasteboard
to store items you
want to reuse.

The Out-of-Place Editor

With the support of client-side imagemaps, the role of the Image
View editor has changed substantially in PageMill 2.0. Adobe has
renamed the Image View editor as the Out-of-Place editor to
indicate its new, more limited role. In PageMill 2.0, you can create
client-side imagemaps (where the pixel location information
resides with the HTML file on your server) directly on the content
area by double-clicking the image to display the imagemap tools
on the toolbar. (See Chapter 6 for a discussion of client-side
versus server-side imagemaps and the use of this window.) The
newly named Out-of-Place editor also lets you work with images to
create server-side imagemaps (the older version of imagemaps
that require separate imagemap files). It also lets you:

- Make an image's background transparent so that it blends in
  with your page.

- Specify if an image is to appear as an interlaced GIF for
  faster displaying.

To activate the Out-of-Place editor from within PageMill on the
Mac, press the Command key while double-clicking an image (see
Figure 2.18). On the PC, press the Ctrl key while double-clicking.
You can also open any GIF file into the Out-of-Place editor while
PageMill is running by double-clicking its icon on the desktop.

 Note

For more information about using graphics and interlaced GIFs
see Chapter 6, "Creating Active Images and Imagemaps."

Image icon

Hot spot tools

Transparency wand

Imagemap Layering tool

Hot spot color menu

Hot spot label toggle

Interlace Image toggle

Mac

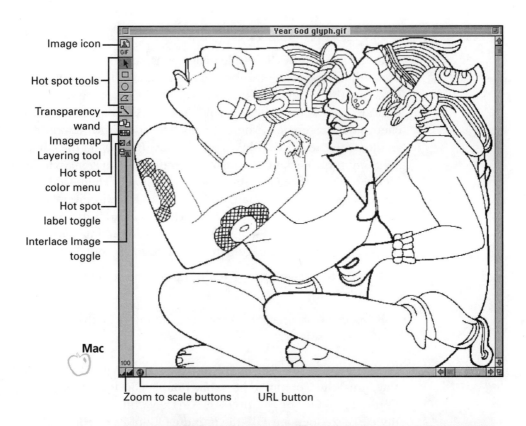

Zoom to scale buttons   URL button

Windows

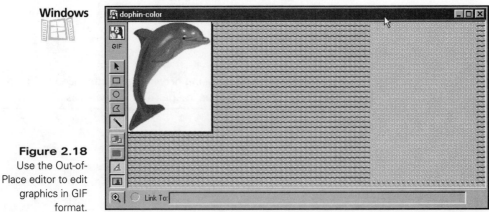

Figure 2.18
Use the Out-of-Place editor to edit graphics in GIF format.

The Color Panel

On the Mac select the Color Panel (see Figure 2.19) from the Windows menu to display a palette of eight colors used by the Web. On the PC, select the Show Color Panel from the View menu (F6). Select an object (text, an image, a table, an element on the Inspector, and so on) and drag a color from the panel onto the selection. The selected object changes to the color you selected. Note that the Font Color menu in the toolbar also changes to indicate the color selected.

Figure 2.19
Drag and drop colors from the handy Color panel onto objects.

Summary

Congratulations! You have just completed a quick tour of PageMill. This chapter discussed the main PageMill Edit window, the Inspector, the Pasteboard, and the out-Of-Place editor. You reviewed the menus and toolbars available for your use in formatting your pages and learned how to toggle between Preview and Edit modes to see your progress.

You've now navigated through most of the basic functions you need to create a Web page. You're ready to dive into PageMill's advanced features and build even cooler Web pages.

Chapter 3

Getting Started

PageMill is a tool. You use PageMill to ease your development of electronic publications. But, electronic publications are still publications and need to be planned before they are executed. Without planning, your Web pages will just be disjointed bits of data that no one will want to read. Because you are not just developing a single document, but rather a collection of interrelated information (called a Web site), you need to visualize your goals before setting cursor to screen. This chapter describes how to plan your Web pages, design efficient graphics, file organization strategies, and layout your Web site as a whole.

The Internet is in its infancy. There are organizations dedicated to setting standards for the tools used to manage the World Wide Web, such as HTML, security issues, and so forth, but browser developers, commercial artists, and businesses are rushing in to use the Web way ahead of the planners. The result is a tower of Babel where you must plan your site to please users of browsers that support every whiz-bang extension to HTML while catering to users whose browsers cannot display graphics, and whose modems will not support large file sizes at adequate speeds.

There are two parts to the design of a Web site:

■ **Content Design.** What are you going to publish? What is the purpose of your site? Who is its audience? How will you structure the site to enable that audience to move efficiently through its pages? Call this the strategic step.

■ **Appearance Design.** When you have determined the contents of the site, you need to design the themes, look, and methodology of the site. You must take into account copyright laws, the logistics of downloading your graphics and how it affects the readability of your site, and other issues dealing with the tactics of site building.

Content Design: Determining What to Say

The goal of a Web site is to communicate. How you communicate is based on what it is you want to communicate and who you are speaking to. So, when you plan your Web site, first answer the following three questions:

■ **What is the intended purpose of your site?** For example, will you be using it to train new personnel in your company across the U.S., or to let people know what is being done about animal cruelty issues in New Hampshire?

■ **Who is the site's audience?** For example, as the Webmaster of Apple Computer, you know your audience consists of well educated, computer-savvy, urban professionals seeking information about computer updates and computer-related news.

■ **How will you construct your site?** Given the site's purpose and the audience, how can you design the site to meet your goals? For example, should your site be one long page or should you break your content into several pages? Will it be in database form or be very graphical, but not contain much information?

We'll take these planning considerations one by one in the following paragraphs.

Intended Purpose of Your Site

A good design rule is "Form follows function." The first thing you have to do is figure out what you are doing. Why are you building this site? What do you want to say? People surf the Web looking for many things. Sometimes they are doing research for a book they are writing. Other times they are looking for a specific piece of information about a subject, such as discipline issues in child rearing, and other times they want to buy something, such as a piece of software. And sometimes, they are just looking around to have fun.

Each type of purpose uses different ways of navigating. For example, if you are researching, you probably use a search engine, such as Yahoo or Alta Vista to locate Web sites by URL that cover the topic you are seeking. If you are looking for people who have answers to specific questions you are asking, such as should you use "time outs" for disciplining a 2-year old, you would start with a search engine and then use hypertext links within sites that describe other sites to jump to those destinations that meet your needs. If you are shopping, you look for a catalog or store site that uses forms and databases to present products that you can order online. So the purpose of the site drives how its navigation features are designed (in other words, how people move around your site).

So, the first task of Web site planning is to figure out what you want to be. Do you want your site to be a catalog, a store, a public relations vehicle introducing a product, a library that points to other sites, a newspaper, or an artist's studio? Each type of site has a different content and way of presenting information.

One way of figuring out what you want to be is to surf the Web and look at other people's sites. By researching what's out there, you can determine how jazzy you want to make the site, where you want to take the reader, how often the site will need updating (how current is the information you are providing?), and so forth.

What the site is about dictates how it looks. (A site dedicated to listing a compendium of other sites is different from a site that shows off a company's products because the first site will have a lot of text and linked headings with very few graphics and the latter will probably be more artsy with lots of images linked to descriptions of products and services you are selling.)

Use a search engine, such as Yahoo or Alta Vista, to identify sites from your industry. The search engine lets you search by keywords and categories, and displays a listing of hypertext that fits your search criteria. Go to each identified site and bookmark those that appeal to what you want to say. Note how the home pages of other sites in your industry work: are the sites attractive, well-organized, with up-to-date content (so the browser will stay to see what is on the other pages)? Note the purpose of the site; for example, if the site's purpose is name recognition, it will present a concise home page that leads to pages stating the mission state-ment, company history, and so forth. If the site is a store, note the use of images to lead readers to the products they want to buy. Also note technical issues, such as how fast the site downloads to your browser.

 ## Tip

It is OK to take the ideas behind such sites. You can even copy the source HTML to see how a site was constructed. Save the source document and open it in PageMill to display its WYSIWYG image and underlying HTML.

When you dissect the site, replace its text and pictures with your own. Do not take any content, such as pictures or text, without permission.

 ## Caution

A good rule of thumb is that every image you find on the Web or take from a clipart collection is copyrighted material. Get permission to use anything that you do not create yourself. Even photographs in the public domain are copied from something that may have a copyright.

Speak to a lawyer if you have questions about using an item. Check out the InfoLawAlert newsletter at `http://www.infolawalert.com` for information about electronic copyright and patent law issues.

Throughout this book we use Adobe's tutorial pages as examples, so let's continue here, and be a company's public relations vehicle advertising our products, called "Earth&Ware."

Now that we have figured out what we want to be, we have to determine who we are speaking to.

The Audience

Your audience might be the most important consideration when creating Web pages. After all, you're publishing information for the public. Understanding characteristics of your audience helps you make smart decisions when designing your page. For example, your Mac-savvy, upper-income, educated consumer will be looking for snazzy, up-to-the minute plug-ins, such as fading text, animations, frames, an so forth.

The "newbie" (someone who is just starting out) doesn't know what to look for and needs more navigation aids and less "noise:" Researchers want quick, no-frills connections to what they are searching for and often turn off the graphics to speed up their searches (they are also under monetary constraints and time on line costs plenty, depending on the service provider).

If you are designing the site for people who know your industry, in our case Earth-friendly household items, you should give them good visual cues to quickly move where they want. Humor and up-to-date information are good ways to keep these people coming back to your site. Your goal is a Bookmark—readers that mark the URL of your site so that they can return again.

Thus, the audience dictates both the content and the appearance of your site. If you determine, as in our example, that you want to attract buyers of environmentally friendly products, you have to then determine whether you want existing customers to come to your site, or are trying to attract new customers who never thought of the subject. Existing customers will not require as much advertising via special effects as do new customers who you want to remember your site through its visual impact.

Other important issues include deciding what browser capabilities and what type of Internet connection (modem, ISDN, T-1, and so on) your audience will have. This helps you decide what information you serve, how you serve it, and how big or how many graphics and images you place on your page.

The Structure of Your Site

Now that you have determined what you want to say and who you want to say it to, you get down to what tools you will need to attract and keep your audience and communicate your information to them. Different types of sites require different appearances. For example, the simple library site uses hypertext links to other URLs outside of the site and a single home page. Informational sites may use graphics that are imagemapped or buttoned (turned into links) to divide the page into subject areas, and break up a long document into shorter pieces that can be navigated using these buttons and visual cues. An example of this type of site is A Space Made For Moms site (see Figure 3.1) at (`http://www.cs.cmu.edu/afs/cs.cmu.edu/user/jeanc/mom/space.html`).

Show room sites such as the Internet Shopping Network (see Figure 3.2) at (`http://www.isn.com`) use the metaphor of a shopping catalog to advertise special sales, and lead customers to products through the use of imagemaps and buttons, as well as indexed lists.

Corporate presence sites, such as the Apple Computer, Inc. site (`http://www.apple.com`), use splashy graphics, textual effects, frames, and other new technology plug-ins to get people's attention.

Figure 3.1
This site uses a bibliographic approach to provide information on child rearing issues for working moms.

Figure 3.2
This is an interactive shopping network site that requires CGIs for database retrieval, imagemaps, and forms.

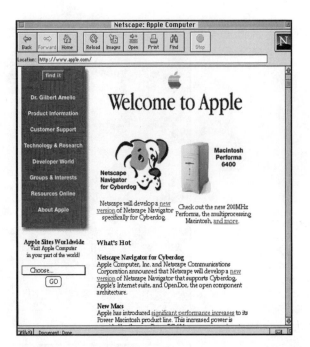

Figure 3.3
Corporate sites use a more commercial art approach to get noticed and provide easily accessed information about the company and its products.

Another factor to consider in designing how your site will operate is what technical tools you will need to make your site function. Catalog sites, such as the ISN site shown in Figure 3.2, use fill-in forms for credit cards and require special security encryption software, CGI (common gateway interface) form processing programs on the server, as well as database CGI programs to search and retrieve information about products. You have to speak to your Webmaster about what CGIs are available and whether you can add others, if needed (such as server-side imagemap CGIs). Many Webmasters will not allow you to place foreign programs on the server, or to reserve a special place for these intruders so that the rest of the server remains safe from any corrupting influences.

One last consideration is the fact that you do not know what lies on the other side of the Web. Do not assume that what you see in PageMill is the same as what you will see in a Web browser. Items such as fonts, colors, and graphics will look different because each browser can interpret HTML differently and each reader can set his or her browser to read documents differently.

There are as many different Web site design philosophies as there are Web publishers, so create your Web sites in a form that feels right for your anticipated browsers.

For More Information

Check out Microsoft's Site Builder Network site (`http://www.microsoft.com/sitebuilder/site06.htm`) for a wealth of white papers, tools, how-to-guides, standards, and software you can use to plan the conceptualization and tactical phases of your site design project. A great article you can find there is "So You Want to Build A Web Site? Everything You Need to Consider From Initial Planning Through Launch," by Dominick J. Dellino.

Appearance Design

Now that you have figured out the purpose of your site, who the site is for, and how to get there (the structure of the site), it is time to actually design the physical layout of the Web site. The act of designing the physical body of the site is called "prototyping." Set up a specification for the site that includes seven pieces of information:

- **What information are you going to include in the site?** Collect a list of all of the information you want to include, such as mission statements, product descriptions, product pictures, URLs you want to link the site to, history you want to include, other graphics, and so forth.

- **How is the site supposed to work?** Create a thumbnail sketch of all of the pages in your site. Place arrows where you want your readers to be able to move. These storyboards create a visual picture of the site on paper that you can use to ensure that you don't forget anything, and that everything is properly positioned so that the links will work.

- **Determine where you are going to place links, and what they will link to.** PageMill makes creating links almost effortless (see Chapter 5), but you do have to identify both sides of a link before actually creating the hypertext, button, or imagemap. Your storyboard will help you make sure that you have given your reader ways to return to the Home page, move up and down long documents, move horizontally between pages, and jump out and back into your site easily.

■ **Collect your materials.** Create a resource file (both paper and electronic) containing all of the text and graphic images you will use on the pages. Make sure that you have permissions to use any copyrighted materials (including photographs, clipart, documents, and other previously published works).

■ **Build the Site.** Construct non-working prototypes of your pages in PageMill that include all of the technologies, such as hypertext links, frames, form parts, tables, in-line graphics, splashsheets (titlebars), imagemaps, buttons, and so forth, you will use. This builds the HTML you need and gives you a list of CGIs you have to check out with your Webmaster. You can also determine where you may need actual HTML programming to accomplish your ends (such as special Java or ActiveX parts, or non-supported HTML such as style sheets).

■ **Test the site.** Check out what the site looks like under a number of different browsers, such as Netscape Navigator 2 and 3, Microsoft Internet Explorer 1 and 2, or Mosaic. Check out the site with beta versions of these browsers, as well. Look at the sizing of text and graphics on different computer platforms, such as Macs and PCs, as well as on different resolution monitors. Check the speed of graphic image downloads on different modem models and speeds.

■ **Upload your site to your Internet provider's server.** Find out how to upload the HTML document(s) to the Web server. Different providers have different methods and requirements for uploading. Some providers use FTP protocols, others let you have direct access to the server. Set up your PageMill Preferences accordingly (setting up the Resource folder, Remote Servers, and so forth). See the end of this chapter and Chapter 11 "Putting It All Together" for more details.

Collecting Your Data

Go back to the strategic decisions you made on what the site is about, who its audience is, and what it will look like. Now, create an outline or flow-chart that diagrams all of the parts of the site: their subject matter and related art work. Outlining lets you see the big picture to ensure that you do not forget anything. In our example of Earth&Ware, this means collecting a list of all of the products we want to include in the site, as well as descriptions, pictures, prices, and so forth. We might also like to include a description of our company's philosophy (being environmentally sound and all that), a description of our employees, including photos and URLs to any home pages they may have produced, a way to write to our company (an email address), ways to order information or products from our company (does the site require a database connection or form?). As you are outlining, you will discover what PageMill tools you will need, such as forms, tables, frames, and so forth. These can be marked on the outline.

Determining How the Site Will Work

The next task is to take this conglomeration of data, pictures, plans, and so forth and list every page you plan to develop and its contents. In other words, break down the outline you just developed into discrete pieces (consider each piece as a page or file) and show how the page will relate to other pages in the site. You can determine these interrelationships by drawing a flow chart. Figure 3.4 illustrates a functional schematic outlining the separate pages and their interconnections of the My Maya Web Site, a site I planned and worked up to learn the features of PageMill 2.0.

Note that the schematic displays different levels, illustrating where various imagemaps or buttons point, not only on the home page, but on all pages. Keep revising the schematic and adding details, such as which pages hold forms, which images are imagemaps, which images are buttons, whether you are including sound files, QuickTime movies, or virtual reality maps, and so on. This schematic will grow with your site. You can later include the schematic as a *site map*, such as the one produced by Progressive Network's

RealAudio site (`http://www.realaudio.com/sitemap.html`) shown in Figure 3.5, as a page on your site to assist your readers in gaining a "bird's eye view" of your site.

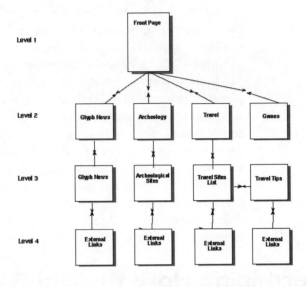

Figure 3.4
Draw a flow chart showing the various links from your home page to outlying pages at your site.

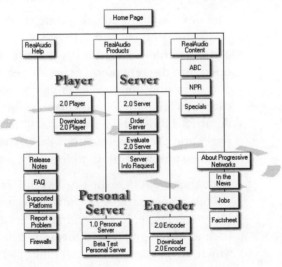

Figure 3.5
Draw a site map to help visualize the relationships of pieces of your site. Then use the map as a page.

Determining Your Links

There are several rules of thumb to remember when designing the navigation features of your Web site. Joseph O. Holmes clearly enumerates these points in his article "How to Organize a Web

Site" in the August 1996 inaugural issue of *MacADDICT* (`http://www.macaddict.com`). Pages from Apple's new Personal Internet Launcher (`http://myhome.apple.com/home/welcome/[yourname]`) are used to illustrate Joe's lessons. Note that not only does Apple create a personalized home page for each subscriber, it also lets you select the subjects you want on your page, the art style used, and buttons to further customize the page by creating links to your own favorite sites.

■ Use the home page as a table of contents (as shown in Figure 3.6) directing your reader to the various subjects on your site.

Imagemaps link to other pages

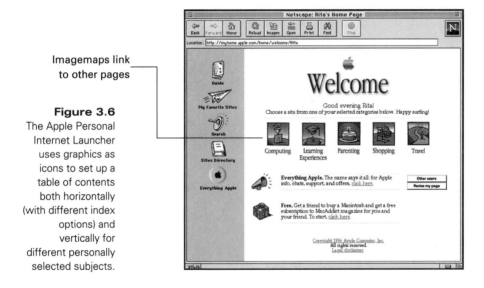

Figure 3.6
The Apple Personal Internet Launcher uses graphics as icons to set up a table of contents both horizontally (with different index options) and vertically for different personally selected subjects.

■ Make sure that your pages fit on standard browser windows and that the pages are not too long. A good rule of thumb is to allow no more than two to four 640×480 pixels-wide screens per page to limit the need to scroll.

■ Most information should be no more than two clicks from the home page. Get rid of pages that serve only to point to deeper information. Direct the reader to that information from the home page.

■ Limit your load time by limiting the size of a page and its image sizes.

■ Provide a "Return to Home" link on every page but the home page (as illustrated in Figure 3.7).

Hotspot back to Home

Figure 3.7
Selecting a graphic image on the Home page jumps you to its linked page. Note that the index hotspots are carried across to each linked page to help you navigate.

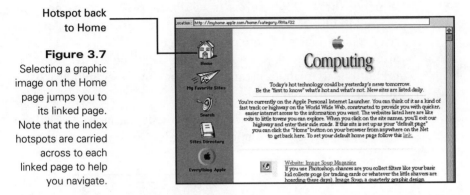

■ People can leap into the middle of your site and get lost. Use repeating icons to point readers back to information on other pages (see Figure 3.8).

■ If you do create long pages, break up the page with links to the top or bottom of the document after each logical section.

■ Go ahead and break these rules, but keep the goal of easily accessed content in mind at all times.

Figure 3.8
At the bottom of the page are the same graphic images letting you jump to other pages on the site.

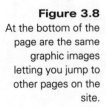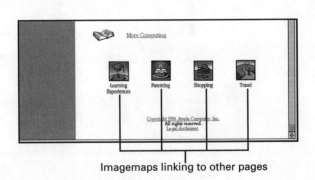

Imagemaps linking to other pages

Keep in mind how you want your reader to move around the site. The headings of the different sections also serve as destination markers linked via hypertext bookmarks later in the process.

Streamline your text and provide keywords to allow readers to "scan" through your data to get its meaning without deep reading.

Collect Your Materials

Now you are down to the nitty-gritty of creating those "wow!" visuals, buttons, splash banners, and so forth. Because HTML does not specify any specific fonts, if you want any creative use of fonts, shows, drop caps, and so forth, you must create them. Your best tools are an image processor, such as Adobe Photoshop, an illustration package, such as Fractal Design Painter, Adobe Illustrator, or Macromedia Freehand, and a word processor, such as Microsoft Word or Corel WordPerfect. In preparing your files for inclusion on the Web page, you must be cognizant of how each image will appear (its width on the computer screen) as well as how long the image will take to download. Remember, almost everything you place on a page will be a graphic, whether it is a background image (such as a tiled pattern), a inline image and layered text, or future images for image maps and buttons. Since each image is a file, and each file must download separately, the most important issue to consider when designing your files is color management (lessening the time it takes to download a page).

Most readers of your page will be using computers that lack power and modems that lack baud rate. Most users are running 14.4K or 28.8K baud modems. With this tool, a 60K file takes about a minute to download (1 second per kilobyte). A good target size for your files is half of that, or 30K, which will download in 30 seconds with a 14.4K baud modem. Get those file sizes as small as possible.

Here are some hints on how to manage file sizes.

Select the Right File Format

There are two image formats supported by the Web: JPEG and GIF. Both have pluses and minuses in terms of file size versus image quality. JPEG (Joint Photographic Expert Group) compresses color bitmapped images (scanned images such as photographs are bitmapped). JPEG enables variable rates of compression (called *lossy* compression). With this compression scheme, images tend to lose some of their quality when compressed and decompressed by browsers. Use JPEG formats for soft photographic images continuous in tone (avoid gradients and three dimensional pictures). Don't use the JPEG format for line drawings or images with wide areas of flat colors. These line drawings and broad color-based drawings will appear distorted after decompression.

Set your image compression at Maximum in Photoshop to get the lowest compression factor so that little data is lost during compression. JPEG produces smaller files with 24-bit images (16.7 million colors) than GIF format can produce with its 8-bit image (256 color) limit.

When selecting compression factors for JPEG images, remember that most of your readers only have 8-bit (256 color) monitors available for viewing your pictures. In addition, each browser interprets higher color bit rates differently. Try to limit your colors to under 256 by removing colors from your images in Photoshop. In fact, even if your file is smaller using JPEG than GIF, because the browser performs the decompressing of JPEG images, these take longer to download than larger GIF images.

CompuServe's GIF (Graphics Interchange Format) is the industry standard for Web pages. GIF supports moving just about any type of graphic between computer platforms without a loss of quality. It does this by supporting only 256 colors (8-bit images). Use the Indexed Color setting in Photoshop to save a graphic with 256 colors. GIF uses LZW compression (also called *lossless* compression) and thus does not lose any quality when compressed and then decompressed. The compression is performed by looking for repeating patterns of color along each horizontal line and compressing those pixels (deleting them but keeping track of the location of the deletions so that the colors can be replaced during decompression). Those images with the most repeating patterns horizontally create the smallest files. Thus, flat colored images are small in GIF format without losing quality. One way to limit the amount of vertical pixels is to turn off dithering (a way of increasing the detail in an image by adding intermediate colors) in Photoshop before converting your images to 8-bit color. You need to tune your graphics (add and subtract colors) and visually determine where degradation begins to occur. Stick right on the edge to keep your files small (under 40K).

Tip

Use Lynda Weinman's Browser-safe Palette (available on the Web at `http://www.lynda.com/hex.html`) in Photoshop to ensure your images are optimized at 216 colors so they look good on both Macs and PCs. This palette works best on images with flat colors or that use a lot of a single color.

GIFs have a benefit over JPEG formats in that you can create transparent images. Transparency provides the illusion of irregularly shaped computer files that you can use to lay a graphic on top of a background and let the background shine through the image. This is also called *masking*. Avoid transparency if you see a halo effect when laying the graphic on top of another color (this is an area of colored edge around a picture, also called *anti-aliasing*). Web technology does not provide a way to avoid anti-aliasing. If you are using a solid background without a pattern, make sure to create an image with the same color background. This creates the illusion of an aliased edge on the graphic (no halo).

More Tips for Speeding Up Download Times

Here are more tricks for speeding up download times.

■ Reuse your images on a page. The first time an image is used, it is stored on the user's computer. That stored version is displayed any subsequent time the image is called for.

■ Use textured or gradated background images so that you can make your GIF files transparent and avoid anti-aliasing effects.

■ When using tiled patterns, make the tiles small so that they load quickly.

■ Use specific color schemes on your pages. The fewer colors used, the better the compression and faster the downloading.

■ Try to use 6- or 4-bit color in your images to create smaller files.

For More Information

Check out the Microsoft Site Builder Network site at `http://www.microsoft.com/sitebuilder/site06.htm` for more articles and tips on Web construction. Read the article called "Decreasing Download Time Through Effective Color Management" by Kate S. Knight.

Construct Your Site

Now that you have created all of these beautiful graphics, amazing movies, animated GIF files, sound effects, and so forth, you need to put them together on a document called a Web page. A series of linked pages is called a Web site.

The first page your reader sees when going to your site is always named index.html (if working on a Mac) or index.htm (when working on a PC that only supports 3-letter suffixes). This page becomes the default document and can be your actual home page or an entrance vestibule enabling your reader to choose between a text-only version or advanced browser version of your site (should you decide to create these options).

The following paragraphs introduce the components of the Home page and Supporting pages.

The Home Page

Web sites are broken into sections and pages. Sections are parts of a page, often divided by headings (type larger than the rest of the content), rules (horizontal lines), or graphics.

A home page can introduce the reader to your site, give some information about what is offered at the site, or tell who created the site and why. Of course, all this information depends on the type of site you are creating.

Home pages can have a clickable imagemap with pictures, icons, or images that are navigation guides for the Web site (see Figure 3.9). A simpler way to display this is to offer a table of contents that links viewers to specific places on the Web site.

Figure 3.9
A home page
enabling you to
navigate through
the Web site via a
clickable imagemap.

Support Pages

Support pages, on the other hand, can include a common graphic
as a header to give the site consistency and identity, but the
information within delves deeper into the Web site's topic. The
following figures use the site I built for myself using Apple's
Personal Internet Launcher (`http://www.apple.com`). The home
page of the site uses a series of graphics you select to indicate
various Web site groups you can travel to. Each button leads you
to a supporting page that lists these sites. You then use hypertext
links on the supporting pages to jump to those sites (see Figure
3.10).

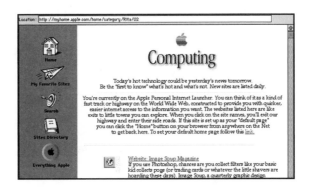

Figure 3.10
Clicking the
Computer icon on
the Home page
leads you to the
Supporting page on
Computers.

Design Your Graphics for Navigation

Graphic images are not just pretty pictures, but ways to find your way around a Web site. Some graphics advertise important subjects in a site. These images can be imagemapped (where hypertext links are added to designated portions of a graphic, which when selected jump you to a supporting page describing the subject of the image). Some graphics are used as stand-alone icons—representations of ideas. These graphics can be placed in a toolbar and linked, directing readers from any page to other areas concerning the subject of the image (such as back to the Home page, to a Feedback page, and so forth). The more redundant your application of toolbars and icons, the better, because your goal is to let your readers know exactly where they are in your site and where they can go at all times.

Figures 3.11 through 3.14 are from a Web site called "Rabbit in the Moon," (www.he.net/~nmcnelly/) by Nancy McNelly, which illustrates the use of images as maps, icons, and art.

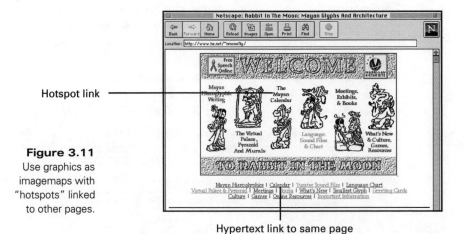

Hotspot link

Figure 3.11
Use graphics as imagemaps with "hotspots" linked to other pages.

Hypertext link to same page

Note that each graphic on the imagemap is a hotspot pointing to a separate page.

You can also jump to the page by clicking the words beneath the map. Each page has hypertext links to assist you in navigating up and down, in and out.

Lastly, each page presents you with a way to return to the home page.

Hypertext links ───────

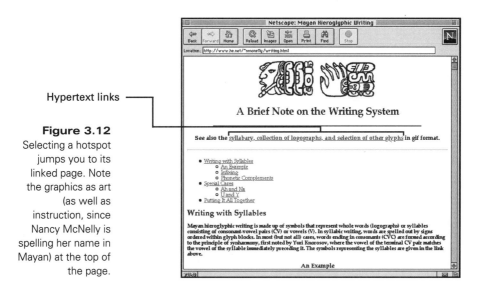

Figure 3.12
Selecting a hotspot jumps you to its linked page. Note the graphics as art (as well as instruction, since Nancy McNelly is spelling her name in Mayan) at the top of the page.

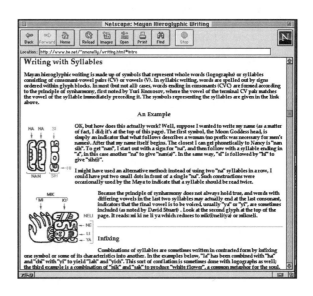

Figure 3.13
Clicking the hypertext table of contents jumps you to that location in the document.

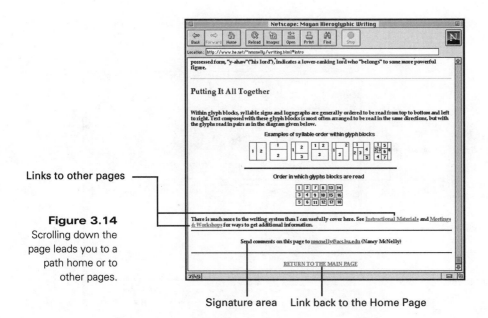

Links to other pages ——————

Figure 3.14
Scrolling down the
page leads you to a
path home or to
other pages.

Signature area   Link back to the Home Page

Testing Your Site

When you have placed all of your art work, text files, hypertext links, advanced plug-ins, and so forth, into your pages, you need to make sure that not only do they all work, but also that they appear and work consistently under most browsers. To do this, open your Web pages using different versions of Netscape Navigator, especially the oldest (version 1) and the newest (version 3). If you can, get a hold of a beta version of Netscape Navigator to ensure that the page remains compatible. Also, do the same testing for Microsoft Internet Explorer (Versions 1 and 2). Make sure to click all links to see if you go where you are supposed to, and check the appearance and download times of your images. You need to test your browsers on both the Mac and PC platforms to see if your site operates cross-platform.

You need to correct all bugs in hypertext links and imagemaps. Go back to Photoshop and tweak those images that load slowly or appear compromised on either the Mac or PC platforms.

Setting Up Your Resources

One of the most important tasks you must do while constructing your site is to set up the folders holding each type of image and text. The best time to do this is when you are collecting materials and producing your Photoshop images.

Most servers run under some flavor of Unix, including Macintosh network servers. Set up your folders under Windows 95 or the MacOS by grouping files according to type (GIFs with GIFs and HTML with HTML). PageMill creates a separate Image folder to store files it converts from other file formats to GIF or HTML. Then, place these format-based folders into folders by location, such as News page, Gallery page, and so forth. The folder system you devise on your Mac or PC will be converted to a system under Unix that uses "directories" and "subdirectories" equivalent to your top folder (the root directory) and all nested folders (the subdirectories) in the hierarchy. (You can recognize directories and subdirectories in Unix locator names—the URL you see at the top of the browser—by the use of back slashes and files by periods.)

Because Unix is unforgiving (meaning move a file, lose a link), it is a good idea to organize your Web resources carefully. Try to limit the number of items in a folder (or directory) to 15 to 25 files or pages. Try to limit the number of subdirectories (or subfolders in your folder hierarchy) to a depth of two because numerous directories create complex URLs as well as file management problems. Draw a map of your file structure (as illustrated in Figure 3.15) ensuring easy access to your files when you update your site. Add a button for "What's New" and a folder where you store updates to make it easy for a reader to scan what is new on the page prior to navigating around your site.

Organizing Your Files

PageMill assists your file organization by providing a pointer to the first folder in your Web site folder hierarchy (termed the *root folder* or *directory*). This folder becomes the lowest level in the directory on the Web server. PageMill and the Web server need to know where to look to find all of the images and text you use in your site. The folder name you place in the Preferences dialog box of PageMill identifies where your resources are stored and later tells the Unix server where to look to find your directories and subdirectories. The following task shows you how to tell PageMill where your files are stored, including any imagemap files (see Chapter 6 for a discussion of imagemaps and imagemap files) and plug-in files.

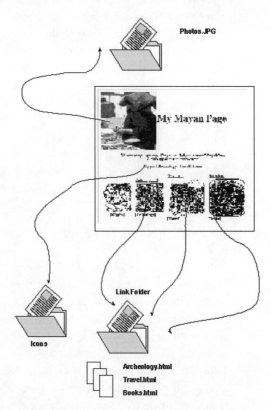

Figure 3.15
Draw a map of the files for each portion of your home page that ensures you have all of the images, links, PDF, and so forth, you need in the right places.

 ## Setting Up a Root Resource Folder

1 Select the Preferences command on the Edit menu. (On the PC you can also press the F2 function key.)

2 In the Mac Preferences dialog box, click the Resources icon on the left-hand frame In the PC Preferences box, click the Resources tab.

3 Click the folder icon in the Resource folder window (see Figure 3.16).

4 Select a folder location for your images in the Open dialog box. Click In Here.

5 Click OK in the Preferences dialog box to return to PageMill. Note in Figure 3.7 that the complete path for the image folder is now listed in the dialog box.

Mac

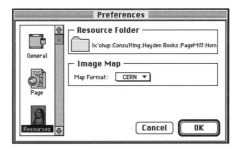

Windows

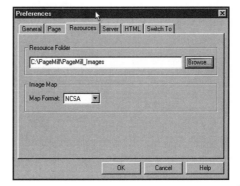

Figure 3.16
In the Resources window, click the Folder icon to identify the location of your image folder (also called a Resource folder).

If you are not going to manage your Web page yourself on a personal server located on your computer, you need to tell PageMill and the Web server how to find your top folder (the root directory). This is done by giving the folder (directory) a name that includes all of the directories the server must pass through to reach it. This is called the folder's *pathname.* You must type the complete pathname for the root directory of the remote server. Place this name in PageMill's Server window of the Preferences dialog box. Ask your Webmaster or the System Administrator for this name if you do not know it.

Summary

You now know how to plan the appearance, file structure, and graphics for your Web site. You know the importance of using pen and paper (or computer screen and program) to develop a design for your site and its accompanying documents prior to actually laying hands on PageMill.

Proper planning before constructing the actual Web pages saves you time later by preventing bugs from occurring due to missing files, too large files, improper color management of images, wrong file formats, or the wrong filing scheme.

In Chapter 4, you will begin the process of adding items to a Web page, including text and graphics.

Chapter 4

Text and Graphics Basics

PageMill makes entering and modifying text on a page easy. With features such as drag and drop, cut, paste, copy, and item selection using the mouse, PageMill feels like a mini-word processor. All the basic WYSIWYG features of the File and Edit menus, as well as window parts such as the close box, zoom box, resize box, and horizontal and vertical scroll bars exist in PageMill. This familiar interface enables you to get up and running quickly.

A PageMill Practicum

Now that you know where everything is located (having read Chapter 2), and you know how to design a Web site (having read Chapter 3), let's get familiar with PageMill in a more hands-on manner. Launch PageMill. If this is the first time you've launched the program, refer to the last page of the book for installation information. If not, close any open windows in PageMill and create a new page by selecting New Page from the File menu.

 Practicing With PageMill

1   At the blinking insertion point, type **Welcome to my first Web Page!**

2   Highlight the text.

3   Let's apply a logical style to our sentence. Select the Emphasis style from Style menu. The highlighted text is italicized, indicating emphasis.

4   Turn off the style by reselecting Emphasis in the Style menu. (You can also apply logical and physical styles at the same time by keeping Emphasis turned on and performing step 5.)

5   Now, let's make the sentence bold-faced. Select the Bold style from the Style menu or click the Bold button on the toolbar.

6   Center the sentence you typed. Click the Center Text alignment button in the toolbar. Click to the right of the exclamation point to deselect the text (see Figure 4.1).

Figure 4.1
You have started your Web page by using the word processing features of PageMill.

7   Move down the page one line by pressing the Return key on your keyboard twice.

8   Type **Welcome to My World**.

9   Highlight the text.

10 Let's make this sentence our title for the Web page by apply-ing a Heading paragraph style. Choose Heading from the Format menu and then select Largest Heading from its hierar-chical menu; or select Largest Heading from the Format pull-down menu on the toolbar. Figure 4.2 displays the results.

Figure 4.2
Your Web page now has a heading.

11 Click at the end of the text string to deselect the text.

12 Move down one line by pressing the Return key twice.

13 Let's make the next text you type a simple paragraph. Select Paragraph from the Format menu. (You can also select Para-graph from the Format pull-down menu on the toolbar.) Make sure that the toolbar shows that the Bold button is turned off, and type a "0" in the text size selector box (or use the arrows to move the number from its current "+3" to "0."

14 Make sure that the text you type is not centered, select the Left Text alignment button on the toolbar.

15 Type the following:

You've reached the home page of <Your Name>. Welcome! I'm just learning how to create Web pages using this great, new program called PageMill. If I had known it was this easy, I would have started long ago. This page is all about me. I hope you like it. Here's a picture of me.

16 Move down one line by pressing the Return key twice.

Placing an Image On Your Page

1 Now, let's place a graphic image on to the page. Click the Place Object button on the toolbar.

2 In the resulting Open File dialog box, select the file milkhead.gif from the Images folder from the Earth&Ware Tutorial folder on the accompanying CD-ROM.

3 Click Place. Figure 4.3 displays the results of your efforts.

Figure 4.3
The image is placed
at your cursor
(left-aligned).

Adding a Horizontal Rule to Your Page

Let's divide the paragraph and graphic from the bottom of the page by adding a line (called a horizontal rule). Click the Horizontal Rule button in the toolbar. PageMill adds a line. You can resize the line (and make it thicker or thinner) by grabbing its size handles and pushing and pulling the rule.

Giving Your Page a Name

1   Move the cursor to the Page Title text box.

2   Delete any text (such as the word "Untitled") by highlighting it and pressing Delete. Click to place the insertion point in the text box.

3   Type **The <Your Name> Home Page** and press the Return key (see Figure 4.4).

Looking At the Results Of Your Work

Click the Edit Mode toggle button in the upper-right corner. The screen changes to a mock-browser and the toggle button changes to the Preview button (see Figure 4.4). Click the button again to return to the Edit mode window.

You have just used most of the text editing and image placement features of PageMill to create a Web page. The following sections describe each step in detail, adding tricks and formatting techniques to your basic knowledge.

Figure 4.4
Here is your Web page as others will view it with their browsers.

Page Formatting

A *page* on the Web is a document in word processing parlance. It can be as long or short as you want it to be, but generally keeping them to one or two screenfuls of information is a good idea. (See Chapter 3 for hints on how to create page sizes that load fast and are easy to navigate.)

PageMill provides tools to set the overall appearance of your page, such as adding text or hypertext link activity colors, background images, and set the parameters for your Web site. You arrange how the overall page will appear in the Page screen of the Inspector.

See Chapter 3 for a discussion of how to use patterns to work with anti-aliasing problems of graphics (where halos appear around graphics when they are set against a background), as well as keep graphic image files small by making their backgrounds transparent.

Creating a New Page

1 Open a new PageMill document by choosing New Page from the File menu (or by pressing Command-N).

2 When starting a new page, give your document a title; enter text in your document's Title text box. For this example, type **I'm a Web Publisher** (see Figure 4.5), and it will appear in the title bar of a Web browser's window when someone loads your page.

3 Save your page by choosing Save (Command-S on the Mac, Ctrl-S on the PC) from the File menu. After your page is saved, you'll notice that the Page icon (at the left of the tool bar) is no longer gray, but is usable (see Figure 4.6). The Page icon is used for creating drag-and-drop hypertext links.

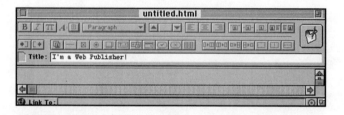

Figure 4.5
Entering text into the document's Page Title field.

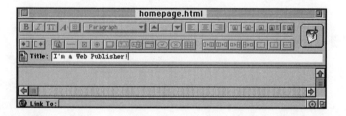

Figure 4.6
The Page icon becomes active after you save your document.

Naming Your Files

To avoid the dreaded "File Not Found" message keep these three main conventions in mind when naming your files:

■ If you know that your site will be residing on a Windows-based server, make sure that your filename is no more than or fewer than eight characters in length. Even though Windows 95 supports longer file names, older Windows 3.1 and DOS-based operating systems do not.

■ Avoid placing any spaces between words. Use the underscore
(_) character to indicate spaces between words. For example,
if you want to name your file "My Home Page" call the file
"My_Home_Page.html".

■ Use .htm as a suffix rather than .html. DOS can only read
filenames in the 8.3 format—eight characters with a three-
character suffix. homepage.htm, for example, would be a
correct filename, but homepages.html would not (nine
characters and a four character suffix).

You can have PageMill save your files with an .htm suffix by
selecting Preferences from the Edit menu and choosing .htm
from the file suffixes pop-up menu. Alternatively, you can make
the change each time you save the file.

Make it a habit to place the file type as a suffix in your filename.
For example, if you create a graphic called "my Dog Spot" in GIF
format, call the file my dog spot.gif. If the same file is in JPEG
format, call it my dog spot.jpg. It is a good practice to document
types, because you may not be the one maintaining the Web site
after it is placed on the server and the future Webmaster may not
be able to tell from your file names what format your files are in.

When you save your document, PageMill adds the .html suffix to
your filename. It's a good idea to keep this suffix because the
.html suffix is how Windows and Unix servers recognize that they
are dealing with a Web page.

Using the Inspector to Format the Page

Use the Inspector palette to set up background and foreground
colors for your page, as well as how your text and hypertext links
are colored. Use the Background Image box to add patterns or
pictures to your page's background. When you open a new document and the Inspector palette, the Page tab is selected and its
screen is displayed (see Figure 4.7).

Tip

The Inspector remains open but is not active when the document is in Preview mode. If the Inspector doesn't seem to be working, make sure your document is in Edit mode.

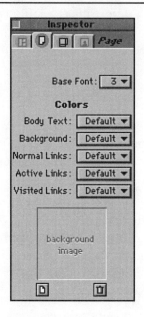

Figure 4.7
The Page screen in the Inspector.

Manipulating Body Text Color

In the Inspector you can adjust the color of both the body text and the page background.

 Tip

There are ways to get around a major shortcoming of HTML, namely that you can have only one color on a page background. For example, create a table with a single horizontal cell and give that cell a separate color. You can add a vertical column in a second table and make it another color. See Chapter 7 for a discussion of the many ways to use tables as layout enhancement tools in your pages. Although any color change you make on the Page screen affects the total page, you can get around this shortcoming by using tables and frames and inserting text into these areas. This text you can give a separate color.

Changing Body Text Color

1 With Page mode active in the Inspector, select Custom on the Body Text pop-up menu. The standard Windows 95 or Apple Color window appears.

Mac

2 If the wheel appears black, slide the horizontal scroll bar up to change the hue. When you have the colors at the brightness level you wish to use, click the desired color in the circle (see Figure 4.8).

Windows

You can use the Custom Color button to change or add to the basic colors. See your Windows 95 help page for more information

3 Click OK.

Mac

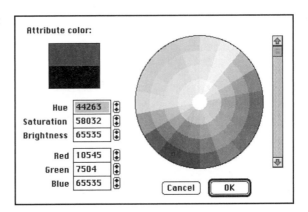

Windows

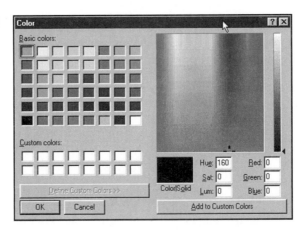

Figure 4.8
Use the Apple Color Wheel to create a custom color for body text, Background, and Hyperlinks.

Tip

Try to limit the number of colors you use to under 216 (8-bit) colors so that your page looks good on both Mac and PC monitors. Use Lynn Weinman's Browser Color Selector mentioned in Chapter 3 to make sure you are using colors that most browsers can display.

Manipulating Background Color

PageMill enables you to change the background color of your page (the color of the window displayed to the viewer). A Web page's default background color is light gray.

Background color is changed the same way text color is (see previous section). There is an easy alternative way to change the colors of your body text, backgrounds, and hypertext using the Color Panel.

Changing Background Color Using the Color Panel

1   Open the Inspector and select Page Mode if it is not selected.

2   Select Show Color Panel on the Window View menu.

3   When the Color Panel appears, drag the color you want onto the options box in the Inspector you want to alter (in this case Background).

4   The new color is copied on to the options box and is reflected on the page (see Figure 4.9).

To revert to the original color of the background or text, select Default from the appropriate pop-up menu. To customize a color, select Custom from the pop-up menu and follow the procedure you used to change the body text color using the Color Wheel.

Tip

When you use the Color Panel to apply colors, you can only drag and drop colors dilineated on the panel. You can change colors by replacing an existing color with a new customized color from the Color Wheel. To display the Color Wheel, double-click color. You cannot add colors to the Color Panel beyond the 16 available. You will lose a color to add a color. Be careful that you only use colors contained in the safe color palette for Netscape and Internet Explorer. See the CD-ROM for a copy of Lynn Weinmann's safe color palette for Photoshop.

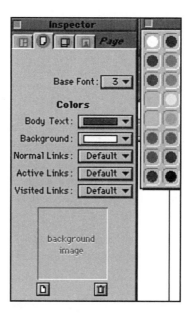

Figure 4.9
Use the Color Panel to click and drag colors onto the Inspector (or directly onto the PageMill page).

Manipulating Background Images

Sure, changing the color of your background is cool, but that's only the beginning. With PageMill, you also can use an image, tiled in the background, for the background of your document.

In the Images folder of the Earth&Ware Tutorial Folder, find the file called paper1.gif. (When you do this, arrange the windows on your screen so that you can see the Inspector.) Drag paper1.gif onto the square with the words background image in it in the Inspector. You can also use the Open File dialog box to insert an image by clicking the Document icon under the Background box. This dialog box works like the Place Object process described earlier in the this chapter's practicum. Figure 4.10 displays the result.

Figure 4.10
The background changes to reflect a tiled version of the GIF file you inserted into the Inspector.

The paper1.gif file is about 96 pixels wide and 96 pixels high. When you drag this file onto the Inspector, a few things happen.

- The Inspector checks to make sure that the file is a GIF.

- If the file is in any other format, PageMill converts it to GIF format or rejects the image. (PageMill accepts PCX and PICT file formats and automatically converts them to GIF format. The program does not accept encapsulated PostScript (EPS) format files.)

- PageMill tiles the image across the background of your document. Because paper1.gif is relatively small, it gets tiled quite a few times across the background.

- You can see the results on the content area of the PageMill window and in the Background Image box.

Note

If you are working in the window where you changed the background color, you'll notice that the image you dragged to the Inspector has completely covered the background color. PageMill tiles background images so that they fit perfectly with the background and dynamically change to fit the size of the browser windows.

Try not to use dark or busy backgrounds (such as the one shown in Figure 4.11) because it makes your text difficult to read on top of such a pattern. Also avoid using all black backgrounds for the same reason. Black backgrounds have recently been used to protest Senator Exon's Internet Decency Act and support free speech on the Internet. Since the bill is currently frozen in the courts, you don't need to bother people's eyes with this startling background. Use a neutral pattern or watermark, such as is shown in Figure 4.12, to assist the reader in following along with your thoughts on your page.

Figure 4.11
Avoid dark or busy patterns in your background because they are difficult to read through (and sometimes slow to download).

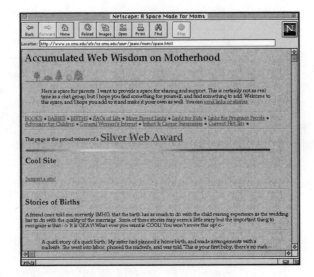

Figure 4.12
Use a neutral
pattern that assists
the reader in
following along your
page.

 ## Deleting a Background

To delete a background image, click the small garbage can beneath the image in the lower-right corner of the Inspector. Your old background returns, including any color adjustments you might have made.

Manipulating Hypertext Link Colors

Earlier you read that changing the color of the text affects text on the total page. This is not completely true. You can adjust the color of text designated as a hypertext link.

Three types of hypertext links are available:

■ Normal: Hypertext links that have not yet been explored

■ Active: Hypertext links that are currently selected

■ Visited: Hypertext links that have been explored

Changing the color of links is not something you should do without forethought. Most browsers display normal (unvisited) links in blue text, active links in red, and visited links in purple. This means that when you come to a new Web page, you see blue links. These are links not yet explored. When you click a blue link, it becomes active and turns red (links are only active while the mouse button is down). From that point on, that page's link will be purple because you have already visited it. Most users have come to expect links to be displayed in these colors.

If you create a page where all normal links are displayed in red, you run the risk of someone visiting your page and thinking he or she has already been there. Or, if your visited links are displayed in blue, users will think the links lead to new information. So, as a rule, if you are going to change link colors, you should change all three types and choose colors that are different from the three default colors. Make normal links yellow, active links green, and visited links aqua, for example.

Adjusting Hypertext Link Colors

To adjust hypertext link colors, find the Normal Links, Active Links, and Visited Links options on in the Page screen of the Inspector. There are two ways to adjust the color of links: select Custom from the pull-down menu next to each and adjust the colors using the color wheel, or use the Color Panel to drag and drop colors on to the visible box next to each option.

Applying Existing Colors Using the Color Panel

Select the Color Panel command from the Windows menu. Drag the yellow color from the panel and drop it onto the Normal Links option box. The box and any existing links turn yellow. Now adjust the colors of the other links by dragging and dropping colors into their associated boxes.

Customizing Colors with the Color Wheel

If you want to change the color of a link, open the Color Wheel by selecting the Custom option from the links pop-up menu. When the wheel's dialog box appears, slide the scrollbar up to select the hue and brightness you want and click on a color (yellow, for example) on the wheel. Click OK. The color is displayed in the option box of the Inspector and all Normal Links appear in that color on your page.

But now you have a problem, because the Active link's default color is red, and red is similar to the new yellow color you selected for the regular links. You should pick a radically different color for Active Links so that they can be easily differentiated from your Normal Links. I'll pick green for Active Links. Drop the green spot from the open Color Panel on to the Active Link's option box to change this link type to green. You can also use the Color Wheel approach.

Lastly, adjust the Visited link color. You already used yellow and green. To really make Visited links stand out, make them black. Drop a black spot from the Color Panel on to the Visited Link option box or use the Color Wheel with the scroll bar pushed all the way down to the bottom so that the wheel appears black.

Now, in your document window, create a link to a file called link.html by typing **link.html** in the link location bar. The text you designate as a link should turn yellow. When the link becomes active, it turns green and when it is visited, it turns black.

Your Web page is set up. It is time to enter text and images to create the page. PageMill offers several toolbars to assist you in this task: Paragraph Formats, Character Formats, Insert Rules, and Place Object. We'll look at each type of formatting in the following paragraphs.

Paragraph Formatting

PageMill's toolbar and menus provide buttons and commands that let you apply styles, such as different size headings, paragraph style, various list styles, and an address style. In addition, you can justify and align your paragraphs around images or other objects.

Headings represent different sizes of text used to create titles for the sections of your Web page. A paragraph is defined by a hard return character at its end. Pressing the Return key on your keyboard starts a new paragraph. Therefore, paragraphs can be single lines, such as headings, or multiple lines.

Tip

If you want to apply formatting to an entire paragraph, click the mouse to position the cursor within the paragraph and apply the format. The entire paragraph changes to your selection.

Applying Heading Styles

Headings come in six sizes—Smallest through Largest, as shown in Figure 4.13. To turn text into a heading, highlight the text and choose the heading you want from the Heading submenu on the Format menu (or select a heading size from the six sizes shown in the Format pull-down menu on the toolbar).

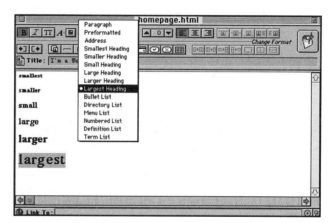

Figure 4.13
PageMill offers six heading sizes.

Applying Alignments

The toolbar in PageMill provides several options for aligning paragraphs: Left (text aligned on the left margin), Right (text aligned on the right margin), and Center (text centered). The default alignment is Left. PageMill won't let you *justify* text (right and left align, or align on both sides of the page at the same time). The Web does not support justified text.

Aligning Paragraphs

1 Open a new PageMill document.

2 Type the following text into the new document:

Greetings from Asbury Park, N.J.

The Wild, The Innocent and the E Street Shuffle

Born to Run

Darkness on the Edge of Town

3 Highlight the text and click the Center Align Text button from the toolbar (see Figure 4.14).

 Note

All objects, such as images and PDFs, as well as rules can also be aligned in this manner.

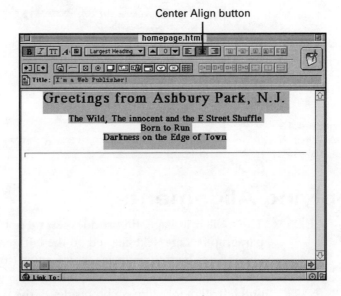

Center Align button

Figure 4.14
Center-align the text.

Adding Indentations

You can tell PageMill to add space on either side of your paragraph by using the Indentation buttons on the toolbar. (Note that they look slightly different on the PC but are located in the same place on the tool bar and act the same.) Clicking the Indent Left button removes space between the paragraph and the left side of your screen. Clicking Indent Right adds space between the paragraph and the left side of the screen.

Indenting Paragraphs

1 Open a new PageMill document and type the following:

Hieroglyphics
Mayan archeological sites
Mexican and Guatemalan travel
Books about the Maya

2 Select the text.

3 Pull down the Format menu and choose Indent Right (Cmd-+ or Ctrl-+) or click the Indent Right button on the toolbar. You can also press the key combination Command +] (see Figure 4.15). The text is moved to the right (see Figure 4.16).

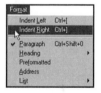

Figure 4.15
Using the Indent Right command...

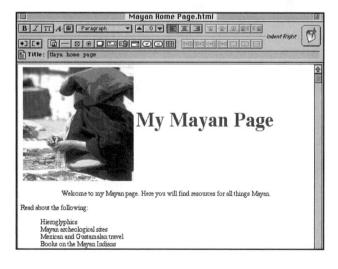

Figure 4.16
...moves text or a paragraph to the right.

Tip

Paragraphs are always indented left as a default.

You can keep moving text to the right by clicking the Indent Right button (think of it as a Tab button). Use the Indent Left button to move the text back toward the left side of the window.

Character Styles

You can change the appearance of individual words or letters within a paragraph by using the character style tools on the toolbar or menu bar. There are two ways to format characters in PageMill:

- **Logical styles.** Logical styles are assigned by the browser (in other words, how characters appear depends on how the Web browser interprets the data). You don't know in advance how the characters will look. Use logical styles if you are formatting text objectively. (You might notice that logical styles are rarely used any more, being the older and more academic approach to HTML tagging and one that you cannot control in your design.) Types of Logical styles you can assign include the following (the listed styles are shown here in the physical appearance that PageMill will use in their display):

  Strong. The Strong attribute makes text stand out. For most browsers, text with the Strong attribute is displayed in bold.

  Emphasis. The Emphasis attribute is similar to Strong, except the text is displayed in italics.

  Citation. This attribute is used when quoting (or citing) text from another source. Most browsers show text with the Citation attribute in smaller font and italics.

  Teletype. Choosing Teletype sets the text in a monospaced font (also defined by the user in the preferences of their browser). Monospaced fonts give the same amount of space for each character and don't try to conserve space between letters.

The following style attributes are an integral part of the original use of HTML: a way to display technical and scientific papers. Most of the following codes are not used outside of academic circles, but PageMill supports them because they are established HTML attributes.

Sample. The Sample attribute is used to display a series of characters taken as a sample from another source. Most browsers display text with the Sample attribute in a monospaced font.

Keyboard. The Keyboard attribute is used to display text meant to be typed. Text with the Keyboard attribute is usually displayed in a monospaced font.

Code. The Code attribute is used when displaying portions of computer programming code. Text with the Code attribute is usually displayed in a monospaced font.

Variable. The Variable attribute is meant for displaying a variable name within a block of computer programming code. Text with the Variable attribute is usually displayed in italics.

 Note

In practice, Logical styles have not been popular with Web publishers because it is impossible to know how a browser will interpret them. You may apply emphasis to a sentence, for example, and one browser will make it bold, another will display it in italic, and so on.

■ **Physical styles.** Physical styles are assigned by the literal application of a font style; all browsers will interpret them in the same manner. Types of physical styles include:

Plain. Choosing Plain is the default style, as defined by the reader in the Preferences file of his or her browser. This is usually a proportional font, which means letters are kerned, or pushed together, on the screen.

Bold. Choosing Bold sets your text in the bold version of the font used with plain text.

Italic. Choosing Italic sets your text in the italics version of the font used with plain text.

To assign a certain style to text, highlight the text to which you want to apply the style and choose a style from the Style menu (see Figure 4.17).

Mac

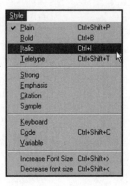 **Windows**

Figure 4.17
Assign a style to
your text.

 Tip

If you do not know which style has been applied to selected characters, look on the Style menu. There will be a check mark to the left of the style in use. You can combine physical and logical styles, such as Bold and Emphasis for bolded italicized text. Just remember that not all browsers will display the logical elements of your style in the same fashion. Use character styles with paragraph formatting, because the styles do not change the line feeds or spaces between paragraphs.

Try combining styles with headings to create interesting heading effects.

Creating Lists

Lists are special type of paragraph format (and so you'll find them listed on the Format pop-up menu on the toolbar) or in a hierarchical menu on the Style menu under Lists. Lists are commonly used in Web pages because they make a document easier to read by breaking up text and giving the eyes some white space to rest upon. Use lists for describing items such as a table of contents, a series of steps, outlining a topic, and indexing. Lists combined with hypertext links create a powerful and orderly way to organize information on a Web page. You can create the following types of lists with PageMill:

- **Bulleted lists.** These lists use bullets to separate items. You can replace the generic bullets with images or animated GIFs for a more dramatic look.

- **Directory lists.** This creates a bulleted list that looks identical to the Bullet formatted list.

- **Menu lists.** This is another way to create an unordered, non-numbered list.

- **Numbered lists.** This type of lists automatically adds numbers next to your text in the list.

- **Definition lists.** This list formats text with an indentation to indicate that you are creating a definition. Use this style with the Term list style to create dictionary-type lists.

- **Term lists.** This style is used to indicate a word or phrase that is being defined. The style automatically adds bold and left alignment to the text.

Making Bulleted Lists

Bulleted lists are used to present items that can be described briefly—usually in 10 words or less. Each item in a bulleted list is preceded by a bullet(•). The type of bullet appearing on a browser is controlled by the browser's font. Do not assume that your bullet will appear as a solid black circle on every browser.

 Tip

You can jazz up your page by replacing the bullets with graphics. A benefit of placing an image next to a bulleted item is that you can link the image to another page, thus creating an index or table of contents for your site. When the reader clicks the graphic, he or she is jumped to its listed subject at your site. Using images for bullets also lets you control what the bullet looks like, which is not possible with the standard bullet list bullets.

Creating a Bulleted List

1   In an open PageMill page, type the following items (press Return after each word):

Writer

Lawyer

Beggarman

Thief

2   Highlight all your text.

3   Choose Paragraph from the Format menu to make sure that you do not have any heading or alignment formatting applied to the text.

4   Select List from the Format menu and choose Bullet (Command-Opt-B) from submenu.

You can also create a bulleted list by highlighting your text and selecting Bullet List from the Format pull-down menu on the toolbar (see Figure 4.18).

Mac

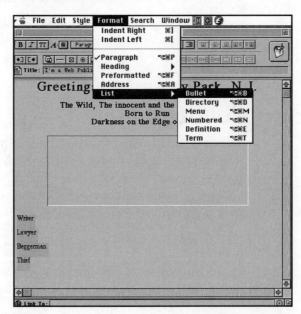

Figure 4.18a
Creating a bulleted list on the Mac.

Windows

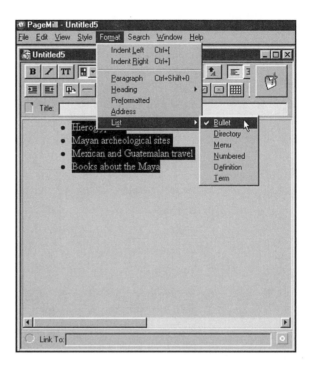

Figure 4.18b
Creating a bulleted
list in Windows.

 Note

Paragraphs formatted as a list have a blank line automatically
inserted above and below each time you press the Return key
(indicated in the HTML with the <P> tag before and after the text.)
If you want to create a list of items and not have a blank line
between each item (in other words create "soft returns"), press
the Shift key while pressing Return. This places a <BR> tag in
place of the more standard <P> tag into the HTML.

Making Directory and Menu Lists

The Directory list style is another way of automatically adding
bullets to your lists. It is identical to the Bullet format. Use the
Menu format for creating indented lists that do not have any
separators (in other words, an unordered list). These two types of
list formats are rarely used anymore.

Making Numbered Lists

Each item in a numbered list begins with a numeral. Numbered lists are great for step-by-step instructions and ordered rankings. Note that all you will see next to an item in a numbered list is a number sign (#) in either Edit or Preview modes. You can't see the numbers until you use an actual browser.

Creating a Numbered List

1 Type the following text. Press Return after each name:

Stephanie Marie

Jillian Leigh

Emma Leanne

Terrie Jo

2 Highlight your text.

3 Select List on the Format menu and select Numbered on the submenu (see Figure 4.19).

4 Notice PageMill inserts #. before each item while in Edit mode. When viewed by a browser, these characters are translated into numbers.

Mac

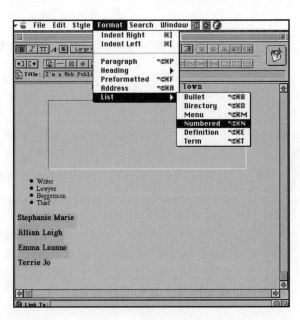

Figure 4.19a
Creating a
numbered list on a
Mac.

Windows

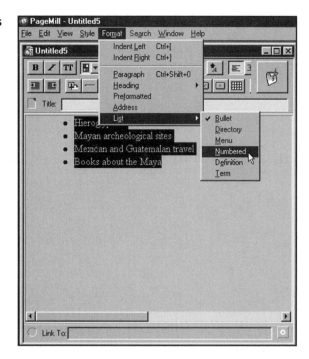

Figure 4.19b
Creating a
numbered list in
Windows.

Tip

You can create a nested or hierarchical list by selecting the list
items you want subordinate and pressing the Right indent button
on the toolbar. The bullet or numbering scheme changes to
accommodate the nesting.

PageMill easily converts numbered lists to bulleted. To do so,
highlight the entire numbered list. Then select List from the
Format menu and choose Bulleted List from the submenu. Voilà!
To convert from a bulleted list to a numbered list, choose Numbered from the submenu.

Making Definition and Term Lists

The Definition and Term list components work together to
introduce a term and then provide a definition. The most common use of Definition and Term elements is in glossaries. Instead
of bullets or numbers preceding a term, the term is listed at the far
left of the page and the definition is indented (see Figure 4.20).

Creating a Definition and Term List

1 Type the following text. Press Return after each line.

Shovel

An excavating machine

Pot

A rounded or earthen container

Basket

A receptacle made of interwoven material

2 Highlight your text.

3 Select List from the Format menu and then select Term from the submenu (see Figure 4.20). Everything you typed should now be styled Term. You can also apply the Term format from the Format pop-up menu on the toolbar or by pressing the key combination Option-Command-T.

4 Next, highlight a definition. Select List from the Format menu and then select Definition from the submenu. You can also apply the Definition format from the Format pop-up menu on the toolbar or by pressing the key combination Option-Command-E. Repeat this for each of the definitions.

Mac

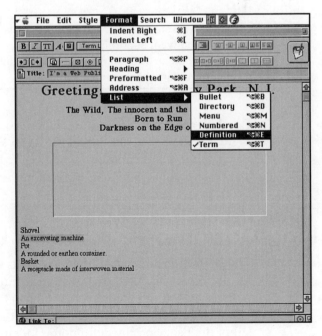

Figure 4.20a
Creating a
Definition/Term list
on the Mac.

Windows

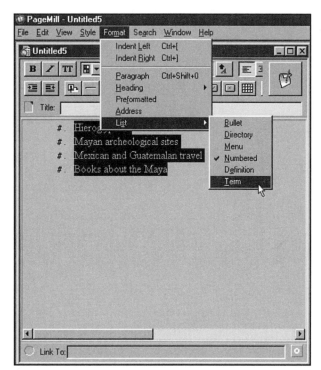

Figure 4.20b
Creating a
Definition/Term list
in Windows.

Using Rules

Adding a horizontal rule to your Web page is an excellent way to break up text and add a graphic element to your page. To add a horizontal rule to your text, click the Insert Horizontal Rule button in the toolbar (see Figure 4.21). By default, the rule stretches across the page and is left-justified.

Figure 4.21
Click the Insert
Horizontal Rule
button to create a
3D line across your
page.

Insert Horizontal Rule button

To manipulate the size and appearance of the horizontal rule, place the cursor on the horizontal rule so that the cursor turns into an arrow. Click the horizontal rule. An outline appears around the rule (see Figure 4.22). Notice the dark boxes at the lower right, far right, and lower middle of the outline. These dark boxes are sizing handles enabling you to adjust the width and thickness of the rule.

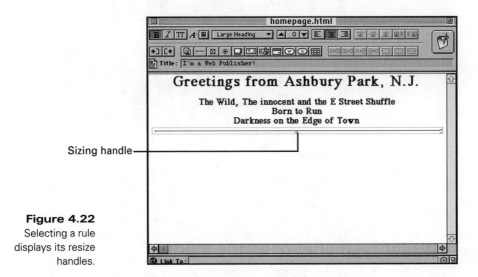

Sizing handle

Figure 4.22
Selecting a rule
displays its resize
handles.

To resize the width of the rule, drag the far right handle to the left. To resize the thickness of the rule, drag the lower middle handle down. To resize the thickness and width of the rule at the same time (see Figure 4.23), drag the lower right rule down (or up) and to the left (or right).

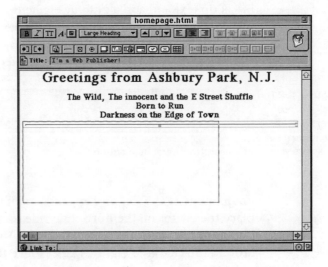

Figure 4.23
Adjusting the width
and thickness of a
horizontal rule.

You also can control whether the rule is left justified or centered by selecting the rule and clicking the toolbar's alignment buttons.

Adding Graphics

Graphic images make a Web site more appealing and up to date with the latest changes. A picture really can be worth a thousand words when you're trying to convey information. In this section, you'll learn the various ways to get graphics into PageMill. Graphics also are presented in Chapter 7, "Frames and Tables." The images referred to throughout these lessons come with *The PageMill Handbook* CD-ROM. The images are located in the Images folder within the Earth&Ware Tutorials folder.

Tip

Viewers can turn off automatic graphic loading on their browsers. You can (and should) enter a label for the graphic in the Inspector's Object screen's Alternate Label text box so that viewers who turn off graphics will see a descriptive label instead of a blank space.

Adding Images Using Drag-and-Drop

You can drag the icon of an image file right into PageMill from your desktop, and it will be inserted on your page.

 Mac

 ### Placing an Image Using "Drag and Drop"

1. Open the PageMill page where you typed your terms and definitions. Place the mouse at the end of the definition for "shovel." Click to place the cursor.

2. Open the Images folder within the Earth&Ware Tutorials folder. Set the folder on the desktop so that both it and the PageMill window can be viewed side by side (see Figure 4.24).

3. Find the file shovel.gif and drag it into the PageMill document (see Figure 4.25).

Mac

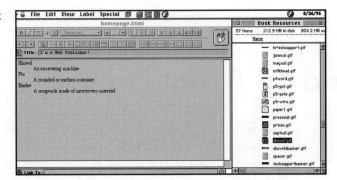

Figure 4.24a
Arrange your desktop so that you can drag the shovel.gif file to the Pagemill window

    Tip

Click and drag the resize button on the bottom-right corner of the PageMill window to resize the window so that you can place the other window next to it.

Windows **Placing an Image Using Drag and Drop in Windows**

1   Open the PageMill page where you typed your terms and definitions. Place the mouse at the end of the definition "shovel."

2   Open the PMImages folder on the CD-ROM.

3   Find the file Tools.gif and drag it into the PageMill document (see Figure 4.24 b).

The WWW supports two file formats for graphics: GIF and JPEG. PageMill converts PCX and PICT graphics into GIFs when you drag-and-drop a graphic onto a PageMill document. GIF formats are best used for solid colored items because GIFs tend to loose information and hense the quality of the image when compressed. Use JPEG formats for photographs or other images with gradiations of color because this format's compression formula is more sophisticated and therefore better capable of handling multiple colors without losing quality.

Windows

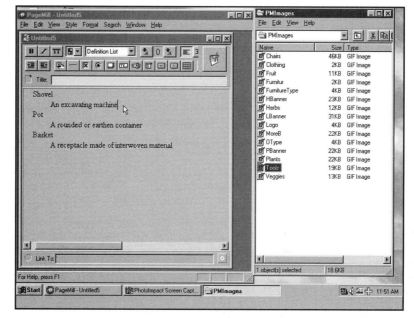

Figure 4.24b
Drag an image from
the desktop on to
your page.

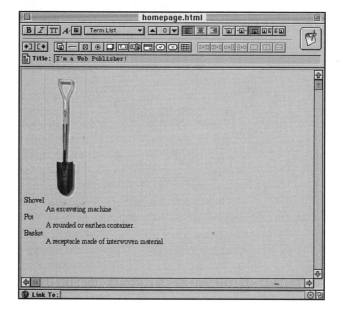

Figure 4.25
PageMill places the
image into your
document at the
cursor.

The converted GIF file will be placed in the folder you specified as your default root resource folder using the Resources screen of the Preferences dialog box.

 Note

Whenever you drag or insert alien-formatted objects (such as a PCX or PICT image) into a PageMill page, PageMill automatically creates a GIF version of the file and places this new file into a special folder on your root directory (desktop) called PageMill Resources. Images placed in this folder are given numerical names based on when they were created. Thus, if you have your 5pot.pict file, PageMill actually links the image on the page to a new file called Image1.gif (or Image2.gif and so forth) located in the PageMill Resources folder. You can easily lose track of where these files are stored or think you are altering the correct version of the image only to have its image disappear from your page or not change.

Even if you find your gif files, when you edit the new gif image by Command-double-clicking on its PageMill image to interlace it or make it transparent for faster downloading, the Image1.gif file is altered. If you locate the PageMill Resources folder, then move its contents and then rename its files to something more descriptive, PageMill breaks the links. You must reconnect the image to its file using SiteMill or by manually re-inserting the renamed file after you move it to its proper folder.

To avoid having PageMill create a default PageMill Resources folder, be sure to set up a root resources folder before creating your page. You set up the folder by creating a folder (call it images, gr, or resources, for example). Open the Preferences dialog box from the Edit menu. Click the Resource screen icon on the left of the box. In the resulting Resources screen, click the folder icon and in the resulting Open dialog box, open the resources folder and click the In Here button. PageMill registers your Root Resource folder in its Preferences file. (See Chapter 3 for a more detailed description of how to use the Preferences dialog box to set up resources.)

Adding Images Using the Pasteboard

Images can be stored on the Pasteboard for easy retrieval. The PageMill Pasteboard serves as a place where you can put items that you may want to use on other pages. Think of the Pasteboard as a library or store house for objects. Display the Pasteboard by selecting Show Pasteboard (Command-/ or F5) from the Window (View) menu.

Changing Pages on the Pasteboard

Click the images of the page fold to move forward through pages 1 through 5. Click the triangle at the bottom left corner (under the page fold) to flip pages backwards to page 1.

Copying Items to the Pasteboard

Click to select the object you want to copy to the Pasteboard and drag the object on to the Pasteboard.

You can copy multiple items on to a single page of the Pasteboard. To copy tables and their contents (including maps), click the table once and drag the entire table marqueed outline on to the Pasteboard. Make sure that the table is outlined with a single line marquee before dragging to ensure that its entire contents is copied.

Copying Items from the Pasteboard

You can either move (remove) items from the Pasteboard or copy items from the Pasteboard (leaving a copy behind to use again). To Move objects, simply drag the item off the Pasteboard on to your page. To Copy objects, press the Option key while dragging (see Figure 4.26).

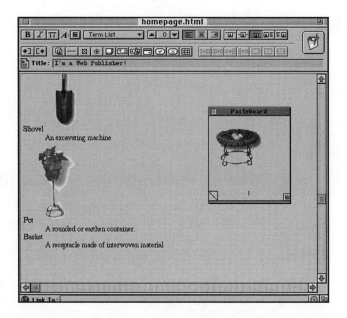

Figure 4.26
Dragging a file from
the Pasteboard into
your document.

 Tip

One of the great uses for the Pasteboard is to copy navigation buttons across a site. Because you can copy an image and its links to the Pasteboard, simply drag the button linked to your Home page to each page in your site to create a link back to your default page (or any other page). This is a way to avoid having to continually retype URLs or open pages and drag page icons to create links.

Images also can be pasted into PageMill from the Macintosh Clipboard.

Adding Graphics Using the Place Object Button

You can use the Place Object button, shown in Figure 4.27, to place a graphic. Pressing this button presents you with a dialog box you can use to identify the file you want to place.

Figure 4.27
The Place Object
button on the
PageMill toolbar is
used to insert
graphics, PDFs,
QuickTime movies,
animated GIFs, and
so forth, into your
page.

Place Object button

 ## Using the Place Object Button

1   Still using our Terms and Definitions document, place the cursor at the end of the definition for pot.

2   Click the Place Object button (see Figure 4.28a).

Mac

3   In the resulting Open File dialog box, find the file p5-pot.gif in the Images folder within the Earth&Ware Tutorials folder and select it.

Windows

In the resulting Place Object dialog box, select the "tools" file from the PMImages folder (see Figure 4.28b).

4   Click Place.

Mac

Figure 4.28a
Choose the
p5-pot.gif file.
Clicking the Place
button places the
image into your
home page.

Windows

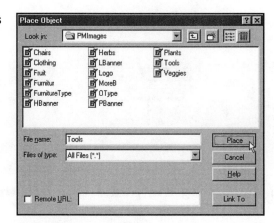

Figure 4.28b

Aligning Text

You have some control over the alignment of text beside an image. You can align the text to the bottom, middle, or top of the graphic.

Aligning Text to Images

1 Click the graphic.

2 Click the Top Align Object button in the toolbar. The definition text now will be aligned with the top of the graphic (see Figure 4.29).

3 Click the Middle Align Object button in the toolbar. The definition text will now be aligned with the middle of the graphic.

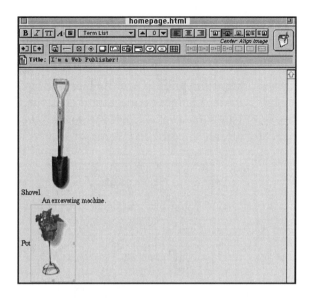

Figure 4.29
Clicking an Align Object button on the toolbar causes your text to flow around the graphic in the manner you specify.

Manipulating Images

You can use the Inspector to manipulate your images. The Object mode of the Inspector palette provides you with precision tools you can use to:

■ Create a placeholder for browsers that do not support graphics

■ Resize your graphic image to scale

■ Define the purpose of your graphic (a picture embedded in a document, an imagemap, or a button in a form)

These tools are discussed in more detail in the following sections.

Creating a Placeholder for Your Image

Open a new page in PageMill and insert the boots.gif image located in the Images folder of the Earth&Ware Tutorial. (If you are using a PC, place the Herbs.gif image from the PMImages folder.) Select boots.gif and click the third button in the Inspector (the same one you used when you defined variables earlier). Your screen will look like Figure 4.30.

 Mac

 Windows

Figure 4.30
Use the Object mode of the Inspector to manipulate your images with precision.

The first box, Alternate Label, is a hold-over from HTML. Alternate Label provides text that will be displayed in the place of your graphic if your image does not load, which happens surprisingly often, especially if your image takes a long time to transfer because of its file size. (We'll look at some ways to reduce the size of your image in Chapter 3.) Type **This should have been a picture** in the Alternate Label box (see Figure 4.31). If your image fails to load to a viewer's computer, this text appears. In the future, enter text that provides the reader with more information about what should have loaded.

Figure 4.31
The Alternate Label provides text as a stand-in for an image in those browsers that do not support graphics.

Resizing Graphics

You can use two methods to resize a graphic:

■ Drag the graphic to the size you desire by using your eyesite.

■ Use the Inspector to enter precise dimensions for the graphic.

 Resizing a Graphic Using the Drag Method

1 Select the graphic you want to resize.

2 When the graphic is selected, sizing handles appear (they should look like the sizing handles you used when resizing the horizontal rule). Click and drag these handles to size the image (see Figure 4.32).

Clicking and dragging a sizing handle is a fast way to adjust your image size, but if you need to be more exact you should use the Inspector.

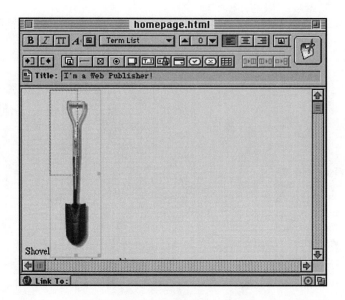

Figure 4.32
Resize an image by
dragging one of its
sizing handles.

When you invoke the Object mode of the Inspector while selecting an image, a series of numbers appear in the boxes next to the "Width" and "Height" headings. Pop-up menus let you choose between pixels and percentages. To adjust the size of your image, click inside the box, type a new number, and press Return (one of the scale checkboxes must be unchecked to modify image size).

 Tip

You can't tab between the boxes or click another one to select it. You must press Return for PageMill to accept the changes you have made.

Remember that the size of most Web browser windows is about 480 pixels. You can make images that span more than 480 pixels, but many readers will need to widen their window to see the entire image. If they have a (gasp!) small monitor, they will have to scroll to see everything.

If you decide to adjust your image based on percent, understand that you are adjusting the width and height independently. This means that if you enter 50 percent for the height, and your image is 2 inches high and 4 inches wide, you will get an image that is 1 inch by 4 inches.

When you place an image on your document, either by drag-and-dropping or by clicking the Insert Image button, PageMill reduces the size somewhat. You'll notice this when you click your image and look at its height and width percentages.

You can maintain the original proportions of an image by holding down the Shift key while you drag the corner of the image. With the Inspector, you gain even more control over resizing your images while keeping the proportions intact.

To keep the image's proportions intact while resizing, choose to constrain proportions based on either height or width. You can choose to do this in either pixels or percentages. Two checkboxes are to the left of the height and width values. Scale to Height is next to the width box and Scale to Width is next to the height box. For now, click the Scale to Height box.

When you click the box, an adjustment takes place and the number changes. PageMill looks at the height and adjusts the width so that your image stays proportional. If you click Scale to Width, PageMill looks at the width and adjusts the height. Notice that after you click the Scale to Width box you can't change the height and vice versa. These checkboxes lock one dimension. That's not to say the dimension can't be changed; it just can't be changed manually. The dimension is adjusted with a PageMill calculation based on how high or wide you want the other dimension.

Did that make sense? Imagine that an image is 200 pixels wide by 300 pixels high. Let's say you want the image to be only 150 pixels wide. Enter 150 in the Width box and the image changes, giving you a squeezed look. To get rid of the squeeze, adjust the height proportionally. In Figures 4.33 and 4.34, you see two versions of the same image. The first was resized proportionally; the second wasn't. The squeezed effect is what you're trying to avoid.

You can determine the correct height and width of the image in pixels by doing the calculations in your head (according to Italian Renaissance artists, your proportions should be around 2:3), eyeballing it until it looks right, or checking the Scale to Width box. If you check Scale to Width, PageMill considers the width of the image (in this case, 150) and adjusts the height to eliminate the squeeze and make your image proportional.

Figure 4.33
An image sized
proportionally.

Figure 4.34
The squeezed
appearance of an
image.

Changing Image Borders

Whenever you place an image in a PageMill document, a default border is created. The border is measured in pixels, and you can make it thicker or thinner by adjusting its number of pixels. Chances are, unless you opened the Inspector, you would never know this because the default border is 0 pixels.

 Note

A pixel is one dot on your computer screen.

The border is controlled with the Border box in the Object mode screen of the Inspector. The thickest you can make the border is 50 pixels. Select your image, and enter 5 in the box at the lower left in the Inspector. You should see a solid black border around your image (see Figure 4.35).

Why would you ever want to do this? For a few reasons, all having to do with making the image a separate element in your document. If, for example, you make the background of the image transparent to keep the file small (and for speed transfer time over the Web), but want the image to be a separate visual element from the rest of the page, you can create a border around it. Or, if you left the image's background intact, but changed the background color to something that matches it (for example, if your image has a blue background, and you changed your background color to blue), a border can help distinguish the image.

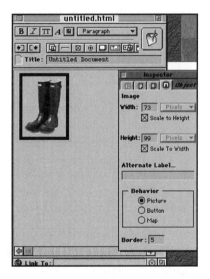

Figure 4.35
A solid black border
is placed around
your image when
you type a number
in the Borders box.

Controlling the Behavior of Your Image

Images can be used in three ways: as inline or embedded graphics (they just sit there and look pretty), portions of the graphic can be selected as hot spots to link to other locations (called an imagemap), or the image can be designated in total as a link (called a button). You designate what you want your graphic to be by selecting the image and clicking one of a trio of radio buttons at the bottom of Inspector's Object mode screen (see Figure 4.36).

The radio buttons are used as follows:

■ **Picture.** This means you want an in-line image to be displayed by the browser. Inline graphics are just pictures that illustrate your page. You can wrap text around a picture. This is the default button.

■ **Map.** You can designate a total graphic as a link to another location. This is a powerful feature because you can replace bullets with linkable images, as well as create independent graphics that jump your readers to other locations.

Another cousin of the map is the "active image." You can turn your image into a series of clickable areas. This enables a reader to select different sections of the image, and by clicking, activate links to different URLs. To create an active image, see Chapter 6. Chapter 6 explains the tools PageMill provides to create the hot spots on your image.

■ **Button.** Buttons are special images that send commands to the server. Buttons work with CGIs to do something, such as submit a form. Any graphic can be used as a button, but buttons require extra software on the server side to work. Read Chapter 8, "Working with Forms" to learn how to add buttons.

Any graphic can be designated as a button or map. You differentiate the purpose of the image by designating different HTML tags using the Inspector's Object screen. You can augment your button images with Java scripts to similate a button click, a spinning top, a sound, and so forth by dragging ready-made Java applet objects on to your page and designating them as buttons, or by writing your own scripts. The important thing is that the object will not work as a button until you connect it to the proper CGI in the Forms screen of the Inspector.

Make sure that your buttons look like buttons and your clickable images look like icons or pictures so that your reader understands the purpose of clicking the area. Note that nothing overt on the page will alert readers to the different between a button and a map unless you put it there.

Figure 4.36
Use the radio buttons to designate how you want your image to behave. In this case, the selected image is an inline graphic or picture.

 Note

You can create a graphic button that doesn't shout "I'm a button!" Go to the border box, enter 0, and press Return. The border disappears. You now have a link that isn't noted in any way. Right about now, that why-would-I-do-this feeling is washing over you. Again, this is a design decision you have to make. Removing the border makes the button less distracting. Most browsers indicate links by displaying the destination URL whenever a reader passes the cursor over a linked object. If it's obvious that the user is supposed to click the image (say, for example, that it's an image of a button with "click here" on it), having a blue border might be distracting and redundant.

Using Find and Replace

A new feature in PageMill 2.0 is the ability to search for and replace items on your page. The Find and Replace commands are useful because if you need to make changes to your page you can find all occurrences of an object and replace it with another. The most powerful feature of Find and Replace is the ability to drag and drop images, form elements, tables, and so forth into the Find and Replace dialog box, and PageMill will find the original object and replace it with the new one. Find and Replace works in both the Edit mode window (WYSIWYG) and in the HTML Source mode (which I'll discuss in Chapter 9). You can also search for link addresses to ensure that they correctly point to where they should.

 Finding and Replacing an Object

1   Pull down the Search menu and select Find (Command-F or Ctrl-F).

2   In the resulting Find and Replace dialog box (see Figure 4.37), select Page Content from the Find What pop-up menu at the top of the box.

3   Select Object from the Scope pop-up menu at the bottom of the dialog box.

4   Check the Deep and Wrap check boxes to ensure that PageMill searches all objects for your image, including within tables and frames and searches the total document from the top to the bottom, no matter where your cursor is pointing.

You can select from four levels of searching: Find Page/not Deep (which searches only the text on a page and not within any object), Find Object/Deep (which searches either through all objects and text, or only within tables and form elements, if the find item is an object), Page/Deep (which causes the search to be performed through the entire page, including all objects), or Object/not Deep (which limits the search to top level tables without looking at nested objects within tables or frames).

5   Drag and drop a copy of the GIF file you want to locate in the Find box (in other words the version of the image you want to change).

6 Drag and drop a copy of the GIF file you want to replace the original with into the Replace box.

7 Click Find to activate the other buttons and find the first occurrence of the object, then click either Replace (changes one item), Replace and Find (replaces the item and goes to the next occurrence), or Replace All (changes everything all at once), to indicate how thorough you want the find and replace task to be accomplished. You can also find each occurrence of an object by clicking the Find Next button and manually replace only those objects you want by clicking the Replace button each time.

The object in the Find box is replaced by the object in the Replace box. A message is displayed on the dialog box giving the status of the search process.

Mac

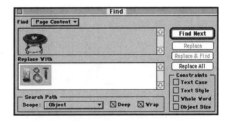

Figure 4.37
Use the Find and Replace dialog box to search for and replace any type of object, be it text, an image, a Java applet, a movie, a PDF, and so forth.

Windows

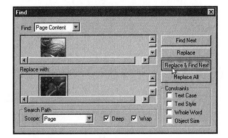

Using the Spelling Checker

New in PageMill 2.0 is a full-bodied spelling checker. Choose Spelling Checker from the Search menu to display its dialog box. You can check the spelling within text only, or deeply to include objects such as form elements, applets, tables, and so forth. You can also teach the spelling checker new words by adding these words to a user dictionary. The spelling checker works like most word processor versions—it finds a questionable word and makes a suggestion for a correction. You can tell the checker to ignore the word, change that occurrence, change all occurrences of the misspelling, or add the questioned word to the user dictionary. The spelling checker provides the same Page/Object scope levels as the Find and Replace dialog box, as well as the same four levels of searching: Page/not Deep, Page/Deep, Object/not Deep, and Object/Deep selected by checking or unchecking the Deep check box and selecting Page or Option from the Scope pop-up menu. By default, the spelling checker will perform a total page search and include text in form elements and tables in the checking process (Page/Deep). Figure 4.38 displays the spelling checker in action.

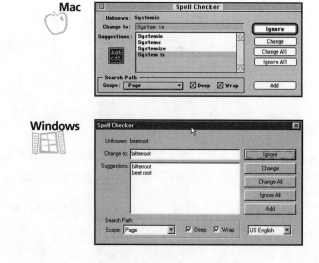

Figure 4.38
Use the spelling checker to audit your page's text and objects for misspellings.

Saving Your Work

Saving your page is very important. The first time you save the page, use the Save Page As command from the File menu. Two things happen: your document is identified as an HTML file (or HTM if working with DOS servers) and a Page icon is created for linking the page to other pages or sites. Save the document in the default Images folder you are using to store your other documents. Figure 4.39 displays the Save As dialog box.

You should use the Save command from the File menu often so as not to lose your work.

Mac

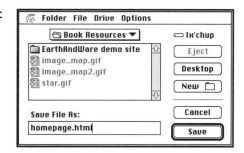

Windows

Figure 4.39
Saving a page gives
the file an HTML
tag, identifying it as
a Web page.

Tip

You should not add an identifying suffix to Windows 95 files
because Windows automatically identifies the file type for you.
You can change the file type by selecting a new one from the
Save As pop-up menu.

Summary

You have now learned the basic functions of PageMill. You can

- Set up your page's appearance (its background color, text color, and images)

- Enter and format both characters and paragraphs using the toolbar buttons and the commands on the menu bar

- Insert graphics using either drag-and-drop or the Open File dialog box

- Use the Inspector to fine tune your page setup, paragraph layout, and graphic image sizes

The next chapter builds on these basic skills, showing you how to link your page, and words within your page, to other pages in your site, other sites, or locations within a single page.

Chapter 5

Working with Links

The power of the Web is generated by the physical connections created between ideas and information. These chains of thought are called *links*. They let someone reading your Web page connect from a location on your page to another idea somewhere else—be it on your page, in another page at your site, or halfway around the world at someone else's site. The key to these links is called *hypertext*—a way of storing the address of a piece of information within HTML codes associated with a piece of text or a graphic.

Just keep two concepts straight:

■ Where are you coming from? This is called the *source* document, the one containing the link.

■ Where are you going? This is called the *destination* or *referenced* document, the one displayed when you invoke the link.

The source document's hypertext link is indicated by color and style (typically blue underlined text or a color border around an image).

Tip

The destination address (called a URL or Universal Resource Locator) appears in some browsers (Netscape, for example) when you pass your cursor over a linked object.

Understanding Links

Hypertext, also called links, is a way to define a path through a series of pages at a site, or connecting concepts within a page. The idea is that the user of the page is making the decisions of where to go next. Hypertext links are the heart and soul of the Web. Hypertext is based on the concept that documents can be linked to other documents by way of shortcuts (addresses) within each file. Both text and images can serve as linking points on the Web. With links, readers can navigate to:

■ Another part of the same Web page (see Figures 5.1a and 5.1b)

Figure 5.1a
Clicking the phrase "Back to the Top"...

■ Another Web page at the same site (see Figures 5.2a and 5.2b)

■ A page on an entirely different Web site (see Figure 5.3)

Figure 5.1b
...takes you back to
the top of the page.

Figure 5.2a
Clicking the basket
graphic or its linked
text...

Figure 5.2b
...takes you to a
new page within the
site, called "Home
Accessories."

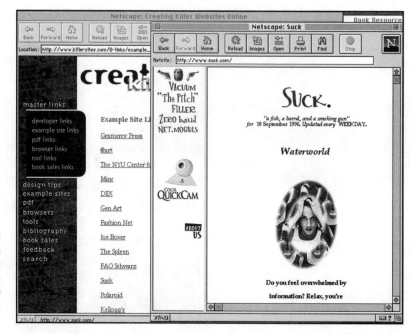

Figure 5.3
Clicking the link called "Suck" at the KillerSites home page takes you to the Suck.com home page.

 Tip

In Preview mode, PageMill's cursor turns from an arrow to a pointing finger when it passes over a hypertext link. In Figure 5.2a, notice that holding down the mouse opens a pop-up menu similar to those in most browsers that lets you decide whether you want the new page to be displayed on a separate window, or to replace your current page on the existing window.

URLs

A URL is a standardized address system used to identify files/pages/sites on the Web. It is, in a sense, an address much like your street, city, state, country, and ZIP code.

URLs have three parts:

■ The name of the Internet service (or protocol) being used; for example: http, ftp, telnet, gopher, and so on.

This tells the browser what tool to use to reach the file your are seeking. If the address contains an @ sign, it indicates an e-mail address.

- The domain name of the computer to be accessed (also called a *host*); `www.mactivity.myserver.com`, for example. The domain is broken down into three parts: the organization or company (in this case "Mactivity") and the type of domain (in this case "www" for the Web), the machine or server's name, here called "myserver," and lastly, a three-letter suffix indicating the type of domain (whether "com" for commercial organization, "edu" for a college or university, "net" for a network provider, or "org" for a non-profit organization).

- The directory path for the file to be viewed; `/conferences/macweb.html`, for example.

When you put these together, you get `http://www.mactivity.myserver.com/conferences/macweb.html`.

This particular address has been specified to use the `http` protocol to connect to the Web-based organization named `www.mactivity.com` and the server named `myserver`, to find the file `macweb.html` in the `conferences` folder.

URL addressees cannot include any spaces, backslashes, or international characters because backslashes are reserved to connote directories and subdirectories (think of nested folders), and some servers, especially Unix ones, cannot interpret blank spaces.

You should know the following about URLs:

- The various notations and symbols of the technical world don't always fit into the concise rules of English. URL descriptions are a good example. When a sentence ends with a URL, you need to end the sentence with a period. URLs *never end in a period*—so ignore any periods at the end of sentences when typing URLs into your Web page or browser.

■ The proper way to define a site's URL is to end the host name with a backslash (/). When a Web server sees a slash at the end of a URL, it knows to serve a page designated as a default page for that site. This is why when you tell someone to check out your Web site and give them a URL with just a server name (that is, `www.mymachine.com`) they will see the default home page for that site.

Relative vs. Absolute Pathnames

PageMill supports the use of relative pathnames to make hypertext links. A relative pathname describes the location of a document *relative* to the location of the current document. When creating a link to a document that is in the same folder as the document that will contain the hypertext link, you can specify the filename instead of the complete pathname. For example, say you have a link in your page called Joewebhead's Page that moves your reader back to your home page, called Mac Web Page. PageMill lets you type only the filename, `macweb.html` of the home page in the Link Locator box, because PageMill knows that both files reside in the same folder, `conferences`. That is why, later in this chapter, you'll see that you can drag and drop .html files from the same folder on to links and PageMill records only their relative pathnames on the link.

By contrast, an *absolute* pathname describes the complete path from the root of the server to the file: `http://www.mactivity.`
`myserver.com/conferences/macweb.html`. This absolute pathname is used when you want to link to a remote URL that resides on a different server, because you must tell the browser and server where to look for the file. You'll see absolute pathnames when you drag and drop pages from the Web on to a selected link in your PageMill page.

PageMill automatically uses relative pathnames when you save your site's pages in the same resource folder. (See Chapter 3 for directions on setting up the local resource folder in PageMill.) This way if you ever move your files and folders to another computer, the URLs will be correct. In general, relative pathnames are more efficient, because the browser can access the page faster when it doesn't have to go to another directory (folder) with less help from the server (providing speedier service to your reader).

Working with Hypertext Links

Every PageMill document you create contains a page icon on its top left corner of the toolbar (see Figure 5.4).

Figure 5.4
When you save a PageMill document, information about the page is stored with the page icon.

When you save your page and give it a name with the .html suffix, the relative path to your page and its name are saved and stored with the page icon (or in the HTML at the top of the page and connected to the icon so it can be used to transfer information about the page in a link) (see Figure 5.5).

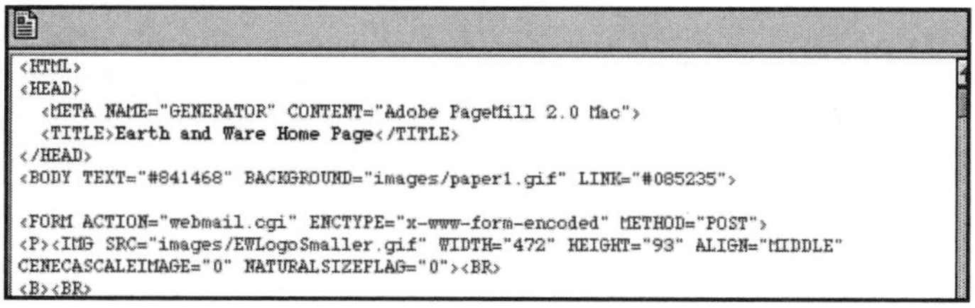

Figure 5.5
Your page's relative path is contained in the HTML at the top of the page.

```
<HTML>
<HEAD>
    <META NAME="GENERATOR" CONTENT="Adobe PageMill 2.0 Mac">
    <TITLE>Earth and Ware Home Page</TITLE>
</HEAD>
<BODY TEXT="#841468" BACKGROUND="images/paper1.gif" LINK="#085235">

<FORM ACTION="webmail.cgi" ENCTYPE="x-www-form-encoded" METHOD="POST">
<P><IMG SRC="images/EWLogoSmaller.gif" WIDTH="472" HEIGHT="93" ALIGN="MIDDLE"
CENECASCALEIMAGE="0" NATURALSIZEFLAG="0"><BR>
<B><BR>
```

There are two ways to connect items using HTML with PageMill: the page icon and the anchor.

Adding Links Using the Page Icon

The page icon is used to create hypertext links between pages at a site, or to create a link from your site to some other site or page. Using the page icon to drag and drop a link always takes you to the top of a page.

Creating a Link Between Pages

1 Open a PageMill document that you want as the source document.

2 Open another PageMill document that you want as the destination document.

3 Click and drag the page icon of the source document on to the destination document. A link is created (see Figure 5.6). Notice that PageMill created the link using the name of the source page. You can edit the link just like any other text (see Chapter 4 for a description of how to work with text).

Figure 5.6
You can create a link between pages by dragging the page icon from one page to another.

 Tip

On both the PC and Mac, make sure that you can see the destination object as well as the page icon of the source page. You must be able to drag and drop between windows. The PC is especially sensitive to incorrect window placement and will not drag and drop if the destination is obstructed.

You can also create a link by copying and pasting links between pages. Create a link by dragging the page icon on to selected text on another page. Select that newly linked text and select the Copy command from the Edit menu (or press the key combination Command-C). The link's text and link information are copied to the Clipboard. You can select other text or open another page and select Paste from the Edit menu (or press Command-V). The text and link are placed at your insertion point.

You can also manually type a link address in the Link Location Bar after selecting the text or image you want to use as the source of the link.

Adding Links Using Anchors

Anchors are a way to use the information from the page icon within a page to link concepts any place on a page to any other place on other pages within your site or on another page at another site. Anchors are made from the page icon and can be placed anywhere on a page. Anchors are a good way of assisting a reader in navigating down a long page. Create a table of contents and create an anchor link from the table of contents entry to its subject on the page.

Creating a Link to an Anchor

1   (On a Mac) In a previously saved PageMill document, drag the page icon on to the page. (On a PC) Click the page icon to insert an anchor at your cursor.

PageMill creates an anchor icon at your current insertion point. If you have the Inspector open, notice that the anchor is an object that you can name. You can make as many anchors as you wish by dragging the page icon onto the page.

2   Drag an anchor to the destination location you want to jump to.

3   Highlight the text or image you want as the source of the link.

4   Drag the anchor onto the highlighted text or image. PageMill creates a link between the source and destination (see Figure 5.7).

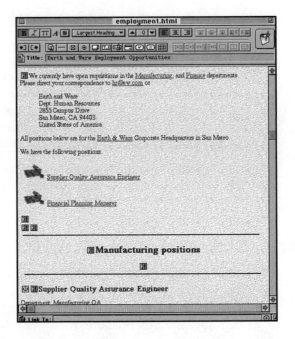

Figure 5.7
Use the page icon
to create anchors,
then drag the
anchors on to the
source object to
create the link.

Use anchors to create tables of contents for long documents by linking a descriptive sentence to its actual location in the document. You can also use anchors to link an image button to a topic in the middle of another page.

 Tip

To name an anchor, select it, open the Inspector, and select the Object tab. A name field appears that enables you to change the name of the anchor. Select the default name, type a new name, and press Return. Be sure to rename your anchor before you start creating hypertext links with it.

You can open another page in your site and highlight an object or text. Drag the anchor from the source document on to the highlighted object to create a link between pages. When you click the link, the browser jumps to the anchor. You cannot copy and paste an anchor between areas, since copying the anchor only copies the anchor and not the link. Copy the destination linked object to use the anchor again on another page. If you move the anchor to a new position, any links that reference that anchor will reference its new location.

Tip

If the source text and destination anchor are not visible on a single screen, use PageMill's autoscrolling feature to help create the hypertext link. A hot scrolling area is provided along the edges of each PageMill page. The autoscrolling region is a 16-pixel-wide border at the left, right, top, and bottom edges of the Page view. If you drag an item to this area and wait for a second, scrolling will begin. You also can use the Pasteboard as a temporary holding area for the anchor.

More About Links

As stated earlier, you can create several types of hypertext links:

- Links to topics within the same page. For this type of link, you use an invisible marker, called an *anchor*, placed at the destination location. You then create the link between the source object and the anchor.

- Links to the top of another page within your site. You can create a text or image-based link to move to the top of a page, no matter where it is located.

- Links to topics somewhere within another page. For this type of link you also use an anchor.

- Links from somewhere within your page to the top of a new page in your site or another Web site. You can create these types of links without anchors.

 Tip

Drag any commonly used hypertext links to the Pasteboard for easy access when creating other pages. Dragging places a copy of the hypertext link, with associated URL intact, onto the Pasteboard. You can then Option-drag from the Pasteboard into the new page. Option-dragging from the Pasteboard places a copy of the hypertext link on your page.

There are three ways to create links—select the source object and either:

- **Drag-and-drop.** Hypertext links are one of the areas where PageMill's use of drag-and-drop really shines. You can drag-and-drop the Page, Anchor, and Image icons to create hypertext links. PageMill takes drag-and-drop a step further by maintaining relevant information. When you drag a PageMill link to the Pasteboard or among PageMill documents, PageMill retains the hypertext associations for that object.

■ **Copy and paste.** After a hypertext link is created, you can cut and paste it to another area on your Web page or to another page. PageMill preserves the URL associated with the linked text when you cut and paste. Select a link by triple-clicking it.

■ **Manually type a URL.** Type a link address into the link location bar.

 Tip

When you are in Edit mode, selecting a text link causes its destination address to be displayed in the link location bar on the bottom of the PageMill window. You can copy this link by dragging the Globe icon next to the link location bar to another location (such as the Pasteboard) (as shown in Figure 5.8).

Figure 5.8
Drag the link location bar's globe to copy a destination address of a hypertext link.

Linking to the Outside World

What good is a Web site if you cannot connect it to other Web sites? PageMill lets you link to remote sites before you upload the page to the server. Use the link location bar at the bottom of the PageMill window to type URLs, or drag and drop links from active Netscape Navigator pages.

Creating a Link to Another Web Site Outside of PageMill

1   Select the text or image you want to use as the source document.

2   Activate the link location bar by clicking in the gray area at the bottom of your PageMill document (to the right of the Globe icon). A white text area appears.

3   Enter the URL of the destination site in this link location field and press Return. The selected text is linked to that URL address.

Tip

You can edit the name of the link in the source document. Highlight the name and type it in the link location field.

You can link your PageMill page to an existing Web page if you are using Netscape Navigator as a browser. With both PageMill and Netscape opened, select the text or a graphic in PageMill you want to use as the source document. Place the cursor over the linked text or graphic in Navigator and drag the link onto the selected object in PageMill. You can also drag links from Netscape Navigator into PageMill's link location bar and press the Return key on your keyboard. Open Netscape Navigator's Bookmark window and drag a bookmark into PageMill in the same two ways.

Tip

PageMill helps you type URLs quickly and accurately in the link location bar. When you type the first letter of a protocol, such as http or ftp, and press the Right Arrow key, PageMill completes the protocol's name. Type the domain name and press the Right Arrow key, and PageMill adds the site type to the name (such as .com, .edu, and so forth).

Deleting a Link

You can remove a hypertext link from your document using one of the following three methods:

- Delete the text representing a hypertext link.

- Highlight the text representing a hypertext link and select Remove Link (Command-R) from the Edit menu.

- Click the link location bar to activate the link, and then delete its contents using the Delete key on your keyboard.

You also can move a copy of linked text to a new location by selecting the text and Option-dragging it to a new location. The link will now appear in both places.

Testing Your Links

One of the most important things you can do when you are finished creating your links is make sure that they work. Any typo, even the slightest, when manually typing URLs on the link location bar makes the link worthless. Anchors may not be placed correctly for where you want the reader to jump. URLs are case-sensitive, meaning capitalization counts. Links to external Web pages go out of date. All of these issues make it very important to test your links.

PageMill's Preview mode supports testing of local hypertext links—hypertext links to documents on your computer. To test links, make sure PageMill is in Preview mode.

When you place the cursor on top of text or graphics that have a hypertext link associated with them, the cursor changes from an arrow to a pointed finger. When you select a hypertext link that links to another page, the other page launches on top of your existing page.

Note

PageMill does not support testing links to URLs on the Internet. You can test external links by opening your Netscape Navigator or Microsoft Internet Explorer browser. Use the Open command on the File menu to open the PageMill document. Click all links to make sure that they really work. If you are actually dialed onto the Web, the browser will jump to the external sites, if you entered the URLs correctly and if the URLs are still valid.

Summary

You now know how to create a Web site by linking text on one page to text on another page. You know how to drag and drop Page icons, anchors, and URLs to create these hypertext links.

The next subject builds on this chapter: creating and using imagemaps as source documents for hypertext links.

Chapter 6

Creating Active Images and Imagemaps

Have you ever visited a Web site that had a graphic with hotspots that, depending on what part of the graphic you clicked, took you to different parts of the Web site? These are called *imagemaps*. In Chapters 4 and 5, I spoke about inserting images and creating hypertext links. Let's review a little bit about images. Images are objects, like Java applets, QuickTime movies, sound files, PDFs, or animated GIFs. You learned how to make a hyperlink to an image in Chapter 5. Single pictures with links are termed buttons in PageMill language. Now, let's introduce an added complexity: *active images*. Active images are images with hyperlinks to more than one destination.

Active images contain *hotspots*—areas within the image that hold separate hyperlinks. The hyperlinks enable your readers to click the hotspot on the picture to go to different URLs on or off your site. Active images are also sometimes called *clickable maps, active maps, sensitive maps,* and *imagemap.*

 Note

Let's not use the term *imagemap* for your Web page's pictures with hotspots, and talk about it separately, because an imagemap is both a special file used to activate clickable maps on the server prior to Netscape Navigator 2.0 and Microsoft Internet Explorer 2.0 and the name of the special server application used to do the interpreting.

A Short History of Active Images

When the Web first was developed in the late 1980s–early 1990s, all of the work of interpreting mouse coordinates, translating their location onscreen into a hotspot, locating the URL linked to the hotspot, and moving to that destination was performed on the server. Imagemaps are also sometimes called server-side image-maps because in order for the hotspots to work, the server re-quired the use of an application called a *common gateway interface* (CGI) to interpret the maps. To confuse things further, the CGI that came with the server used to do the interpreting was called *imagemap.*

In 1995, James Seidman of Spyglass, Inc. devised a new way to embed the mouse coordinates and URL information within the Web page for the Spyglass proprietary browser. These client-side mapping conventions were shared with the public and soon incorporated into the HTML 3.0 standard and accepted by both Netscape Navigator 2.0, and higher, and Microsoft Internet Explorer 2.0, and higher. *Seidman mapping* does not require a CGI on the server or coordinating with the Webmaster to ensure that your imagemap file is understood by that server's CGI software. It does require the conversion of mouse coordinates to HTML (which PageMill does for you).

Your readers' browser and the server knows you are using a client-side map because PageMill adds an HTML attribute called USEMAP to the <IMG> tag and a pair of <MAP> </MAP> tags enclosing the hotspot coordinates into the HTML.

 Note

Because the map information is either embedded in the Web page (indicated by giving the USEMAP attribute the value of the name of the imagemap file that is the same as the HTML file) or is another HTML file residing in the same folder as the image (indicated by a value for USEMAP that provides the name of the additional HTML file), you can test the results of your hotspots in the Preview mode of PageMill. You cannot check the results of server-side maps because the data needed for the link is not present. This is one of the many reasons client-side mapping is easier to implement than server-side mapping.

The caveat is that not all mapping tools or browsers can interpret client-side maps. It is polite to include both client-side and server-side map information on your pages to accommodate all browsers, so this chapter discusses both client-side and server-side mapping techniques.

How Client-Side and Server-Side Mapping Works

All maps begin with an image or images you mark into areas. When you click this area, the browser jumps to another URL. Setting up the coordinates is done using four graphics tools: a square, a circle, a triangle, and a polygon. (Where you draw these hotspots is how PageMill differentiates client-side from server-side maps). The end result of your drawing work is a file, called an *imagemap file*, containing, in text, the mouse coordinates of the hotspots and their associated URLs.

Now the fun begins...

If you decide to draw your hotspots in PageMill using the Hotspot tools on the toolbar (accessed by double-clicking the image), you create a *client-side map*. This tells PageMill to either embed the imagemap file in the same HTML file as the image itself or it is saved in a separate file and an attribute tag value of USEMAP= maps.html#outfilemap is added with an HREF tag locating the imagemap file. The important thing is that the imagemap information remains local. The data is saved in the same folder as the image or in the page with the image. When your reader clicks a hotspot, the browser looks up the link location in the local file (or on the page) and contacts the Web server containing the linked page. This local processing enables client-side maps to load faster than the older server-side maps.

Server-side maps use an older system based on software on the server interpreting the coordinates. You create server-side maps to ensure that browsers based on HTML earlier than version 3.0 can use your active images. PageMill knows you are making a server-side map because you perform your work in the Out-of-Place editor (accessed by Command-double-clicking the image). The Out-of-Place editor contains the same shape tools as the Hotspot toolbar but adds the ability to create a link between the resulting imagemap file and the HTML page. You use the Out-of-Place editor because server-side maps require an extra step. PageMill sets up the server-side map by using a special attribute tag called ISMAP with the <IMG> tag that tells the server to look for an imagemap file to use for collecting the coordinates. PageMill also uses information you provide in the Inspector to tell the server which CGI (in NCSA servers this is typically and confusingly also called imagemap) will perform the coordinate translation work.

 Tip

Depending upon the age of the server software, there may be a helper program available that identifies the CGI needed, or you may have to identify the CGI. Check with the Webmaster to see what your server requires.

When the reader clicks the hotspot, the browser sends the click coordinates to the server, the server looks up the linked location in the imagemap file, contacts the server storing the linked page, and then sends the correct page back to the browser for displaying.

Server-side maps make the server work harder because the browser passes the translation work to a CGI. In addition, you cannot check to see if the hotspot connects to its referenced URL because the coordinates are not yet translated in server-side maps. You can test your hotspots if you are using client-side mapping because the coordinate translations are embedded in the HTML or located in a local HTML file. In addition, systems administrators must work with you to ensure you are making the proper references to CGIs, directory names, and so forth, prior to your uploading the active images. You can see that client-side maps are the way that Web page publishing is heading. But today we are half-in and half-out of the woods. It is still polite to give your readers both types of maps by first creating the active image in the content area in PageMill using the Hotspot tools, and then again in the Out-of-Place editor using its tools. The end result is HTML that names both imagemaps embedded in the page using the USEMAP tag and locates the imagemap file using the ISMAP tag and an HREF pointing to the CGI.

What Is an Active Image?

As stated earlier, an active image is a picture that points to more than one URL through the use of "hotspots.". Go to Nancy McNelly's Rabbit In the Moon site (`http://www.he.net/~nmcnelly`) for an example of the use of an active image.

Active images are different from the buttons you created with the Inspector in Chapter 4. On a button, the URL is attached to the entire image, and you are always taken to the same URL no matter where you click on the image. In an active image, when you click a hotspot (specially designated area of the image) you jump to a different URL.

Note

Remember, URLs can point to anything on the Internet, including pages on your own Web site or another Web site entirely. You can even point a hotspot to a larger version of a thumb-nail picture you used as the hotspot.

How Do Active Images Work?

As stated earlier, there are two types of active images: client-side and server-side maps. Client-side maps store all of the mouse coordinates and associated hyperlinks locally and let the browser link with the connected site directly. Server-side maps use the server's services to translate the mouse coordinates into screen locations with associated hyperlinks, and link with the connected page, via a CGI.

Figure 6.1 is the home page of Steve Mulder, Web guru at Hayden Books (`http://www.mcp.com/people/mulder/`). The page consists of a large image with several clickable "hotspots" indicated by overlaid words. Each hotspot is a clickable area linked to another page at Steve Mulder's site.

Figure 6.2 shows the source HTML code for this page. Note that some active images contain coordinates embedded into the page. These are client-side maps. Other hotspots point to imagemap files. These are server-side maps. Yet, when you return to the actual Web page, the images do not look different—only their behavior behind the scenes when you click a hotspot differs.

 Tip

If you are not sure your visitors are using browsers that support any imagemapping at all, be sure to provide an alternative method to link to the intended page (such as a line of text links beneath the map). In PageMill, the Alternate text box in the Image screen of the Inspector provides a place to give the image a name that can be clicked to jump to the associated URL.

Figure 6.1
Steve Mulder's
home page contains
both client-side and
server-side maps.

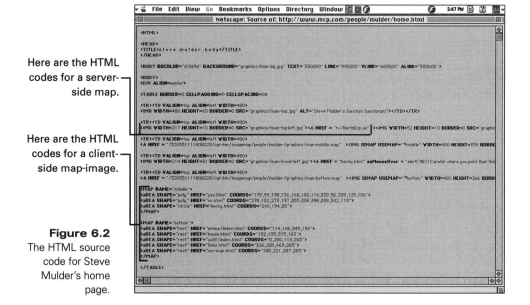

Here are the HTML
codes for a server-
side map.

Here are the HTML
codes for a client-
side map-image.

Figure 6.2
The HTML source
code for Steve
Mulder's home
page.

Preparing Your Site To Use Active Images

The server recognizes two formats for active images: CERN and NCSA (named after the research facilities that developed the formats). Before you create an active image, you must tell PageMill which format your server accepts. In addition, if you are still planning to use a server-based CGI to process your map, you need to identify the absolute path name of your map file (identified by the .map suffix). PageMill creates the .map file for you, or you can write your own using a text editor. Both versions of the file should be saved in the same folder as the clickable image. The last thing you have to do is tell PageMill where to find the clickable image. All three things are done using the Preferences dialog box.

Setting Up Preferences

1 Select the Preferences command from the Edit menu. (Press F2 on the PC.)

2 On the Mac, select the Resources icon on the left frame to display its window. On the PC, click the Resources tab.

3 Under the Images section, select either CERN or NCSA from the Map Format pop-up menu (see Figure 6.3).

Note

Find out from your Webmaster which formatting method your server is using and select that standard from the Images pop-up menu. Map files are text documents that describe the regions you defined in your hotspot, as well as the URLs attached to them. Hotspots and their map files can be formatted as either NCSA or CERN files. NCSA is the National Center for Supercomputing Applications. CERN is a French abbreviation for the European Particle Physics Lab. Both organizations are largely responsible for the standards of the World Wide Web, and both have a format for creating active imagemap files.

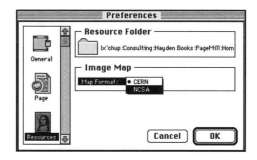

Figure 6.3
Select a map format
from the Map
Format pop-up
menu prior to
creating any active
images.

Mac

Tip

If you are serving your hotspots from a Macintosh and using the
imagemap.acgi, choose NCSA.

4 Click Save and close the Preferences dialog box.

Setting the Local Resource Folder

1 Select Preferences from the Edit menu.

2 On the Mac, select the Resources icon on the left frame to display its window. On the PC, click the Rources tab.

3 In the Resource section, click the Folder icon.

4 In the resulting Open dialog box, select a folder to store your
imagemap files and images. Click the Open button to open the
folder and then click In Here (see Figure 6.4). Click the Browse
button in the Resources Folder section to open the Browse folder.
Select the folder to use as your Local Resource folder.

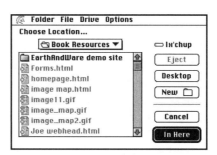

Figure 6.4
Identify the location
of imagemap files
by selecting a folder
here.

Setting the Remote Server Location

1 Select Preferences on the Edit menu. You'll have to scroll down to see it.

2 Select the Server icon on the left frame to display its window.

3 On the Mac, in the text area, type the absolute pathname next to the Globe icon. On the PC, type the URL of your Website (as provided by your ISP) in the text box. Use the clear button to start over if you make a mistake.

4 Click the folder icon beneath the text you typed to identify the location of your site.

5 In the resulting Open dialog box, select a folder to store your imagemap files and images (by clicking Open) and then click In Here. On the PC, type the pathname for your local folder where your site is currently saved or click Browse to select a folder from the Browse for Folder window.

6 The pathname of your site folder is entered into the Server Preferences window (see Figure 6.5).

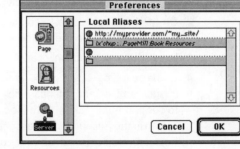

Figure 6.5
Identify the location of the server-side map in the Server Preferences window.

Understanding Hot Spots

Both client-side and server-side maps rely on a set of coordinates created when you delineated the hotspot with your hotspot tools. When your reader clicks a hotspot, the coordinates of the spot clicked (such as 14, 160, meaning 14 pixels over from the upper-left corner of the image and 160 pixels down) are converted to a URL and passed back to the server (in server-side mapping) or saved with your HTML file (in client-side mapping). The coordinates are determined based on where you click the mouse.

To create an active image, you need to identify different sections of the image you want to use as "hotspots" and assign different URLs to each spot.

Object-Oriented vs. Bitmap Images

Computers have two ways of understanding shapes onscreen. One is called *bitmapped*. The other is called *object-oriented*. Bitmapped means the computer knows there are a bunch of pixels onscreen. Object-oriented means, if you draw a circle, the computer knows it is a complete object. With object-oriented applications, you can draw an object (an object being line, dot, polygon, circle, and so on), and then select it with the pointer and resize it or move it to a new location. PageMill is object-oriented.

Defining a specific region of an image involves identifying the coordinates of specific pixels in a pre-determined area of the image (namely, the "hotspot"). Remember, everything displayed on a monitor, from a picture of the Mona Lisa, which you can download from the Louvre Web site (`http://www.paris.org/Musees/Louvre/Treasures/`), to the letters in a word are made up of pixels.

 Note

Pixel is a combination of the words *picture* and *element*.

If you understand that the graphic you plan to use as an active image is handled by the computer as a series of dots arranged in rows and columns, you can imagine that there is a grid overlaying the image where each pixel has a corresponding set of coordinates. Using this imaginary grid, you can refer to individual pixels by their coordinates—the number of pixels across and down the screen. The top-left pixel then is 0,0.

Let's say that this image is 450 pixels wide and 200 pixels tall. The lower-right pixel, then, is 450, 200. (Coordinates are always given as number of pixels across, number of pixels down.) Figure 6.6 shows the coordinates mapped onto the image. When you did graphing in geometry or algebra class, the number of pixels across was always copied into a variable called x; the number of pixels down was copied into a variable called *y* (oh no! variables again!). The main difference here from algebra or geometry is that the coordinate 0,0 is the top-left corner. In algebra and geometry 0,0 is the lower-left corner.

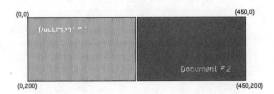

Figure 6.6
Image illustrating the coordinate system.

URLs are activated when certain pixels in a hotspot are clicked. In Figure 6.7, the graphic is shown with the middle line at pixel 225, 0. The bottom of the line is 225, 200. If the user selects a pixel to the left of that line (with an x variable less than 225), you want the server to access the URL to retrieve document #1. If the user clicks a pixel to the right of the line (with an *x* value greater than 225), you want the server to access the URL to retrieve document #2.

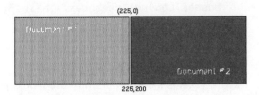

Figure 6.7
The division of the two areas by the coordinate system.

Creating the Hotspot

Active images can be created from any GIF image, but your graphic should have some visual clues showing what each one of the regions does or where they take you.

It is very easy to tell PageMill the coordinates of a hotspot. Use the Hotspot tools on the toolbar or Out-Of-Place Editor tool palette to draw geometric shapes on top of the image. The coordinates of the pixels composing the shape tells PageMill where to put the hotspot.

Let's make some hotspots.

Open a new document in PageMill. Drag the image_map.gif file from the CD into a new document (see Figure 6.8). When you have placed it in the PageMill window, double-click the image to invoke the Hotspot tools on the PageMill Editor window's toolbar so that you can delineate hotspots on the image directly on the Content area (or you can Command/Control-double-click the image, which opens the Out-of-Place editor window. You use the window's tools to label hotspots by drawing shapes around the area you want to be "hot" when you want to create server-side active images).

Figure 6.8
A single graphic image with two sections.

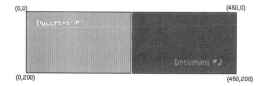

If you have ever used a drawing program, these should look familiar to you. They are as follows:

- **Pointer tool.** Used to move objects around.

- **Rectangle hotspot.** Used to define areas with four right angles.

- **Circle hotspot.** Used to define areas of circular objects.

- **Polygon hotspot.** Used to define areas objects with multiple sides, all made of straight lines.

 Note

You cannot draw with PageMill. All of your images need to be created in another application. The Circle, Rectangle, and Polygon hotspots are used to map the regions to which you want to attach URLs.

To create a rectangular region to which a URL can be attached, select the Rectangle hotspot and drag it diagonally across the area of the graphic labeled Document #1. This specifies a particular group of pixels; all the pixels within the rectangle. Now you need to attach the URL.

Click the link location bar at the bottom of the PageMill Editor mode's window to turn on the text field. Enter the URL to be attached to this group of pixels. Type `http://your_web_site/ document_one.html`, for this example, and press Return/Enter. This URL now appears inside the rectangle (see Figure 6.9). If the URL is not there, click the checkbox with the letter A (on the left side of the Out-of-Place editor or the last button on the Hotspot toolbar). With this checkbox, you can either have the URL displayed in the hotspot or be hidden.

 Tip

> You can also assign URLs to hotspots by dragging the Page icon of the destination page (or its anchor) onto the hotspot to create the link. See Chapter 5 for a further discussion of how to create links.

Figure 6.9
The link address of the destination document is displayed in the hotspot and on the link location bar.

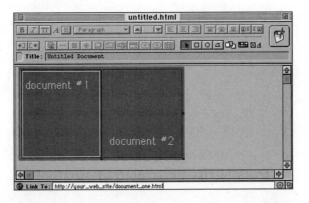

The default color of the URL and the area you defined is blue, but you can change this with the Color Palette icon. You don't have many choices. The important point is to make the URL a color that stands out from the image so that it is easier to see.

 Changing the Active Color of a Hotspot

1 Double-click the graphic to activate the Hotspot toolbar.

2 Create a hotspot using one of the hotspot tools.

3 Create a link to the hotspot.

4 Select the Color Palette icon to open its pop-up menu.

5 Drag the mouse to a color and release the button. The URL changes to the color you selected (Figure 6.10).

Figure 6.10
Click the Color Palette button to open the palette. Drag the mouse and release its button to select a new hotspot active color.

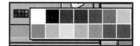

Now, do the same for the other side of the dividing line. Create a rectangle that extends from the dividing line to the edge of the image. Type `http://your_web_site/document_two.html` in the text box in the link location bar (or drag the destination page's Page or anchor icon onto the mapped image) (see Figure 6.11).

Figure 6.11
When you are finished, both sides of the image will be linked to separate pages via independent URLs.

You have created two hotspots on a graphic and attached URLs to them. If you are using client-side mapping, your work is done when you save the HTML file containing the hotspots. PageMill converts the pixels to coordinates and embeds the numbers in the HTML file.

 Note

URLs can point to anything on the Internet. Try experimenting with the URLs you are putting into the Location box. Try linking to other Web sites, email addresses, or FTP sites.

More about Defining Clickable Regions

PageMill can create clickable regions in shapes other than simple rectangles. Open a new document in PageMill. From *The PageMill Handbook* CD-ROM, drag the image image_map2.gif into the new document. Double-click the image to display the imagemap tools on the toolbar. You can use the rectangle, circle, and polygon hotspots to define areas of this image.

Single-click the Circle hotspot. You can use this to define circular regions and attach URLs to them the same way you did with the Rectangle hotspot.

Define a circular area around region #2 as shown in Figure 6.12. Notice you are not drawing ovals with this tool. You cannot define oval regions with PageMill because regions must be defined by a center point and a point on the radius so that proper coordinates can be identified. This is only possible if the region is a perfect circle. When you use the Circle hotspot to define a region, the point at which you click the mouse is the upper-left corner of a square that encloses the circle.

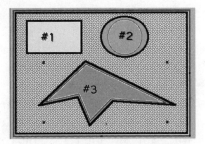

Figure 6.12
A graphic with irregular clickable areas.

The Polygon hotspot is used to define regions with many sides where all lines are straight. When using the Polygon hotspot, the first mouse click becomes the first point of your polygon. You then get a line from that point that you can extend in any direction and any length. The next mouse click becomes the second point, giving you a second line that you can extend any direction and any length. Try to define area #3 in Figure 6.12 with the Polygon hotspot. When you have created the perfect polygon, double-click the mouse. This will draw a line from the last point you made to the first point, closing the polygon. Type the URL into the link location bar and press Return.

Editing Defined Regions

After you have mapped a few regions on the image, you may need to adjust them. Select objects by clicking them. You can drag the region or resize it by clicking one of its corners (see Figure 6.13). You can do this with any of the objects that you have created. Always save your changes to update the PageMill document (and any accompanying map file you may be creating).

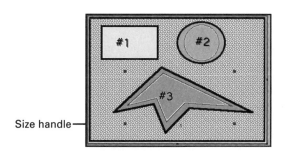

Figure 6.13
Click and drag a size
handle to resize
a hotspot.

Size handle—

Understanding the Map File

As stated earlier, server-side active images need a separate file that describes the pixel coordinates and source and destination URLs of the hotspots on an image. This file, called a *map* file, is used by the CGI to create the hypertext link.

Map files are indicated by the .map suffix. Use the Out-of-Place editor to create an active image using the graphic from the CD-ROM called image_map2.gif. Find the active image map file in the Book Resources folder you identified in the Preferences dialog box. Open the map file. If you chose NCSA format, it should look like this:

```
rect      http://your_web_site/document_two.html 144,0
290,155 rect
http://your_web_site/document_one.html 0,0 144,154
```

This is your map file. If yours does not look exactly like this, don't worry. Your coordinates will, of course, be different and sometimes PageMill puts all the information on a single line.

Each line of the map file consists of three sections. The first section tells you to what type of region the map file is referring (in this case, "rect" is short for rectangle). The next section is the URL, and the last section holds the coordinates attached to this URL. In this case, only two sets of coordinates are needed: the upper-left corner and the lower-right corner. Because this is a rectangle, known from the first bit of information, only two sets of coordinates are needed to draw the complete region.

Upload the map file (.map suffixed file), shown in Figure 6.14, to the same directory on the server where the rest of your HTML files reside.

Figure 6.14
This is the map file created for the 3tools active image.

How the Map File Works

Warning! This section is pretty techno-Web geeky. If you're not interested, skip ahead and leave the rest of us to our propeller hats. Your Webmaster should understand this information. It's not required knowledge if you're creating documents for a server that someone else is managing.

As you recall, the primary function of server software is receiving requests and sending files. All other duties are delegated to the CGIs on the server computer. When a user clicks a pixel inside a hotspot, the browser software sends the coordinates of the mouse click to the server. Those mouse click coordinates get delegated to a CGI that handles active images.

The imagemap CGI contains rules. Rules are the basis of all computer applications, in the form of if…then statements. An application receives information and passes it through its if…then statements. The application then performs actions based on the results.

Note

An if...then statement says if a certain condition exists (such as a number being within a certain range), then perform the action listed next (such as add the two numbers together and place the results in an address area). If...then statements are also called conditionals.

A series of if...then statements helps the imagemap CGI decide which file is being requested by the user. You can imagine that, inside of the CGI, there are some rules that look like this:

If *x* is greater than 144 and less than 290,

and if *y* is greater than 0 and less than 155,

then tell the Web server to send document two.html to the user.

If *x* is greater than 0 and less than 144,

and y is greater than 0 and less than 154,

then tell the Web server to send document_one.html to the user.

So, let's say the user clicks coordinates 18, 95, which are sent to the CGI. The CGI receives this as *x*=18&*y*=95. The CGI then passes these coordinates through the rules above and concludes it needs to tell the server to send out document_one.html.

The way the CGI and Web server software communicate is pretty complex and not within the scope of this book. For our purposes, let's just say that they are able to exchange information freely and with relative ease.

You now have a Web page with a graphic marked with hotspots. Each hotspot is linked to a URL. If you are creating a server side active image, you also have a separate text file named with a suffix .map describing the coordinates and URLs. The best way to understand active images is to compare the HTML for client-side versus server-side active images. I created a Web page called server-side test.html containing a graphic marked with three hotspots for client-side mapping. I copied the graphic and created a server-side hotspot. Figure 6.15 shows the source code for these two active images. Note that the client-side hotspot HTML includes a MAP NAME attribute and the actual pixel coordinates of the hotspot copied from the .map file. The server-side hotspot includes an ISMAP attribute and the name of the .map file.

Figure 6.15
The HTML source
code shows the
different code of a
client-side map.

```
<P><IMG SRC="3tools.gif" WIDTH="111" HEIGHT="65" ALIGN="BOTTOM" NATURALSIZEFLAG=
"3"> <MAP NAME="3tools">
    <AREA SHAPE="rect" COORDS="4,4,37,64" HREF="../formsindex.html">
</MAP><IMG SRC="3tools.gif" WIDTH="111" HEIGHT="65" ALIGN="BOTTOM" NATURALSIZEFLAG=
"3" USEMAP="#3tools" ISMAP>
```

Newer servers, such as the Apache Unix server, can find the map file if it is stored with your other HTML files, and it knows it needs a CGI if it finds a .map filename.

Older servers need to be told where the CGI resides. So, you need to give the server the absolute pathname to the .map file and include the CGI's name, as follows:

```
<A HREF="/cgi-bin/imagemap/~your name/texts/name of
map file.map"><IMG SRC=".../images/name of the graphic
used to create the hotspots.gif" ISMAP></A>
```

In our example, you would have to edit the HTML (See Chapter 9 for information on how to edit the HTML source code) to read:

```
<A HREF="/cgi-bin/imagemap/~my_site/
EarthAndWare%20demo%20site/images/3tools.map"> <IMG
SRC=".../images/3tools.gif" ISMAP></A>
```

To be polite, try having it both ways and edit the HTML source code (See Chapter 9 again) to state:

```
<A HREF="/cgi-bin/imagemap/~my_site/
EarthAndWare%20demo%20site/images/3tools.map"> <IMG
SRC=".../images/3tools.gif" USEMAP="#3tools" ISMAP></
A>
```

This gives the server both a client-side map and a server-side map to work with. Client-side browsers will use the #3tools information and ignore the 3tools.map. Non-capable browsers will use the 3tools.map absolute path to locate the CGI and imagemap file and use server-side processing.

More Information About the Out-of-Place Editor

Inside the Out-of-Place editor window (see Figure 6.15) you can control several aspects of the image, including interlacing the image, making the GIF image transparent, as well as adding the hotspots that when clicked take the reader to another page. Physical size is the only aspect of the image the Out-of-Place editor can't control.

Open a new document in PageMill. Drag the file year_god.gif from *The Adobe PageMill 2.0 Handbook* CD-ROM into the new document. Press the Command key and double-click the image to open it in the Out-of-Place editor (Figure 6.16) You can also open a GIF image in the Out-of-Place editor by double-clicking the image file directly.

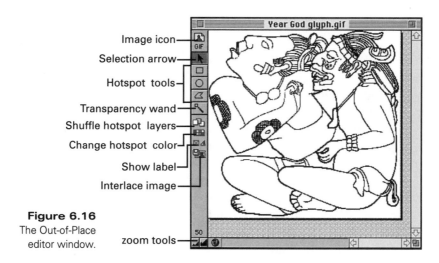

Image icon
Selection arrow
Hotspot tools
Transparency wand
Shuffle hotspot layers
Change hotspot color
Show label
Interlace image

Figure 6.16
The Out-of-Place
editor window.　　zoom tools

Using the Out-of-Place Editor to Create Links

The top-left corner of the Out-of-Place editor contains an Image icon with the word GIF under it. GIF is one of the two image formats that can be served over the Web (JPEG is the other). The icon works like to the Page icon in the main PageMill window in Edit mode. The icon represents the image, and you can drag-and-drop it onto pages other than the one you are working on or onto other elements (images or text) on the page.

Being able to drag-and-drop the Image icon lets you do two things:

- Create links to outside images
- Copy and paste local images on to pages

Dragging and Dropping Images Using the GIF Icon

As mentioned previously, you can copy and paste an image into other pages by dragging and dropping its image icon. You can try this now by opening a new page, clicking the Image icon, and dragging it onto the new page. It should appear on the new page as if you copied and pasted it there. Close the second window.

The Image icon also lets you create links to external images. Before you ask, here's why you would want a link to an external image: images are big. They take up a lot of space on your hard drive, take a long time to transfer, and, on the Internet, time is definitely money. If you have a large image that takes up a lot of pixels or uses several colors, the file is going to take a great deal of memory and a long time to transfer. Although you might have spent hours making sure that every detail of your hamster Joey's image is absolutely perfect, there is a good chance the user does not want to spend his $4.95 an hour access time downloading it. If you place the image in the document, you don't give the user a choice; when he loads your page, he gets the picture of Joey.

A better solution, and one that is more user-friendly, is to give users the *option* of looking at the 120K image of Joey. For example, type the line **Here's a 120K picture of my lovely hamster Joey** and make it a link to the image. If someone wants to see it, they can click the link. If not, you haven't wasted their time.

Let's try this in PageMill. Create a link to the year_god.gif image (located in the Images folder on the CD-ROM). If you don't have the image available from the previous example, open the image in PageMill by selecting Open on the File menu (or type Command-O) or by clicking the Insert Object button on the toolbar. In the resulting Open dialog box, find star.gif in the Finder list box and double-click it to open it (or select the image and click Open). The Out-of-Place editor opens with the image inside it.

Now, create a new page (by choosing New Page from the File menu, or by typing Command-N). In the new page, type **Here is the glyph for the year god** and highlight the text. Go back to the Out-of-Place editor and drag the GIF icon over the highlighted text in the main PageMill window and release the mouse button.

A link has now been created from this text to the image (Figure 6.17). Switch to Preview mode in PageMill and try out the link. Clicking the text will switch you to the Out-of-Place editor window with the picture of the star. Over the Web, this image will be displayed in the window of the reader's Web Browser.

Figure 6.17
The year god glyph image will open when you click the linked text.

Interlacing Images

In the column of buttons on the left side of the Out-of-Place editor is an icon that looks like a disk in front of a person (see Figure 6.14). Click this icon and a series of horizontal bars appear across it. This interlaces the image. *Interlaced* is a type of GIF image. When you have interlaced GIFs on your Web page, the browser displays a very low-resolution version of the image first and then passes over it a few times, refining the detail until the reader sees the finished product (see Figure 6.18).

Figure 6.18
The initial displayed view of an interlaced image.

You should interlace all your GIF images. Interlaced GIFs give the reader a preview of what is to come and show that the server is active and in the process of sending the image. User patience with slow-loading graphics is notorious. Interlaced GIFs are an excellent way to get the reader's attention and hold it during the sometimes arduous process of image loading. Some browsers have the added benefit of loading text before the image's detail is refined, enabling the reader to view text while waiting for the image to appear.

Transparent Images

In the middle of the toolbar in the Out-of-Place editor window is a button with a Magic Wand icon. The Magic Wand is used to make the background of any GIF image transparent. Turning backgrounds transparent is important for images that are going to be displayed over the Web for two reasons: the images will look better and load quicker.

First, an explanation of what is meant by making the background transparent. All GIF images are saved with a background, which is usually white. If you have a non-rectangular image, it displays on your Web page with a white rectangle around it. Because the default background on most Web browsers is gray, this will make your image look out of place on the page (see Figure 6.19).

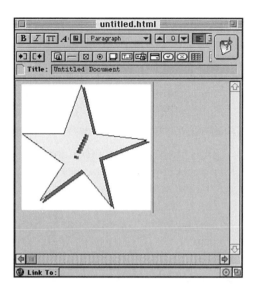

Figure 6.19
An image with a
white background.

When you make the background transparent, the color of the
Web browser's window is the image's background (see Figure
6.20). The image looks more integrated into the page. Changing
your background color will not affect the transparency; the new
color will show through, just like the old one (see Chapter 4 for
details on how to change the background of the window).

Figure 6.20
An image with a
transparent
background.

An image loads faster when the background is transparent because removing the background makes the file size of the image smaller. The image in Figure 6.18 takes 22K of disk space. The image in Figure 6.19—the same image but with the transparent background—takes up 11K. As mentioned earlier, the smaller the image file, the faster it loads. Making an image's background transparent is a quick way to decrease the file size of your images.

Drag the star.gif GIF icon into the content area of PageMill to place a copy of the image on your page. Return to the Out-of-Place editor of the star.gif file and select the Magic Wand tool. Click the white background and your image becomes transparent. You'll need to save the image for it to become transparent on your page.

Zoom Tools

The last set of tools in the Out-of-Place editor is the zoom tools (see Figure 6.21). In the lower-left corner of the Out-of-Place editor window are two landscape icons. The one on the right zooms in to the image; the one on the left zooms out. This doesn't change the size or appearance of the image in your document, just your view of it. You can enlarge your view of the image 800 percent and reduce it to 12 percent.

Figure 6.21
The zoom tools zoom the image in or out, changing its focus so that you can see it more clearly in the editor window.

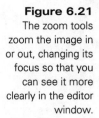

Summary

Creating active images used to be very difficult to achieve because you did not know what would happen when your reader clicked a hotspot (because the processing was all done by the server's software). Today, with the advent of client-side maps, all of the pixel coordinates locating the hotspot and its hyperlink are embedded into the document, obviating the need for a specialized helper program on the server. Suddenly, active images are much more achievable.

In PageMill 2.0, it is assumed that you wish to create client-side maps because they are easier to load, present less overhead for the server software, and jump to their links more quickly than the older server-side maps. PageMill does all the work of translating coordinates and embedding pixel locations and URLs. PageMill also creates the imagemap file that records the pixel coordinates and URLs should you need this file to create a server-side image.

In this chapter, you learned

- How to differentiate client-side from server-side maps in the HTML.

- How to set up PageMill to create client-side and server-side maps.

- How to edit graphics in the Out-Of-Place editor to reduce their size (with the Transparency tool) and speed up their downloading (with the Interlacing tool).

- How to create a hotspot and link it to another page.

- How to work with HTML to ensure that all browsers can use your active images.

Imagemaps are a popular way to spruce up your Web pages. PageMill makes defining them easy.

Chapter 7 increases your skills in advanced page layout. It describes two new features of PageMill 2.0: tables and frames that you can use to control the layout of graphics and text on a page.

Chapter 7

Tables and Frames

This chapter discusses two new formatting commands added to PageMill 2.0 to make WYSIWYG Web page layout more "WYSIWYG": Tables and Frames.

- **Tables.** Tables are ways to arrange information in columns and rows, the intersection of which is called a *cell*. Cells are an excellent way of aligning graphics, areas of color, and separating areas of your page because HTML provides such limited support for basic desktop publishing features as object alignment, multiple columns of text, or layering. You can also actually display spreadsheet information with a table. PageMill 2.0's implementation of tables lets you add colors to separate cells, align objects horizontally and vertically, and change the size of individual cells or the entire table. You can also add borders to individual cells.

- **Frames.** Frames are a way of placing more than one URL location on a page. You can break up your page into horizontal or vertical sections and designate separate URLs for the areas. In this manner, you can create windows that shift URL pages within your page by placing an index in one area and having the other area display the contents of the index subject when it is selected. Each frame set can be named and saved separately to let you add many HTML pages to a single screen.

Creating Tables

To create a table in the "old days" (with PageMill 1.0), you had to go into Raw HTML mode and laboriously type in tags indicating the presence of each cell in a table. PageMill 2.0 introduces a new series of commands on the toolbar that create tables onscreen that can be resized using the mouse for utmost flexibility. After using the Insert Table button on the left side of the toolbar to create the cells of your table, you are presented with an array of table cell manipulation tools on the right side of the toolbar (see Figure 7.1).

Figure 7.1
Use the Table toolbar buttons to manipulate table cells.

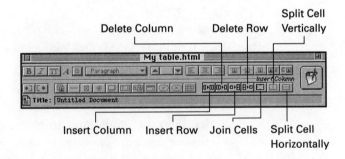

Tip

It is legal and smart to look at the document source code of Web pages you admire. (In Netscape Navigator, select Show Document Source from the View menu. In Microsoft Internet Explorer, select Source from the View menu. Whenever you see the <TABLE> tag, you know there is an invisible table being used as a design aid. You'd be surprised how many good looking Web sites use tables. Figures 7.2a and 7.2b show David Siegel's Creating Killer Sites Home Page (`http://www.killersites.com/core.html`) and its underlying source code to illustrate the use of tables as containers. (The site is a companion to a terrific book on the aesthetics of constructing Web pages, called Creating Killer Web Sites, published in 1996, by Hayden Books.)

Figure 7.2a
Here is David Siegel's "Killer Sites" Home Page. He uses many invisible tables to layout his objects.

Figure 7.2b
Note that the black column, multiple objects, and text reside in separate joined cells that are used as a grid to layout the page.

Tables are not only useful as ways to present columns and rows of text and numbers, such as you get in a spreadsheet, but you can also use a table as a design aid to add blocks of color, align elements, or create multiple columns of text. You can insert another bordered table within the design-aid borderless table or line up images as buttons or active images using this technique. In fact, you can place any object into a table, including other tables, plug-ins such as Java applets, and so forth.

Tables are easy to create—just press a button and drag a picture—but difficult to manipulate because the table functions as an entire object. You have to work with all columns and rows when sizing the table and realize that each column's width affects all of the other columns. Cell padding and Cell spacing also affect how objects will fit into tables. You should pre-design the measurements of your table's width and the relationship of the cell sizes to this width prior to creating the table. All tables are initially placed across the entire width of a page (640 pixels).

Creating a Basic Table

1 In an open PageMill document, click the Insert Table button on the toolbar and drag the resulting pull-down table horizontally and vertically. The pull-down table numbers the cells horizontally for rows and vertically for columns. Drag the mouse down and across until the number of cells in the table (columns and rows) that you want to use are displayed (see Figure 7.3).

Figure 7.3
Click and drag the table button to create a table.

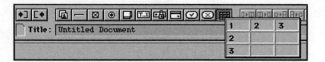

2 Release the mouse. The table is displayed (see Figure 7.4). You are now ready to select horizontal and vertical borders to resize columns and rows, add color to cells and text, change the width of the entire table, and so forth.

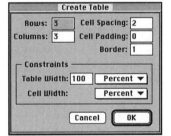

Figure 7.4
When you release the mouse, the table is placed on the page.

 Tip

You can also create a table by clicking the table button on the toolbar. In the resulting Create Table dialog box (see Figure 7.5) type the number of rows and columns in their associated text boxes. Change the cell border thickness, distance between cells, and space between the contents of the cell and its borders (cell padding) by selecting the appropriate text box and typing a new number. Click OK to close the box and display the table. Read more about using borders, cell padding, setting cell height and width, and so forth with the Inspector in the paragraphs below.

Figure 7.5
Click the table button once to display the Create Table dialog box.

 Tip

You can open a Microsoft Excel spreadsheet and copy a selection of cells and paste them into a PageMill document. PageMill will convert the selected table into HTML. If you move large tables from Excel to PageMill, the conversion process may take time and does require large amounts of RAM.

Selecting and Moving Cells

There are three areas in a table where you can select items:

1 **Select the table.** Click the border of the table to select it for resizing. A colored marquee surrounds the entire table. (The color of the marquee is based upon the color settings of your computer desktop. My highlight color is set on pink, so the marquee appears pink on my screen. Yours will be different.) If you want to select the entire table to change Table attributes in the Inspector, click the table. A gray boundary surrounds the entire table. You can double-click the table to open the Table Cell screen of the Inspector for the cell that was closest to the cursor.

2 **Select a cell (or cells).** You would want to select cells to copy or move a cell or change Table Cell attributes in the Inspector (or via the toolbar's buttons). Shift-click on a cell outside of its contents. Drag the mouse while Shift-clicking to select more than one cell at a time. A marquee surrounds the cell or cells (see Figure 7.6). Note that if your cursor is on the border of a cell when you click the mouse, the marquee and cursor changes to a resize box.

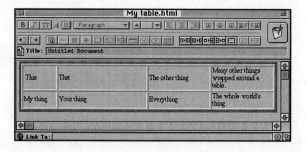

Figure 7.6
Shift-click a cell to select it.

3 **Select the contents of a cell.** You would want to select an object or text to create an active image, edit text, or change the attributes of text using the toolbar and menu bar. Click within the object in the cell (or Shift-click to select more than one item). A marquee with resize handles surrounds the object (see Figure 7.7). Click and drag to select text. Click within text to place the insertion point within the text for editing.

Figure 7.7
Click an object to
select it.

You can copy a cell (or cells) by dragging the cell's marquee off of the table and on to the location of the insertion point. When you release the mouse, the cell is placed across the entire width of the page (see Figure 7.8).

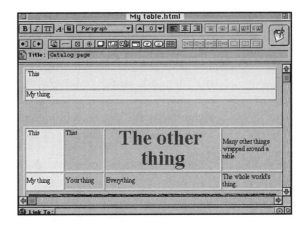

Figure 7.8
Drag a cell's
marquee to copy it
and its contents to
another location.

You add text to a table by clicking inside a cell and typing. Text will wrap around the cell as a default (you can change the default using the Table Cell screen of the Inspector). The cell where you are typing grows to accommodate the quantity of type or the size of the object you insert into a cell.

Formatting Cells Using the Toolbar

Anything placed in a cell, be it text, images, movies, and so forth, can be formatted using the style buttons on the toolbar (see Chapter 4 for a discussion of working with text and images). You can perform the following formatting to things in cells:

■ **Align objects.** You can click the Left, Center, or Right alignment buttons on the toolbar to align objects and text to the cell (see Figure 7.9).

Figure 7.9
Click an alignment button to align objects to cells.

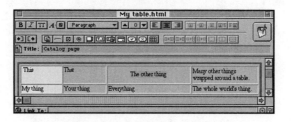

■ **Set up styles and formats.** Use the Format pop-up menu on the toolbar to make selected paragraphs into a paragraph format, such as a heading, paragraph, address, and so forth. (An alternative way to change paragraph formats is to use the format hierarchical menus from the Format menu on the menu bar.) You can also select text and apply character styles, such as Emphasis, Strong, Citation, bold, italic, and so forth from the Style menu or toolbar (see Figure 7.10).

Figure 7.10
Use the Format pop-up menu and Style buttons on the toolbar to change the formatting of paragraphs in tables.

■ **Change the color of text.** Colored text is useful if you want to create a contrast between a dark background and white letters or make the text more legible against bright backgrounds. Headlines in white on a dark background can be very striking. You can also change the color of text in a table by selecting the Font pop-up menu and choosing Custom, then select a color from the resulting color wheel.

 ## Changing the Color of Text In Tables

1   Select the text you want to change.

2 Open the Color Panel by selecting Show Color Panel from the Window menu.

3 Select a color from the Panel and drag it onto the highlighted text. The text changes to the selected color (see Figure 7.11). You can also drag the color on to the Font pop-up menu on the toolbar.

Figure 7.11
Drag a color from the Color Panel on to the selected text to change its color.

■ **Change the size of your text.** Select the text in a cell (or series of cells) and use the arrows on the Relative Font Size box on the toolbar to make the text larger or smaller. You can also type a number into the box.

■ **Wrap text around an image or object.** Select the image or object and click the appropriate button to cause the text to flow around the object, be placed at the top of the object, be placed at the center of the object, or be placed at the bottom of the object (see Figure 7.12).

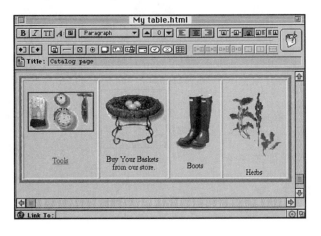

Figure 7.12
Use the Object Alignment buttons on the toolbar to set how text will flow around an object.

Formatting Cells Using the Inspector

Use the Table Cell attributes screen of the Inspector to vertically and horizontally align objects to the cell, set the width of cells, set how text is placed into a cell (for example, whether it wraps around the cell or inserts a single line), and whether the table has a row that serves as column headings. You can also change the background color of a cell (or cells).

Adjusting the Width of Cells

This powerful feature lets you use a column of cells to align objects and create beautiful backgrounds. Tables are composed of columns and rows of cells. Each cell is sized in relation to the entire table, as either a percentage or pixel-size. When you change the size of a column, the entire table structure adjusts to accommodate the change.

Hayden Books (`http://www.mcp.com/hayden/index.html`) uses a hidden table to create a running table of contents of animated buttons by varying the widths and colors of table columns (see Figure 7.13).

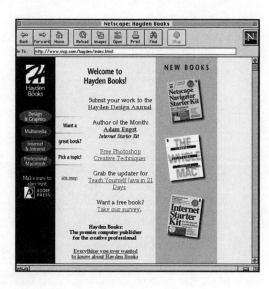

Figure 7.13
Notice how Hayden Books' home page uses horizontal bars of colors which are really table columns to arrange the subject matter of the Web site.

There are two ways to adjust the width of cells:

- **Use the mouse.** Select a cell or cells and pass the cursor over the right border. The cursor changes into a double-arrow. Hold down the mouse and drag the arrows right or left to widen or narrow the cell. Notice that the rest of the table expands or contracts to fit the size of your column to the size the entire table (see Figure 7.14).

Figure 7.14
Resize a column of cells by dragging the column border.

Tip

You cannot adjust the width of a single cell if there is more than one cell in a column. PageMill will move the entire column. The column will also not be widened if the object in another cell is too large to accommodate a wider cell because the overall width of the table does not adjust unless you move the outer border.

- **Use the Inspector.** Select the cell or column you want to resize. Type a new percentage (in this case, 25 percent) in the Width text box in the Table Cell screen of the Inspector. Remember to press the Return key to register your change. You can also change the measurement to pixels for a more accurate size (see Figure 7.15). The table behaves in the same fashion as when you used the mouse to perform the resizing of the column; a column will change size only in relation to the total size of the table.

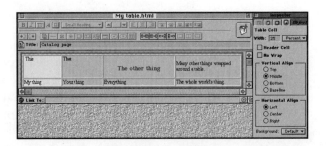

Figure 7.15
Typing a new number in the Width text box resizes a column in relation to the total table.

Another way to change the width of cells is to select the No Wrap checkbox in the Table Cell Inspector. Selecting this option causes any wrapped text in a cell to expand horizontally. The cell expands to accommodate the text. This method lacks precision but will create single-line cells from multi-line cell boxes if you should desire to line up text horizontally across columns.

Aligning the Contents of Cells to the Cells

You can use the Vertical and Horizontal Align radio buttons to set up how text or objects sit in a table cell. Text or objects can be centered vertically and/or horizontally, aligned left or right, top or bottom, or mixtures of these options by clicking the appropriate radio button in the Table Cell screen of the Inspector.

Adding Background Color to Cells

One of the interesting things you can do with the Inspector is to add color to the backgrounds of cells. This option lets you use tables to create borders, boxes, and boundaries on your pages. When accompanied by the alignment features mentioned in the previous paragraph, you have the tools to build attractive indices, such as the object-based one shown in Figure 7.13, Hayden Books' Home Page.

 Adding Background Color to a Cell

1   Open the Color Panel by selecting it from the Window menu.

2   Select the cell(s) you want to color.

3   If you want to use one of the eight colors optimized for browsers shown in the Color panel, drag the color onto the Background pop-up menu. The Background pop-up menu changes to the selected color and the selected cells reflect your selection (see Figure 7.16).

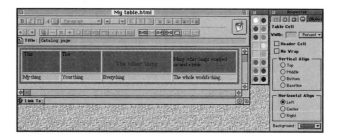

Figure 7.16
Drag a color from the Color Panel on to the Background pop-up menu in the Inspector to add color to a row or column of cells.

 Tip

You can create custom colors by selecting the Custom option from the Background pop-up menu. Use the scrollbar and color wheel in the resulting Apple Color Wheel dialog box to select a color. When you click OK, the color appears in the selected cell(s) and on the Background pop-up menu. If you do not like the color you selected using either method, select Default from the Background pop-up menu to return the cell(s) to their original gray.

As mentioned earlier in the chapter, you can change the color of text within cells using the same method as the one you used to add color to backgrounds, only drag the color from the Color Panel onto the Font pop-up menu on the toolbar.

Formatting Tables Using the Inspector

You can change the entire table's formatting using the Table attributes screen in the Inspector (see Figure 7.17). The Table screen on the Inspector provides three powerful tools you can use to bend a table into a design aid:

▋ Change the width of the total table (and its accompanying rows and columns). Using the Width text box in the Table screen of the Inspector lets you adjust the relationship of columns and rows to the total size of the table. You can use the table width attribute to create single-column, multiple row tables that are very narrow, for a border effect. You can also make a multiple-column, single row table the width of the page to create a toolbar effect. The cells are always sized as a percentage of the total size of the table. Use pixels for additional accuracy by changing the pop-up menu from Percentage to Pixels.

▋ Add or delete borders from tables. If you are using the table as a design aid, you can type a "0" in the Borders text box to remove the border from the table. Fill the table with a color to create an attractive boundary for your page. You can also change the width of the border by typing a number from 1 to 50 in the text box. Typically, avoid using borders as much as possible because the three-dimensional effect provided by most browsers distracts from the information provided in the cell.

▋ Change the way the table holds its data in two ways: cell padding (the distance from the object in the cell and the cell's borders) and cell spacing (the distance between cells). Use Cell Spacing to space cells across or down a page. Type a number from 0 (for no distance) to 50 to increase the distance. Change the number in the Cell Padding text box from 0 to 50 to balance the objects within the cells accross or down a page. (The two attributes are synonymous for design purposes, but add precision when laying out tables containing data with rows and columns of text or numbers.)

You can also add a caption to your table if you are using it strictly as a data container.

Figure 7.17
Use the Table attributes screen of the Inspector to change the formatting of an entire table and its contents.

Changing the Size of a Table on a Page

If you want to create a single column table with multiple rows (to align a list of objects or buttons in a table of contents, for example), use the Width text box in the Table screen of the Inspector. Type a new percentage of the page measurement or state the size of the table width in pixels (remember that a standard computer monitor is 640 pixels wide). When you press the Return key, the table changes to the size you typed (see Figure 7.18).

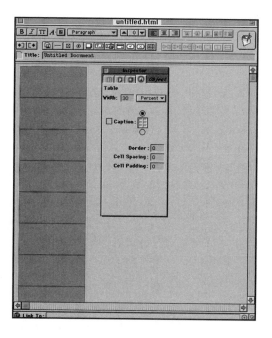

Figure 7.18
Use the Width text box on the Table screen of the Inspector to modify the total width of a table.

Adding or Deleting Borders from a Table

As I have stated repeatedly in this chapter, there are two ways to use tables: as a container for data (such as a spreadsheet) or as a design aid. If you are using the table to hold information, add borders to selected areas of your table and not to the entire table. This makes the table easier to read. If you are using the table as a layout grid, turn off borders completely by typing a 0 in the text box (see Figure 7.19). The fewer lines you have on the page, the fewer distractions for the reader.

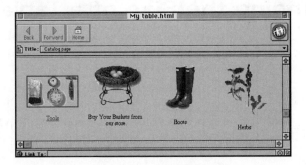

Figure 7.19
The Preview window displays a table whose borders are set to 0.

 ## Changing the Border on a Table

1   Create a table 4 columns wide and 1 row deep using the Table button on the toolbar.

2   Select the entire table.

3   In the Table screen of the Inspector, highlight the Border text box and type the number "0." The border is removed from the table (see Figure 7.20).

Figure 7.20
Set the Border text box to 0 to remove borders from your table.

Changing the Spacing of Rows and Columns in a Table

The Cell Padding text box controls the amount of space within a cell between the object and the boundaries of the cell. The Cell Spacing text box controls the distance between cells. If you are using the table as a layout grid, always set the Cell Padding attribute to 0 to remove any padding because in layout terms Cell Spacing and Cell Padding are the same thing—distance between objects. The Cell Spacing text box controls the distance between cells. Setting this box at 0 places the cells smack against each other (see Figure 7.21).

Tip

Remember to press the Return key after typing a new number into any text box to record your change.

Figure 7.21
Set the Cell Spacing
text box to 0 to line
up cells one against
the other.

If you want to create a box effect to align objects evenly vertically or horizontally, type a number from 1 to 50 in the Cell Spacing text box. Each number represents an incremental increase in pixels between cells (see Figure 7.22).

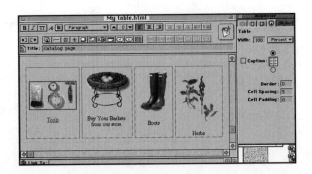

Using the Table Toolbar

PageMill's Table toolbar provides a series of buttons that make it easy to change the structure of a table after it has been created. You can insert or remove rows or columns, merge (or join) rows or columns, or split apart joined cells using the toolbar's buttons. You turn on the Table toolbar by selecting a series of cells in a table. Figure 7.1 displays the Table toolbar.

Adding or Deleting Cells

If you want to add or remove cells from your table, use the appropriate buttons on the Table toolbar. The columns are always added to the right of the selected cell and rows are added below the selected cell.

 ### Inserting a New Row

1   Create a table with five columns and three rows using the Table button on the toolbar.

2   Select a cell or a horizontal series of cells. The Row buttons on the Table toolbar become visible.

3   Click the Insert Row button on the Table toolbar. A new blank row is inserted beneath your selected cell(s) (see Figure 7.23).

You can delete a row by performing the above steps, but by clicking the Delete Row button rather than the Insert Row button in Step 3.

An alternative way to add a row or column is to press the Option key while dragging an outside row or column.

You can insert or remove a column of cells by selecting a cell, or a series of vertical cells, and then click the Insert Column or Remove Column button on the Table toolbar.

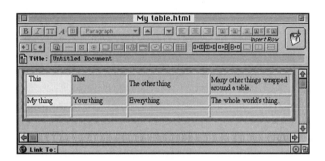

Figure 7.23
Use the Insert Row button on the toolbar to add a row of cells to your table.

Joining and Splitting Cells

Merging or *joining* a row of cells and then centering its contents using the Center Align button on the toolbar is an easy way of centering a line of text or an object over a series of other objects or text. You would do this if you wanted to place a heading off of the center of the page, but centered over other items. You can merge cells in columns to center things vertically, such as a graphic of text that has been rotated 180 degrees. Merging cells also lets you create large areas of horizontal or vertical color on your page. You then can nest another table within the merged cells to add objects on to the colored areas (see Figure 7.24).

Joining a Row of Cells

1   Create a table with five columns and three rows using the Table button on the toolbar.

2   Select horizontal series of cells. The Row buttons on the Table toolbar become visible.

3   Click the Join Cells button on the Table toolbar. The series of cells you selected becomes one large cell (see Figure 7.25).

Figure 7.24
Use the Join Cells button to create large areas of color or to center text or objects over other objects off of the page center.

Figure 7.25
Select a series of cells and click Join Cells to merge the cells and their contents.

 Tip

Any color you added to a cell joined to another is lost in the merge. Add cell background colors after performing a merge.

You can separate merged cells by selecting the merged cell area and clicking the Split Cells button on the toolbar. Note that it is very tricky to select merged cells or to resize their area because the width of the cells remains a percentage of the entire table's width, even if the cell boundaries are now invisible.

Using Objects with Tables

One of the most useful aspects of tables is their use in aligning objects vertically or horizontally on a page. Use table cells as containers for images, animations, applets, and so forth. Go back and look at Figure 7.13 again. The colored ovals on the left side of the page are actually active images and applets that shine when clicked. You can place any object or program into a cell and use it as an active image to jump to another location. Use frames if you want the new page to be presented next to the clicked object (see the following paragraphs on how to use frames).

When you place an object in a cell, the cell expands to fit the object and the other cells in a row contract to maintain the overall width of the table. You can rescale the object to restore cell widths to better balance. The cell will contract to the new object size.

Use the Place Object button on the toolbar to place an object, such as an image, into a table cell (see Figure 7.26). Click inside of a cell to move the insertion point to that cell. If you want the image to span the width of the table, merge the row of cells before placing the image. See Chapter 4 for a description of how to place images and manipulate them once they are placed on the page.

Figure 7.26
Use the Place Object button on the toolbar to place an image into a table cell.

Creating Links with Tables

Just as you can insert any object into a table cell, you can create a hypertext link or active image using an object within a cell. You create the link in exactly the same way as you would for text or objects that reside outside of tables, by highlighting the object or text and dropping the page icon or anchor of the destination page onto the selected item. See Chapter 5 for a discussion of creating links and Chapter 6 for a discussion of how to create acitve images.

The interesting thing about creating links to objects, such as images or applets in tables, is that you can either jump to a new page and carry the table of contents theme over to the new page (such as is done in the Killer Sites site shown in Figure 7.2a) or you can combine the table with a frame to display the page pointed to in the column next to the index (see the section on frames that follows for a short lesson on how to use frames to display multiple page documents next to an index). David Siegel opens up his table of contents on each new page to display the subject matter of that page (see Figure 7.27), and it is all done with tables and hypertext.

Figure 7.27
Notice the use of an expanded table of contents in one cell while the subject matter is displayed in other cells on this Web page.

Using Frames

The trouble with tables as a layout device is that tables do not scale to different screen resolutions. If you create a table 640 pixels wide, it stays that way, even if it is opened on a Sun workstation at 1280 pixels wide. The Frames feature was adopted by HTML Version 3 to remedy this problem (among others). Frames are fully scalable because they are independent windows. Frames are a way to create special areas on Web pages where you can view other Web pages. Each frame has its own URL and is independent of the other frames. Frames come in handy if you want to do the following:

■ Create a *ledge* that does not scroll with the rest of a page. Splashsheet headlines use these static areas.

■ Create a table of contents hyperlink list on a separate area of the page apart from the active area that displays these linked pages selected by your readers.

■ Add a form whose choices display different objects on another window frame.

■ Let the user select options in different frames that result in the display of a page in an additional frame.

Frames are also useful when you are presenting a long document you wish to break up and display in sections. You can place a table of contents in one area of your page with hypertext links to pages displayed in the accompanying frame. Frames are a very new function of HTML and may not be supported by all browsers (although both Netscape Navigator and Microsoft Internet Explorer support frames starting with version 2).

Frames are special types of Web pages that do not contain a body tag. When you create a frame in PageMill, the program writes a pair of tags called <FRAMESET> </FRAMESET> that surrounds the contents of that frame. Each framed area also is identified by a pair of <FRAME> </FRAME> tags. (All of these are written by PageMill when you click and drag margins and select options in the Frame screen of the Inspector.) You can nest frames within frames (for example, to create multiple columns of text). Just like you learned with tables, frames are governed by row and column attributes that define the boundaries of the frame as a percentage of the horizontal and vertical areas of the page.

The creation of frames consist of three parts:

- **Frame.** An area of a page with an independent URL. Each frame is saved with a separate name. You can use these names in the title bar of the frameset.

- **Frameset.** A collection of frames. This is the file containing information about the layout and files that make up the various frames. Consider the frameset as the Page in terms of naming it because this is the name the browser displays.

- **Frame target.** The frame where your linked page is displayed.

Let's look at each step in creating a frame individually.

Making a Simple Frame

Frames are an elegant way of making a single Web page behave like a multiple-page site. The first thing you have to do is delineate where on the page you are going to place your frames.

 Creating a Frame

1   Open a new PageMill document.

2   Press the Option key while dragging one of the window margins (see Figure 7.28). Note that the cursor changes to a single-sided arrow when the margin is first selected. As you drag the margin, the cursor changes to a double-sided arrow to indicate that you can move the margin right or left (or up or down if you are moving a top or bottom margin). When you release the mouse, a frame is placed on the page with the boundaries set as a default with scrollbars.

3   Open the Inspector to its Frame screen by selecting the new frame and choosing Open Inspector from the Window menu.

4 In the Name text box, highlight the text and enter a more meaningful name for the frame. This is the name that will appear in the Title bar of the browser when you activate the frame.

5 Pull down the File menu and select Save Frame As.

6 In the resulting dialog box, give the frame a name without spaces (use the underscore to indicate separate words, if needed). Be sure to add the suffix .html (or .htm for Windows).

Figure 7.28
Press the Option key while dragging a margin horizontally or vertically to create a frame.

Formatting a Frame

Once you have broken up the page into frames, you can use the Inspector to define how the frame behaves. Frames can do the following:

■ Scroll up and down using a standard window scroll bar.

■ Remain static with no ability to move

■ Have borders to delineate where the frame starts and ends. You can also define the color of a frame's border.

■ Have no border and serve as a placeholder for a graphic display or splashscreen.

■ Be able to resize the frame by dragging its margins to a new position on the page. Turning off this capability prevents the frame from moving.

 ## Setting a Frames Format Option

1 Open the Inspector by selecting Show Inspector from the Window menu.

2 Select the new frame. In the Frame screen of the Inspector (see Figure 7.29), select a format for the frame from the Scrollbars pop-up menu (you can select either scrollbars, none, or automatic scrolling).

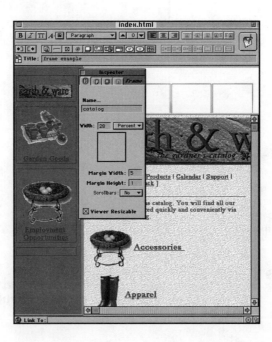

Figure 7.29
Use the Frame screen of the Inspector to set margins, frame width, and scrolling features of the frame. You can also give the frame a name.

To create a table of contents type frame:You want the ability to scroll down the frame, so choose Scrollbars.

To create a splashbar type frame: You want the frame to be invisible, so select None so that the frame does not move.

To create a button selection type frame: You want the frame to be invisible, but possibly mobile so that you can place buttons and links down the margin for navigating, so select Automatic Scrolling.

3   You can adjust the height and width of your frame by manually typing a percentage of the window size or actual pixel count in Width text box.

4   Adjust the space between the frame window and another frame (called the margin) by typing a number from 1 to 10 in the Margin Width or Margin Height text boxes. Note that typing a 1 gives you an invisible margin.

5   Check the Viewer Resizable check box if you selected automatic scrolling to enable your reader to use the cursor to scroll down or across the frame as needed.

Completing the Frame

As mentioned earlier, the goal of building frames is to enable your reader to open more than one page at a time on a screen on the same window. To complete the process, you must tell PageMill which frames to include on the window by saving your frames in a separate HTML file (called a frameset).

Creating a Frameset

1   Pull down the File menu and select Save Frameset As.

2   In the resulting dialog box, give the layout and files that compose the page a name, also keeping the .html or .htm suffix. I named my frameset "Index.html" to indicate that it is the default page.

3   Repeat steps 2 through 5 if you want to create more frames on the page.

Tip

Always name the default page (the page you want opened whenever someone enters any part of your URL) index.html. If this page contains a series of frames, give the frames descriptive names but save the set with the standard default name. In this way, you won't accidentally mess up navigating among frames and their associated page links, and you can manage frame updates in a logical fashion (since their names tell you which one does what).

Adding Targets to Frames

You now have three blank frames in a frameset called Index.html. Add tables, images, objects, and so forth to each frame as you would to individual pages. I created three active images on one frame and another active image on the other frame, each one pointing to other pages on my Earth&Ware Web site. You can also point your links to external Web sites. See Chapters 4, 5, and 6 for a discussion of text, images, links, and active images. Let's use those active images and links to finish our frameset. You must create the links before setting up the frame target.

 Setting up Frame Targets

1   Triple-click a hypertext link.

2   Click and hold the mouse on the top of the link. The pointer changes to a bull's-eye and the Frame Target pop-up menu is displayed. You can also click the Target button on the bottom right corner of the PageMill window to display the Frame Target pop-up menu (see Figure 7.29). (Note that Windows users should always use the frame target button to set up a target frame.)

3   Move the bull's-eye cursor to the picture of the target pane you want to use as the target of the linked page (this is where the link will be displayed).

4   Select Save Frame from the File menu.

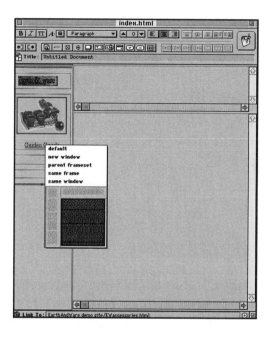

Figure 7.29
Use the Frame Target pop-up menu to choose which frame will display the linked page.

When you close the document or quit PageMill, you will be reminded to save each frame (see Figure 7.30) and the frameset (see Figure 7.31).

Figure 7.30
PageMill reminds
you to save the
frames when you
close the document
or Quit.

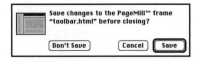

Figure 7.31
PageMill also
reminds you to save
the frameset before
quitting.

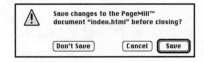

 Tip

You can add a background image or color to frames by clicking
the Page tab on the Inspector. Drag a color from the Color Panel
onto the Background pop-up menu or select Custom to select a
color from the Color Wheel. You can also drag an image onto the
Background Image box to replace the color with an image. See
Chapter 4 for a discussion of setting up the page.

 Note

Frames are tricky beasts because each frame is an independent
page with its own URL. Experiment with scrollbars, jumping to
other windows, and other special effects, but remember to save
the frames and framesets. Search the Web for sites you think use
frames. Look at the source code of these pages to learn how to
use the various options for displaying pages in frames. Often,
you cannot tell by looking at a page whether it uses tables or
frames to move through a site. One hint that frames are in use is
that if you click an active image, the window moves to another
portion of the window if you are dealing with tables and to a new
URL if you are dealing with frames.

Summary

You have learned two advanced HTML tricks, tables and frames, that formerly were difficult to accomplish. With PageMill 2.0, both tables and frames can be created onscreen using the tools you have learned in earlier chapters, such as active images, hypertext linking, formatting, and so forth.

You have now learned all of the functions in PageMill. Chapters 10 through 13 show you how to operate your Web page and site, while Chapter 9 teaches you how to add those HTML tags PageMill does not support, such as blinking text.

Chapter 8

Working with Forms

Forms are special types of Web pages used to collect information about your readers. The use of form elements (checkboxes, text areas, text fields, radio buttons, and so forth) provides a way for you to interact with your users. PageMill provides a powerful and easy facility for creating and manipulating form elements on a Web page.

Forms can be used to perform many tasks, including:

- Receive feedback from people who browse your page.

- Set criteria to use in searching a database.

- Set customized settings for your Web page specifically for each user, such as the view of a map set to a reader's preferences.

- Secure your site by requiring a password to enter certain areas of your Web site.

- Collect data about your readership, such as age, income, and interests.

Creating a Fill-In Form

Forms consist of two parts: what you place on the Web page to collect information and a backend program, called a common gateway interface (CGI), that processes the information by interacting with the server. When the user presses the button on the form to submit its contents (in fact, pressing "submit" sends the information to the server), the CGI script, written in AppleScript, Perl, Visual Basic, MacPerl, or C++, does something with the data. That something can be as easy as filtering the data and dumping it in a file or as complex as jumping to another page based on criteria set by the information in the form. (CGIs are discussed more thoroughly in Chapter 10.) For the purposes of this chapter, all you need to know is that PageMill only presents the form. Acting on the data is the job of a CGI.

 Tip

In PageMill 2.0, every element of the form is an object, just like a graphic, sound, video snippet, and so forth. (In fact, you can liven up your forms by including images that work as buttons, animated GIFs, and so forth.) You use the Inspector's Object mode screen to define the object's purpose on the form. Figure 8.1 illustrates the star image set up as a button.

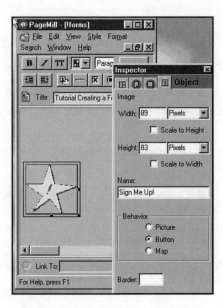

Figure 8.1
Use a graphic object as a button in your form.

Planning is important for good form design. As with Web page design, you have to think through your form before committing it to the page:

1 Figure out what you want your form to do; list all of its actions.

2 Figure out what form elements you will need to best suit your information requirements.

3 Create the form in rough form to make sure that you like the layout and that all of the fields are placed where you desire. The only limit PageMill places on forms is that they must be contained on a single page (which can be very long, as you have learned).

Now you are ready to build the form in PageMill.

To create a form, click one of the form element buttons in the toolbar (see Figure 8.2). Form elements can be modified and edited for your specific needs.

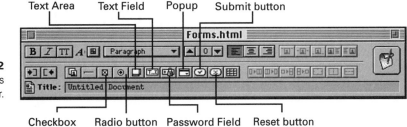

Figure 8.2
The form elements
on the toolbar.

Form Elements

Web page form elements are classified as:

■ Fields, including text fields, areas, and password fields

■ Pop-up menus, which include scrolling dialog boxes

■ Buttons, including radio buttons and checkboxes

Fields

Fields are form elements into which users enter text (see Figure 8.3). PageMill provides three types of fields:

- **Text Fields.** Single-line fields modified by width only.

- **Text Areas**. Multiple-line fields modified by width and height.

- **Password Fields.** A special type of text field. When a viewer types text into a Password Field, bullets appear in place of the actual text being typed. You can use the Password field type to ask your readers to enter a Password (a secret keyword only they and your server know that gives access to special areas of your site).

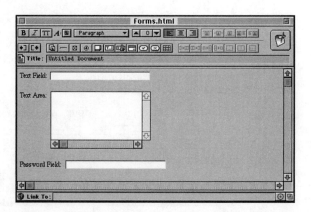

Figure 8.3
The Field elements are used to enter text into the form.

Pop-Up Menus

Pop-up menus are form elements enabling users to select one or more items from a list. You can create scrolling lists or true popup menus in PageMill (see Figure 8.4).

Figure 8.4
Pop-up menus let users select one or more subjects from a list of items.

Buttons

Buttons are graphic elements in which users use their mouse to make selections or to take action (see Figure 8.5). PageMill provides the following types of buttons:

- ▌ Radio buttons are used to select only one item from a list.

- ▌ Checkboxes are used to select multiple items from a list.

- ▌ The Submit button is used to send the data collected on a form to the server.

- ▌ The Reset button is used to reset or clear choices on the form before submitting data.

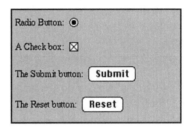

Figure 8.5
Buttons let users click the mouse to toggle selections on or off.

 Creating a Form

1. Create a new page in PageMill.

2. Type **Name:** and press the Spacebar.

3. Click the Insert Text Field button on the toolbar and press Return.

4. Type **Password:** and press the Spacebar.

5. Click the Insert Password Field button on the toolbar and press Return.

6. Type **Street Address:** and press the Spacebar.

7. Click the Insert Text Field button on the toolbar and press Return.

8. Type **City:** and press the Spacebar.

9. Click the Insert Text Field button on the toolbar and press Return.

10. Type **State:** and press the Spacebar.

continues

11 Click the Insert Text Field button on the toolbar and press Return.

12 Type **Country:** and press the Spacebar.

13 Click the Insert Text Field button on the toolbar and press Return.

14 Type **Zip:** and press the Spacebar.

15 Click the Insert Text Field button on the toolbar and press Return.

16 Type **Tell us about yourself:** and press the Spacebar.

17 Click the Insert Text Area icon from the toolbar and press Return.

Your completed document should look like Figure 8.6.

 Tip

You can assist your readers in completing complex forms by inserting text inside a field to show the reader what to type in the field. To do this, enter the text into the field when you create it. Inside the Name field, for example, you could type **Enter name here.** The text will be presented to every reader who loads the form.

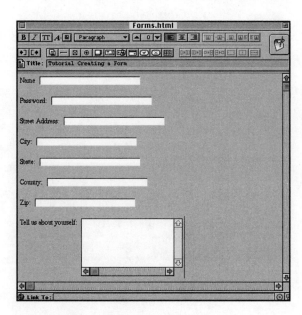

Figure 8.6
Use the Form
Elements toolbar to
create a form.

Modifying Form Elements

1   Adjust the length of text and password fields by clicking the field and dragging the sizing handle on the far-right side of the field right or left (see Figure 8.7).

2   Adjust the length and width of text areas by clicking the field and dragging the sizing handles on the bottom-middle, bottom-right, and far-right sides of the field (see Figure 8.8).

Figure 8.7
Drag the sizing handle to change the length of a text or password field.

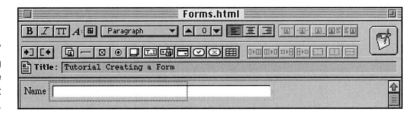

Figure 8.8
Drag the sizing handle to change the height or width of a text area.

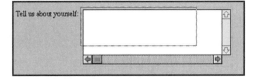

 Tip

Drag frequently used form elements to the Pasteboard for easy access when designing other Web pages.

Working with Radio Buttons and Checkboxes

Radio buttons need to be created as a group to work properly. The first button must be created by selecting the Insert Radio Button button from the toolbar. Subsequent buttons for the group must be created by cloning the original button.

You can clone radio buttons two ways:

■ Select the original button and copy and paste it to subsequent locations.

■ Option-drag the original to subsequent locations. Option-dragging creates a copy of the original button.

When you have cloned the physical buttons, you need to finish the job by selecting each of the buttons in turn, and in the Object mode of the Inspector window giving each of the buttons the identical name in the Name field.

Using Radio Buttons

1 Type **Select your gender:** and press Return.

2 Type **Male:** and click the Insert Radio Button button on the toolbar.

3 Press the Spacebar three times.

4 Type **Female:** Clone the radio button you created by selecting it and then holding down the Option key as you drag it to the right of the text you just typed ("Female").

5 Deselect button and press Return.

Your document now should look like Figure 8.9.

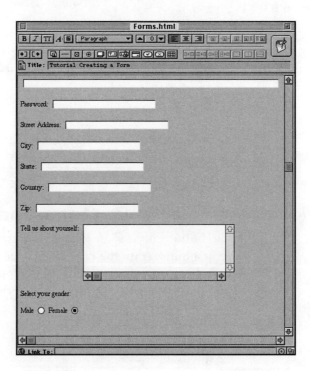

Figure 8.9

Set up your radio buttons in groups so that selecting one toggles off the others.

Using Checkboxes

1   Type **Which of the following do you own:** and press Return.

2   Type **Stereo** and press Return.

3   Type **TV** and press Return.

4   Type **VCR** and press Return.

5   Place the cursor next to Stereo and click the Insert Checkbox button on the toolbar.

6   Place the cursor next to TV and click the Insert Checkbox button on the toolbar.

7   Place the cursor next to VCR, click the Insert Checkbox button on the toolbar, and press Return.

Your document should now look like Figure 8.10.

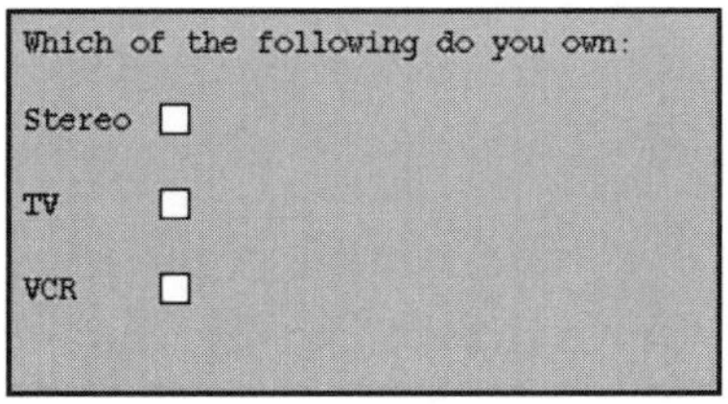

Figure 8.10
You can select more than one check box at a time, so each one is an independent entity.

Tip

To create forms in which the form elements align neatly, use the Teletype style for the descriptive tags and add spaces after the tags to align them. Using the Teletype style ensures a mono-spaced type font is used so that spacing is even. This gives your forms a clean, professional look. Try it.

Select all the elements of your form input area including the descriptive tags. Select the Teletype style from the Style menu. Manually add spaces between the descriptive tags and the text fields to line them up.

Working with Pop-Up Menus

A few things you should know about pop-up menus:

- Pop-ups can have as many items in them as you choose.

- You can select the default item by sliding the inverted triangle in the list next to the item you want to be the default.

- You can determine whether the pop-up is open all the time (a scrolling list box) by sizing the pop-up while in Edit mode. To size the pop-up, select it and drag the sizing handle at the bottom of the pop-up down until all menu items are visible. The menu changes into a box with a scrollbar.

- Using the Inspector, you can specify how many items can be seen before the list is opened.

- Using the Inspector, you can determine whether viewers can select multiple items in the list. Specifying this option places checkboxes next to each item in the list.

 ### Creating Pop-Up Menus

1   Type **Select Income Bracket Menus**.

2   Click the Insert Popup button on the toolbar.

3   Double-click the pop-up menu that appears. You'll see item one, item two, and item three as default selections in the pop-up.

4   Highlight item one and type **$20,000–$50,000** (notice the field width widens to accommodate the length of the text).

5   Highlight item two and type **$50,001–100,000**.

6   Highlight item three and type **$100,001–$500,000**.

7   Add a fourth item to the list by pressing Return and typing **+$500,000**.

Your pop-up menu should look like Figure 8.11.

Figure 8.11
Pop-up menus are
useful when you
want to offer a
specific selection of
responses.

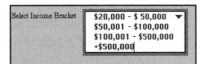

Setting Up the Form for the CGI

When you have completed the physical building process, each object in your form must be named so that the form element can be recognized by the CGI and processed appropriately. If, for example, you have a field asking the viewer for an email address, name that field **email** in the Inspector's Name field (see Figure 8.12). Then the server will receive the email address typed into the text box as `thename@thecompany.com`.

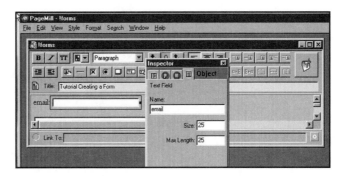

Figure 8.12
Use the Inspector
to name the field in
your form.

Naming fields is the "programming" work involved in creating forms. In fact, what you are doing is declaring variables and assigning values to them. Because the data from the fields is treated differently based on the type of variable it is and the value assigned to that variable, this is an important, and often confusing, step in the form-building process.

 Note

Again, if you are working with a Webmaster who's going to do the background techie stuff, you might need to talk about naming your fields. You might have to give the fields in your Web page the same names as the Webmaster has given fields in the database where the data will eventually go.

Declaring Variables

Let's have a quick computer science lesson to understand declaring variables. Variables are vitally important to almost every computer application ever created. The best way to think about variables is to imagine them as containers for data. If you've ever taken a basic algebra class, you've seen this in equations such as this:

$x = 4$

$8 \div x = 2$

x is the **variable** with a **value** of 4. After x is given that value, you can use it in various ways, such as dividing 8 by it. Why is this better than simply stating $8 \div 2$? Because the value of x can be changed easily to get a different answer. For example:

$x = 2$

$8 \div x = 4$

This is a simple example, but if this were one of those horrible word problems, the need for variables would be more apparent. Forgive me for taking you back to the ninth grade for this next example.

Francine has 8 friends and 16 apples. How many apples will each friend get if she divides them equally? What if she has 24 apples?

$x = 16$

$x \div 8 = 2$

$x = 24$

$x \div 8 = 3$

In this example, x is equal to the number of apples Francine needs to divide among her 8 friends. x's value can be changed easily to get different answers to the same question.

Computers can do this and much more with variables. In this case, you want to assign a user's input as the value of a variable. So, if the variable x contains the data a user entered for his or her name, a mechanism of telling the computer that this is a "name" is needed:

$x = $ Joe User

You are not restricted to using single letters for variables. You can create a variable that looks like this:

name = Joe User

The server can do several things with this little piece of information. In addition, declaring variables is the most efficient way to keep track of data entered into forms (because more than one person will complete the form, the server can use the variables as a way to organize responses to the same variable). Later, this book will take a look at some of the things you can do with that data. First, let's see how to use PageMill to assign user input to variables.

Naming Text, Password Fields, and Text Areas

Let's name the fields (also known as declaring variables) in a vanilla form. Follow these steps:

1 With the Inspector open, create a text field by clicking the Insert Text Field button on the toolbar. Select the field. The words "Text Field" appear at the top of the Object mode window of the Inspector.

2 In the Inspector, double-click the text field to highlight the Name text, type **firstname**, and press Return. This assigns the data entered into that field to the variable "firstname" (see Figure 8.13).

On the Mac after you press Return, the field turns gray, which is PageMill's way of telling you that the name has been assigned to the field. (Note that the field color does not change on the PC.)

Tip

You can do two other things in this panel of the Inspector:

■ Change the size of the field (how wide or long the physical space appears on the page)

■ Set the maximum number of characters to be input (set how many letters or characters a reader can enter in the field, no matter how long it physically appears)

The default size is 30 characters, but you can make this larger or smaller by entering a different number in the Size box. To make the field larger, for example, type **45** in the field and press Return/ Enter. The user can now enter up to 45 characters in the field.

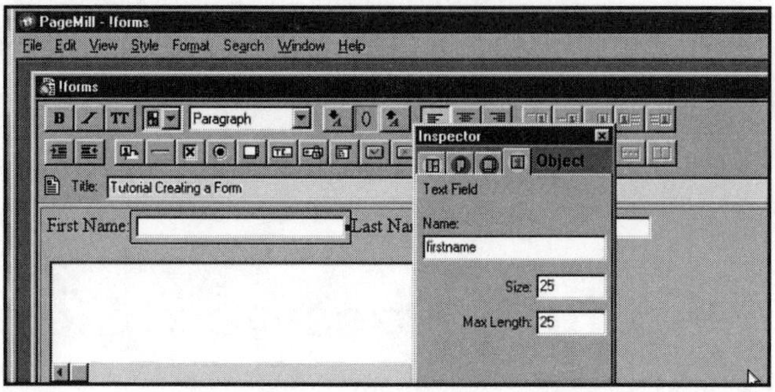

Figure 8.13
Assign a name to a selected text field in the Name text box of the Object window of the Inspector.

3 Let's assign a Password field. Create a Password field by clicking the Insert Password Field button on the toolbar. With the Inspector open, select the password field. The Object mode window now is called "Password Field."

4 Select the text in the Name text field and type **password**. Press Return. Set the size of the field by typing **45** into the Size box and pressing Return.

5 Next, let's assign a text area. Create a text area using the Insert Text Area button on the toolbar. With the Inspector open, select the field. The Object mode window is now called "Text Area" (see Figure 8.14). Notice you are given Rows and Columns text boxes to let you modify the scrollable text area in two dimensions.

6 Before you adjust these, type comments in the Name text field to assign this text area to the variable **comments**, and press Return.

You can change the size of the text area by replacing the row and column numbers or by clicking a corner of the text area and dragging it. The default size is 7 rows by 27 columns. Change this to 5 rows by 45 columns so that the scrolling box lines up with the other Text fields. Remember to press Return after you type the new numbers.

Text fields, text areas, and password fields are the simplest input types available. Essentially, you're creating a container, naming it (or assigning a variable to the information that will be placed in the container), and letting users dump anything they want into the container. This is perfect if you are asking a user for his or her name, or for comments.

Sometimes, though, you want a user to pick from an existing set of items (to limit the number and types of answers you get). Say, for example, you want to know if a user lives inside or outside the United States (a useful bit of information because people from all over the planet will be looking at your work). You could include an input field and hope that he types "inside" or "outside." But what happens if he types "cold cuts"?

The solution is to give users a list and allow them to make selections only from that list. On the Web there are two types of lists you can present: those from which the user can choose one or more options (pop-up menus), and those from which the user can choose only one option (radio buttons).

Multiple Options Lists

Let's take the example of where in the world someone lives (inside or outside the U.S.) and make it more complex. Let's say you want to know what continent the user is on. You need to present seven choices and prevent someone from entering "cold cuts." Because users can only be on one continent, they should be able to choose only one option from your list.

The easiest way to do this is with a pop-up menu. Think of pop-up menus as standard text fields with several options available. If you use the Macintosh or Windows 95 interface, you are familiar with the concept of pop-up menus. Every item in the typical WYSIWYG menu bar is a pop-up menu.

Think about the File pull-down menu in the menu bar of a program such as PageMill. When you hold down the mouse button on the word File a pull-down menu appears with the functions you can perform. When you move the mouse to a command and release the mouse button, a message is sent to Print, Save, Close, Quit, or whatever function you selected.

Imagine if the pull-down menu were replaced with a text field and you had to type Print in the field when you wanted to print. After the computer ignored your command for the third time because you made a typo, you'd be longing for the carefree elegance of Unix.

With PageMill, you can create the same WYSIWYG atmosphere you are used to for your Web page by following these steps:

1 Select the pop-up menu you created previously with the dollar amounts. Double-click the pop-up menu and highlight the items. Press Delete to erase the contents of the pop-up menu.

2 Enter the names of the seven continents and press Return after each entry. When you finish, click elsewhere on the page so that PageMill knows that you have finished putting options into your pop-up menu. Whatever item out of the seven choices provided the user selects becomes the value for the field.

3 Now you need to give this field a name. With the Inspector open, click the pop-up menu. The Object mode of the Inspector displays a screen called Selection Field (which is really what PageMill considers the pop-up menu to be). Click the Name text box and type **continent** (see Figure 8.14).

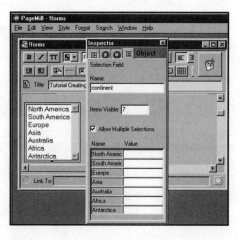

Figure 8.14
Assign a name to a selected text area in the Name text box of the Object window of the Inspector.

4 Press Return after naming the field to save the variable name.

5 Three more options are on this screen: Items Visible, Allow Multiple Selections, and a Name and Value matrix (see Figure 8.15). To keep this a true pop-up menu (where only one item is displayed until the menu is selected, and then only one option can be selected from the list), leave both of these options empty. You'll come back to them later.

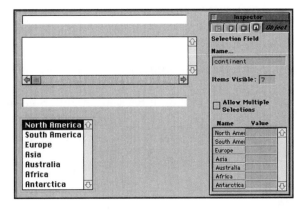

Figure 8.15
Assign a name to a pop-up menu (called a Selection Field) in the Name text box of the Object window of the Inspector.

6 To test your pop-up menu, click the Preview mode icon in the upper-right corner of the PageMill screen. Place the pointer on the pop-up menu and press the mouse button. All of the options appear. You can highlight each option by moving the mouse up and down the menu. Release the mouse button on one of the options and the pop-up menu disappears, leaving the option you selected.

Offering Multiple Selections in a Pop-Up Menu

Say you want users to tell you which continents they have visited. You still want them to choose from the list that you established, but you want them to choose as many continents as they can. You can do this two different ways in PageMill.

In the previous examples, variables were described as containers for data. The data fit perfectly inside the container, leaving no room for anything else. $x = 4$ or $x = $ Joe, for example.

This is totally unacceptable for the task before you. To put several values into one variable, you need to author a document with a variable in it that makes room for as many items as the viewer wants to enter.

Go back to the Continents pop-up menu (see Figure 8.15) and select it (make sure you're in Edit mode). In the resulting Selection Field screen of the Object mode of the Inspector, click the Allow Multiple Selections box.

In Preview mode, you will find your pop-up menu is no longer a pop-up. Click one of the options; it becomes highlighted. Now click another; it becomes highlighted, turning off the previous selection. No difference, right? Now hold down the Shift key and click a few of the options. You can select several options (see Figure 8.16).

Figure 8.16
You can allow the selection of more than one item in the list by selecting the Allow Multiple Selections checkbox in the Inspector.

If you go back into the Edit mode and return to the Inspector, there is a box enabling you to enter the number of options you want visible. This is especially useful if you have a long list of options. You can make just a few options visible and let the user scroll through the list. Enter 4, for example, in this box and press Return. Now only four continents are visible at a time in the pop-up menu and the list box provides a scrollbar for moving up or down the list.

Offering Multiple Options Using Radio Buttons

Another way to offer one and only one option from a list is to use radio buttons. Radio buttons are named after the preset buttons on radios. Think about the radio in your car. You can't be tuned to separate radio stations at the same time on the same radio, right? A mechanism enables you to go from the rock station to the jazz station and not have both stations going at the same time. If you're listening to the rock station, which is preset on button #1, and want to flip to the jazz station, which is preset on button #2, you press button #2, turning off button #1 and switching your radio to the jazz station.

To build a radio button into your Web page with PageMill you need a little variable trickery:

1 Create a radio button by clicking Insert Radio Button on the toolbar. Clone the button six times pressing the Return key after each button. You should now have a column of seven buttons.

2 Now, place the insertion point next to the first radio button and type **North America**. Continue typing until a continent name is next to each radio button.

3 Now you need to determine what each one of these buttons means. As you go into this, remember that you are offering several different responses to one question. If you think about this in terms of variables, you are offering several different pieces (each continent is a piece) that can be put into your container.

4 Click the first radio button and then click the far right button in the Inspector. You should get a screen with two fields: Name and Value. The Name field will have something cryptic in it such as radio206506.

5 Highlight this and press Delete. Name this field **continent**. (And don't forget to press Return after you name the field.)

6 Click the Value field and type **North America**. Press Return (see Figure 8.17).

7 Now click the next radio button. The Name field should change to another cryptic name. Click this field, highlight the name, and press Delete. Type the word **continent** in this field exactly as you did before.

8 Now click the Value field. Highlight the text in the field and press Delete. Type **South America** to give this radio button a different value and press Return to lock in the value.

9 Click the Preview icon in the top-right corner of the page screen to switch to Preview mode. Click the radio button to the left of North America.

10 Now click the radio button to the left of South America. If you built the buttons correctly, they'll toggle back and forth, just like your car radio. To put this another way, there are two options that assign different values to the same variable. Because this variable can only hold one value, when it gets a new one, it tosses the old one out.

11 Go back to the Edit mode. Click the other radio buttons, type **continent** in the Name field (back in the Inspector), and type a value matching the text you typed next to it in the main PageMill window. Each radio button should have the name continent, but a different value (make sure you spell "continent" correctly for each radio button). When you have finished, go to the Preview mode and click any of the seven options, turning off the others.

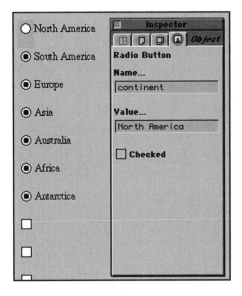

Figure 8.17
Give each radio button the same variable name, but assign it a different value.

Providing Multiple Options Using Checkboxes

Another way to offer a user multiple options is with checkboxes. Checkboxes are a lot like radio buttons, but they do not cancel each other out when one is clicked.

In this example, I use the continent example one last time (I promise). Create seven checkboxes in a column by clicking the Insert Check Box button on the toolbar seven times, pressing the Return key after each box:

1 Type a continent name next to each of the checkboxes.

2 Select the first checkbox by clicking it. In the Inspector, the Checkbox screen of the Object mode is displayed.

3 Click the Name text box to select it, type the word **continentsVisited**, and press Return. This assigns the name (variable) **continentsVisited** to that checkbox.

4 Then, click the Value text box and type **North America.**. When the user looking at your Web site selects this particular checkbox, the value "North America" will be assigned to the variable continentsVisited.

5 Follow these same steps for your other six checkboxes, and make sure you give each one a separate value (see Figure 8.18).

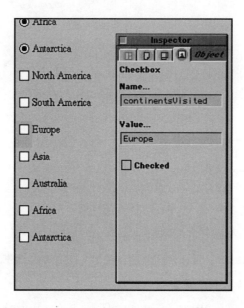

Figure 8.18
Give each checkbox the same variable name, but assign it a different value.

Your next checkbox, for example, will have the name "continentsVisited," but the value "South America"; the next will have the name "continentsVisited," but the value "Europe."

Note that the Checkbox screen of the Object mode of the Inspector has an additional box called Checked. Clicking this box at any time makes the selected value the default. If you are offering your readers choices, though, it doesn't make much sense to have one of them already selected, so this option is not used often.

After you build your checkboxes, switch to Preview mode and test your work. Look closely at how you entered the names, though, to make sure that you spelled the name exactly the same for each. With the radio buttons, it was easy to determine if you named them correctly, because if you didn't, selecting one would turn off another. With checkboxes, however, it's not as easy to tell if you've named them incorrectly because you should be able to click as many as you like.

Setting Password Fields Using the Inspector

PageMill enables you to build a Password field into your document. Return to the Password field you created and select the field (Figure 8.1). In the Inspector, the Password Field screen is displayed. In the Name text box, type the word **secret** and press Return (see Figure 8.19).

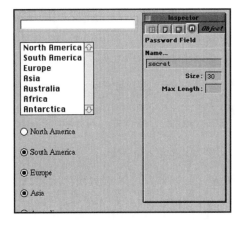

Figure 8.19
The Password Field screen is used to set up a scrambled area to enter confidential information, such as passwords.

Go back to the document window and switch to Preview mode. Click the Password field you created and type a few characters. The text should look like Figure 8.20.

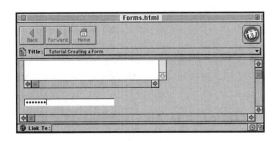

Figure 8.20
Nothing typed into the Password field is visible onscreen.

The Password field works identically to the standard text field, but rather than showing the letters being input, it displays dots. This protects your user from one thing: someone looking over her or his shoulder. PageMill does not do any type of encryption to the data entered into the field. All PageMill does is keep the text from appearing on the monitor of the person browsing your page.

Submit and Reset Buttons

You can include two more buttons in your document. One is optional, the other is absolutely necessary.

The optional button is the Reset button. The Reset button clears all entries in the form. This is helpful if you have a particularly long form. Fortunately, Reset buttons don't have to be named; insert one and you're set. To do so, click the last button on the far right of the Forms portion of the toolbar.

Another button, and the one that is absolutely necessary, is the Submit button. Click the second button to the left on the Forms portion of the toolbar. A button should appear like the one in Figure 8.21.

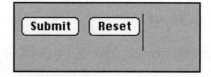

Figure 8.21
The Submit and Reset Buttons.

The Submit button takes all the data your readers enter (along with the individual variable names), packages it, and sends it to your server.

 Tip

You can select a button and rename it by double-clicking the button (whereupon a gray border appears around the button) and typing a new name, such as "Sign Me Up!" (see Figure 8.22). Here is where the variable becomes important. Because PageMill knows Submit is the name for this button, it doesn't matter what appears on-screen; The Submit button's purpose will always be to transmit the data onscreen to the server. You can replace the button with a prettier version, such as an animated GIF, and as long as you indicate that the object is acting as a button called Submit, it will submit the data.

Figure 8.22
Click a button to
select its text and
rename the button.

The big question now is, how does the document know where to send the information? This brings you to the next major topic: capturing data.

Using the Form Mode of the Inspector

At the top of the Inspector's Form mode are the Action field and the Get/Post pull-down menu. These are probably the most technical aspects of PageMill and deal with serving the document.

Although having a series of text fields, buttons, and boxes on a Web page is definitely a good thing, it is only part of the process used to create forms. You need a way to send the information in these forms to the Web server. A form filled out and not sent to the server isn't much good to anyone.

This is where Get/Post and Action come into the picture. For Web servers to do anything with information a viewer has input into a form (such as put it into a database), the form information must be sent to a CGI (Common Gateway Interface) that can manipulate the data. In the Action field, you specify the CGI to which you want to send the form information. This is done with a Universal Resource Locator (URL).

In the Action field, type the URL of the CGI handling the data coming from this form. If you are using a Macintosh Web server, a number of CGI options are explored in Chapter 10. For now, just put the datacapture.acgi in the Action field.

The Get/Post pop-up menu is a little more complex. Essentially, there are two different methods servers and CGIs use to process data from a form. These are Get and Post. Think of Get as the server retrieving data and Post as the server placing data somewhere on the server.

If you are working with a Webmaster who is going to handle the technical details of data coming in to the server from a form, find out the name of the CGI and the method that you should use (Get or Post) from this Webmaster.

 Note

Most of the CGIs in Chapter 10 use the Post method.

Retrieving Form Data

Web server software sits on a computer and waits patiently for file requests. It can act on those requests in a limited manner, and can do a couple of things with the files, but essentially its life follows this cycle:

1 A request comes in.

2 The Web server checks its hard drive to see whether it has that particular file.

3 If the Web server has that file, it ships the file. If it doesn't, the Web server apologizes.

So what happens when users send their name, email address, and a list of continents they have visited instead of a file request? What happens is a CGI.

CGIs are written in a programming language such as C++, MacPerl, or AppleScript (on the Macintosh) or Perl, Visual Basic, or C++ on a Windows-based PC. If you're a programmer, you might want to look into building a CGI yourself—it isn't difficult. If you're not a programmer, several CGIs are available on the Internet as shareware and freeware. CGIs can take the data entered into a form, for example, and place it into a text file, create a new record with it in a database, or put it into an email message and send it to someone.

If you're going to create a form that asks your reader for information, you need a CGI to do something with that form. Point your

Web browser to Maxum Development's Web site (`http://www.maxum.com`), and download a copy of NetForms. NetForms is an application that sits on your server, takes the data sent to it from a form, and dumps the data into a text file or an email message. If you'd like the form information posted to a FileMaker Pro database, point your Web browser to Russell Owen's home page (`http://rowen.astro.washington.edu/`) and download the ROFM CGI. If you want to write your own, go to Jon Wiederspan's Extending WebSTAR site (`http://www.uwtc.washington.edu/Computing/WWW/Lessons/START_HERE.html`) where you will find an excellent tutorial on building CGIs to help you get started.

Summary

You now know how to physically design form elements on a Web page. You have learned how to edit the elements and set them up to become a form. The last information you covered was how to connect the form to the CGI. Chapter 10 discusses the other end of the process: how CGIs are used to create information from the data in your form. Before getting into CGIs and server stuff,

Chapter 9

Working with HTML

Now we get down to the real nitty gritty—what lies underneath the PageMill 2.0 covers. As I have been stating throughout this book, Web pages are composed of a page description language called HyperText Markup Language (HTML). HTML uses *tags* (codes identifying what the following text is doing) to surround blocks of text. These tags do not actually convert the text in any way, but they do tell the browser how you want to display the tagged items. What you have been putting on the PageMill content area with your toolbar and menu commands is translated into these tags.

All Web pages consist of HTML tags. It is the creative use of graphics and tags that make a great page. For example, Figure 9.1 displays the Hayden Books Home Page. As you can see, the Web page is a balanced composition of columns of color and images containing text, plus text inputted on to the Page.

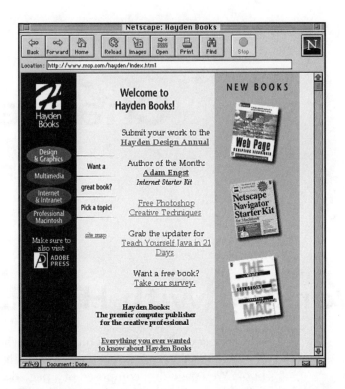

Figure 9.1
The Hayden Books
Home Page is
chock full of
advanced HTML
tags.

In Figure 9.2, is what must be coded in HTML to create the tables, Java applets, hypertext links, active images, and inline images presented on the page.

Notice that most of the text is actually imported into the Web page as graphics files (those <IMG SRC="… things you see). If you want fancy text or colorful logos, you have to create them in separate software packages, such as Adobe Illustrator, Adobe Photoshop, Macromedia Xres, or Macromedia FreeHand (available on both Mac and Windows platforms) and place them on the Page. HTML does not provide any ability to perform advanced desktop publishing, such as rotating text, making things three-dimensional, or even creating gradients of color. HTML does no formatting, but simply tells the viewer's browser how to present the information contained within the bracketed tags. To get HTML to jump through layout hoops takes complicated nested tags within tags. PageMill 2.0 is designed to hide that complication by writing the HTML tags for you for each process you perform.

Figure 9.2
The source code
for the Hayden
Home Page with its
complex nested
HTML tags.

One of the problems Adobe had to tackle when updating PageMill is that HTML is a developing standard half-way between version 2.0 and version 3.2. In addition, commercial browsers such as Netscape Navigator and Microsoft Internet Explorer add their own proprietary extension supports to the mix, further complicating the task of deciding which HTML tags to support in PageMill 2.0. Adobe could not possibly keep up with all of the new uses of tags. So, Adobe did the next best thing: PageMill 2.0 now enables you to see the HTML source code and edit it to add the bells and whistles PageMill cannot provide in a WYSIWYG format.

Although you cannot view such nifty items as Cascading Style Sheets, font specifications, and such from within PageMill, you can hard-code them into the underlying HTML so that they will be viewable with appropriate browsers.

This chapter describes how to work with PageMill 2.0's HTML editor.

How HTML Works

All HTML documents consist of a shell, a basic set of tags that define the parameters of your Page. PageMill bases its total philosophy on this basic template because you can build any page by adding bells and whistles to this basic format:

```
<HTML>
<HEAD>
<TITLE> This is the Title</TITLE>
</HEAD>
<BODY>
        <H1> Major document heading here</H1>
            text and markup
        <A HREF="URL"> anchor title</A>
<ADDRESS>Author and version information</ADDRESS>
</BODY>
</HTML>
```

You can see PageMill's use of this shell if you open a newly saved PageMill document and select HTML Source from the Edit menu (see Figure 9.3).

Figure 9.3
PageMill writes a basic HTML shell when you first save a new document.

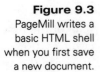

Tip

HTML is not sensitive to case. You can type in all caps, initial caps, or lowercase letters and it is all the same to the markup language. It is smart, however, to differentiate your tags from the text or image it is containing by typing things like tags that don't change in all caps and things that change, such as attribute values (you'll learn about these later) in lowercase letters. PageMill follows a similar practice. This makes it easier to read the HTML source code, should you have to edit it.

Applying Tag Pairs to Format Items

As stated previously, all HTML consists of a pairs of tags, one in the front of the item it modifies, and one that follows the item. Tags are sometimes called *containers* because they come in pairs and "hold text or images" you want to include on the page. For example,

```
<h1>Welcome to Joe Webhead's Home Page!</h1>
```

tells the browser to display the text "Welcome to Joe Webhead's Home Page!" as a first level heading (whatever that is formatted like on that browser). All you know is that first level headers have the largest font size and boldness, and each subsequent heading level (<h2> down to <h6>) is less prominent.

As I introduced in Chapter 4, you can set up different text and paragraph formats to tell the browser how to display the text. The <STRONG></STRONG> pair you see in Figure 9.4, is a tag telling the browser to use the logical format strong to make the enclosed word bold text. Whenever you use the Format or Style menu commands or Format pop-up menu in PageMill, you are telling PageMill to assign HTML tags to the selected item.

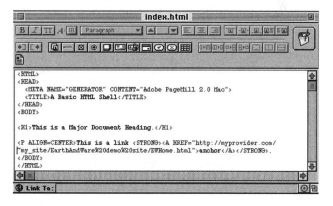

Figure 9.4
PageMill writes a subtag modifying the paragraph tag that aligns the paragraph in the center of the page.

Using Attributes and Values to Modify Tags

Tags are the primary way of telling the browser how to display what the tags contain. Tags, such as <H1></H1> shown above, are modified by attributes, secondary tags that offer layout options, such as center, left align, and so forth. We can add details to how the browser is supposed to display the contained text by adding an attribute/value pair, written *attribute=value*. Figure 9.4 illustrates the addition of center alignment to the paragraph text in our shell document (the <P ALIGN=CENTER> addition to the HTML source code was added by presssing the Align Center button on the PageMill toolbar).

Attributes describe optional specifications, such as height and width of an image, that modify a tag. Values are the different options from which you can select, such as center, right, left, and so forth. Whenever you see a phrase that includes an equals sign, for example ALIGN=LEFT, you are looking at an attribute/value pair. When you use the alignment buttons on the PageMill toolbar or set attributes in the Inspector, you are telling PageMill to add these subtags to the source code.

Creating Hypertext Links

In Chapter 5, I introduced the concept of hypertext links (also called *hotlinks*). The HTML tags for these links use two structures: an anchor (remember PageMill's anchor icon you created to identify links in the middle of pages) and a hypertext reference. So, when you drop the Page icon or anchor icon on to a selected object, PageMill writes the following HTML:

```
<a href="the URL you are linking to"</a>
```

If, for example, you want to point to Hayden Books' Home Page on a link, you select the object you want to use as the source of the link and type the URL for Hayden Books in the link location text box. PageMill writes:

```
<a href="http://www.mcp.com/hayden/index.html"</a>
```

Placing Objects into a Page

As you learned in Chapter 4, you cannot paste graphics into a Web page. When you use the Place Object button on the PageMill toolbar and select a file with a .gif extension, the PageMill writes an image tag (<IMG>) to indicate you want to import a graphic. On the Hayden Books page, for example, the buttons used to jump to other pages are graphics with Java applets applied and the code is written:

```
<IMG SRC="graphics/dot.gif">
```

where "graphics" is the directory and "dot.gif" is the name of the image file being placed.

In fact, PageMill 2.0 provides an elegant way to insert items on to a page. PageMill treats anything you import on to a page via the Place command or button as an *object*, and writes the appropriate HTML tag that identifies what type of object is being placed, be it an <IMG> for a graphic or an <APPLET> for a Java applet. In fact, the only way that PageMill knows how to write the proper tag is if you name your files using appropriate extensions (the two to four-letter addition applied to the end of a filename after a period). It is very important to name your files correctly. Table 1 presents a list of common file extensions and their meanings.

Table 9.1   File Extensions and their Meanings

Extension	Description
.gif	a graphic image
.mov, .moov, .qt	a QuickTime movie
.class	a Java applet
.AIF, .AIFF, .au	a Macintosh sound file
.WAV	a Microsoft sound file
.doc	a text file
.html, .htm	a Web page
.avi	a Microsoft Video for Windows file
.mid	a midi music file
.mp2, .mpeg, .mpg	a video/sound file
.jpg, .jpeg	a photographic image file
.sty	a Style Sheet file

Working with Paragraph and Line Spacing

The only other thing you need to know is how dumb HTML really is. You need to designate all paragraph endings, line endings, and line spaces. So when you press the Return key in PageMill, the HTML is a <P> tag for hard paragraph return, and if you press Shift with the Return key, HTML writes a <BR> tag indicating a line feed or soft return. Anytime you see a <P> tag in HTML, it indicates a paragraph. That is why <P> is used to indicate blank lines as well as actual paragraphs.

Basic HTML

Now, let's add some complication to HTML. When I said that all HTML tags come in pairs, I was lying. Most HTML tags come in pairs. These tags are called *containers* and toggle on and off a function (such as a paragraph style). A specialized type of tag operates as a single. These non-container tags do something, such as create a horizontal rule.

An HTML document consists of two parts: the Head and the Body. The Head area uses Document Structure Tags that identify information about the document, such as its name, its originating application, what type of HTML is being used, and so forth. These tags consist of the <HTML>, <HEAD>, and <TITLE> tags. The Body area uses Content Tags (also called *body elements*). Content tags are every other tag offered in HTML, including <BODY>, <H1>, <IMG>, and so forth. Body elements come in two flavors: block-level elements that cause paragraph breaks, such as <P> or <ADDRESS>, and the text-level elements which do not, such as <STRONG> or <B> for bold text. Block-level elements can act as containers for text-level and other block-level elements. Text-level elements may only contain other text-level elements.

Let's look at our shell HTML once more keeping the basic structure of a page in mind.

This is the Head Area, the stuff that tells the browser what to do with the rest of the HTML source code.

```
<HTML>
<HEAD>
<TITLE> This is the Title</TITLE>
</HEAD>
```

This is the Body Area, the stuff that appears on the graphical browser's screen.

```
<BODY>
        <H1> Major document heading here</H1>
            text and markup
        <A HREF="URL"> anchor title</A>
<ADDRESS>Author and version information</ADDRESS>
</BODY>
</HTML>
```

The Head Area

PageMill generates the Head Area of the document from the information you provide in the Title bar and when you save the document. The Head section of the document provides information for browsers and other applications that access HTML files. The Head section can include the title of the document, the relationship between it and the HTML document, and where its associated files are stored (its file directories). It sometimes provides keywords that can be used in indexes to identify the document. You are familiar the head area of the HTML document because it is contained between two <Head> tags.

 Tip

When you are typing the title of your page into the Title Bar, PageMill writes the <TITLE></TITLE> tag portion of the Head area. This is the name of the page that appears on the browser's title bar. You are not limited as to how long to make the title, but remember that most browser title bars are not large and also contain the name of the browser. Therefore, try to limit the title to 64 characters so it will not be truncated by the browser.

The Body Area

The Body of an HTML document contains all the data you want to show the reader's browser. All the formatting and styles provided by the PageMill toolbars and menu bars reside in the Body, including Headings, lists, forms, tables, frames, applets, inline images, active images, and so forth. The Body of the document is set off by the two <Body> tags.

Table 9.2 presents commonly agreed upon HTML 3.0 tags as well as agreed upon Netscape 1.1 extensions that modify these tags.

Table 9.2   Common HTML 3.0 Tags

Tag	Description
<A> </A>	This is a Body element tag used to define a location that can be linked to, or to define links to other resources.
<Address> </Address>	This is an Address element tag used to identify the author of the document.
<B> </B>	This is a Body element tag that makes what it surrounds bold.
<Base>	A Head section element that identifies the URL of the current document.
<Basefont>	This is a Body element tag that defines the default text size for the document. You can give this tag a value from 1 to 7. The standard setting is 3. This is a Netscape-only supported extension.
<Blink> </Blink>	This Body element tag makes its contents blink.
<Blockquote> </Blockquote>	This Body element tag identifies its contents as a quote from another source.

Tag	Description
<Body> </body>	Used to define the body of your document. You can modify how the page looks with the following attributes: Background Image, Background Color, Text color, Link color, Visited Link color, Active link color.
 	Inserts a soft return (also called a line break) A Netscape 1.0 extension adds the attribute Clear that defines where the content can begin the next line of the document. You can give Clear the value Left, Right, or All.
	This tag is not really supported by HTML standards, but all browsers understand that it means to center the enclosed object or text on the page. Another way to indicate center is as an attribute of a heading: <h1 Align=Center> </h1>.
<Font> <Font>	Marks text to be set with special attributes. Attributes include: color="number" or "name," face="name," size=n.
<Form> </Form>	This tag defines its contents as a form containing input fields (INPUT), Selection lists (SELECT), and input boxes (TEXT AREA). You can modify forms using the following attributes: Action (defines the CGI used to process the form) and Method (defines the procedure used for passing information to the CGI and can be either Post or Get).
<h1> </h1> to <h6> </h6>	Six hierarchical levels of headings.

continues

Table 9.2   Common HTML 3.0 Tags   Continued

Tag	Description
<Head> </Head>	Defines the header section of the document that provides information about the originating program, the level of HTML used, the title of the Page, and other information needed to identify the page.
<HR>	Inserts a horizontal rule. Netscape 1.0 extensions added the following attributes: Width, Size, Noshade, Align left, Align Right, and Align Center.
<HTML> </HTML>	Defines the document as an HTML document.
<I> </I>	Makes everything within its boundaries italic.
<Img>	Inserts an image file. The Img tag uses the following attributes: SRC (source of the associated image file), Alt (provides an alternate text string for browsers that do not support graphics), ISMAP (Imagemap), Align Top, Align Middle, Align Bottom, Align Left, Align Right, Align Texttop, Align Absmiddle (absolute middle), Align Baseline, Align Absbottom (absolute bottom), HSPACE (defines the space along the horizontal edges of an inline graphic), VSPACE (defines the vertical space), Width, Height, Border, and LowSRC (low resolution version of the graphic).

Tag	Description
<Isindex>	This is a Head element tag that lets you set up keywords for simple searches. The tag is used with the Prompt attribute that lets you place a customized message in the search dialog box or window. You need a search engine (CGI) on your server to use this tag.
<Li>	This is a Body element tag that defines a new item in a list. You can modify the listed item using the following attributes: Type (defines what type of dingbat is used as a bullet or number) and Value (that lets you set where to begin numbering the items in the list).
<Link>	This is a Head element tag that defines relationships between the current document (identified by the Base tag) and another document.
<Meta>	This is a Head element tag that lets you present information about the document that is not displayed by the browser.
<multicolor> <multicol>	Marks text that should be set in multiple comlumns. This tag uses the following attributes: cols=n, gutter=n, width=n, where n is the number of pixels.
<OL> </OL>	This tag set identifies an ordered list of items with sequential numbers.
<P>	Inserts a hard return (also called a paragraph break).

continues

Table 9.2 Common HTML 3.0 Tags Continued

Tag	Description
<Table> </Table>	This tag defines its contents as a table that contains rows (TR), cells (TD), Headers (TH), and captions (CAPTION). You can modify tables by using the following attributes: Border, Cell-Spacing, Cell-Padding, Width.
<Title> </Title>	This is a Head element tag. Defines the title of the document (the name that the Browser places in the title bar).
<UL> </UL>	This tag set defines an unordered list of items.

You probably notice by now how the attributes are assigned in PageMill using the various Inspector windows, such as the Table screen with its text boxes for Border, Cell-Spacing, and Cell-Padding.

Adding Special Characters

Because HTML is an international markup language, it accepts the standard ASCII code set called Latin-1 of special characters. The problem in PageMill is that you cannot add the special characters by simply using the keystroke equivalents you are used to because HTML must see an ampersand before the symbol and a semicolon after the symbol to recognize it as an ASCII character. The Latin-1 Extended Character Set uses both literal codes (that spell out what they do, such as add an accent agrave to a letter—typed as à) and numerical equivalents (accent agrave is also Ç). You can use either literal or numerical notations in HTML to get the extended character to appear.

When you type an ampersand (&) in PageMill's content area, the program writes its ASCII equivalent (&) in the HTML. For example, I wanted to add a copyright symbol (©) to my page in

Figure 9.5a. I selected HTML Source from the Edit menu and typed the ASCII literal code *©* in the place I wanted it to appear (see Figure 9.5b). It showed up as a symbol on the PageMill content area. I also could have used the numerical equivalent (®), as I did to insert the registered mark (®) at the end of the sentence.

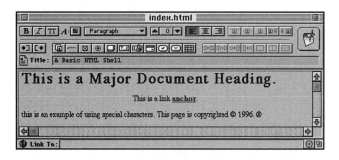

Figure 9.5a
You cannot type special characters directly on to the PageMill Edit window…

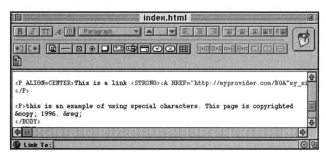

Figure 9.5b
…you must type their ASCII code equivalents in the HTML Source window.

Table 9.3 presents the Latin-1 ASCII character set and the figures you must literally type into the HTML Source window to get them to appear.

Table 9.3   The Latin-1 Extended Character List

Character	Literal	Numerical	Description
^		&#136;	Circumflex accent
–		&#150;	En dash
—	&emdash;	&#151;	Em dash
™		&#153;	Tradmark symbol
			Non-breaking space

continues

Table 9.3 The Latin-1 Extended Character List Continued

Character	Literal	Numerical	Description
¢		&#162;	Cent sign
©	&copy;	&#169;	Copyright symbol
-	&shy;	&#173;	Soft hyphen
®	&reg;	&#174;	Registered tradmark symbol
^{2}		&#179;	Superscript 2
1/4		&#188;	Fraction one-fourth
1/2		&#189;	Fraction one-half
3/4		&#190;	Fraction three-fourths
<	&lt;	&#60;	Less than sign
>	&gt;	&#62;	Greater than sign
&	&amp;	&#38;	Ampersand
º		&#178;	Degree sign

 Tip

You can add extended characters to your PageMill documents in four ways:

1   Manually type the ASCII Extended Character in the HTML Source window.

2   Copy the special character from KeyCaps on the Mac or from the Symbol dialog box in Word 6 on the Mac or Windows Platform and paste the character on to the PageMill content area. PageMill writes the ASCII extended character code into the HTML.

3   Copy the special character and paste it directly into the HTML Source window. The special character also is displayed on the PageMill content area.

4   Copy the special chracters you want to use on to the Pasteboard. Drag and drop the special character either on the PageMill Edit window or HTML Source window.

HTML Version 3.2 and PageMill 2.0

The problem that Adobe had to face when updating PageMill was that the HTML 3.0 standard had already been bypassed, but the Version 3.2 standard had not been fully accepted as the current HTML standard. HTML 3.2 supports many future elements that have not yet been defined, such as Style Sheets, client-side active images, Applets, Font colors, and JavaScript (a Netscape-derived scripting language based upon Sun's Java). Adobe chose to support the more accepted HTML 3.0 standard along with some widely supported extensions, such as <CENTER>.

What HTML PageMill Doesn't Support

PageMill 2.0 is a large step ahead of PageMill 1.0 in its support of HTML 3.0 and 3.2 tags. Yet some tags are not recognized by the program. These are

- IsIndex
- Style
- Script
- Blink
- Font Face

You can add unsupported HTML to PageMill, but you will not see it on the content area in WYSIWYG form. See the discussion of "placeholders" below for a discussion of adding HTML to PageMill.

 Tip

Since the summer of 1995, Microsoft Internet Explorer has supported the ability to specify which typeface should be used to render text on the screen. Netscape Navigator 3.0 now also supports this capability. Although PageMill 2 does not let you view the results of your specifications, you can use the <FONT FACE></FONT > tag pair to enhance your layout without having to resort to the placement of graphics to achieve a certain font.

continues

To add font support to a section of text, enclose the text within the <FONT FACE></FONT > tags. For example, if you want your "Welcome to Joe Webhead's Page!" heading to be displayed in Comic Sans MS, type the following HTML:

<H1><FONT FACE="Comic Sans MS">Welcome to Joe Webhead's Page!</FONT></H1>

You can add attributes such as color or alignment to the font by selecting the text in the content area and changing its color or alignment (see Chapter 4) with appropriate tool option on the toolbar. For example, if you add font specifications to our "Joe Webhead" page from Chapter 4, your HTML would look like this:

<H1><!—NO EDIT><FONT FACE="Impact"</—NO EDIT> SIZE=4 COLOR=#FF0000"ALIGN="center" Welcome to My World!</FONT></H1>

><!—NO EDIT> <FONT FACE="Comic Sans MS"></—NO EDIT>

You've reached the home page of Joe Webhead. Welcome! I'm just learning how to create Web pages using this great, new program called PageMill. If I had known it was this easy, I would have started long ago. This page is all about me. I hope you like it. Here is a picture of me.!</FONT>

Although you can't see the fonts in PageMill (see Figure 9.6a),the result is visible in Netscape Navigator 3.0 (or Microsoft Internet Explorer) in Figure 9.6b.

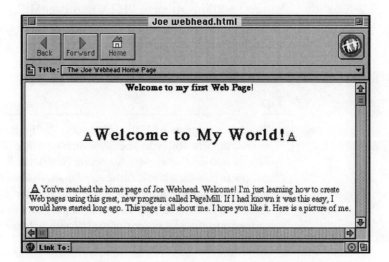

Figure 9.6a
PageMill displays HTML Placeholders where you specified fonts.

Figure 9.6b
...whereas your
browser actually
displays the
specified font.

Be sure to insert your HTML within PageMill Placeholders (see the paragraph on HTML Placeholders below) so that PageMill does not process your codes.

There is a caveat to using a specific font specification is that if your reader does not have that font installed, the text will be displayed in the browser's default font. Make sure that you specify several font options. You can also place a link on your page to Microsoft's site where Microsoft is offering a series of about 30 free TrueType fonts to promote this tag. The URL is http://www.microsoft.com/truetype/iexplor/.

What PageMill Doesn't Understand

So, what do you do when PageMill presents you with the equivalent of a "Huh?" icon (see Figure 9.7) meaning it does not understand the HTML you are inserting?

Figure 9.7
Whenever PageMill encounters an HTML tag it does not recognize, it places an object, the question mark icon, on to the page.

You can click the icon and use the Inspector to edit the misunderstood code or add a placeholder to remove the code from PageMill's notice.You can also use the HTML Source Code View and directly edit the HTML to ensure that non-supported HTML is included in the document but ignored by PageMill's WYSIWYG editor.

The ability to hide tags from PageMill's processor vastly extends the capabilities of the program, since anything you code is usable (although not visible in PageMill). For example, you can insert new objects, such as Java applets or QuickTime VR videos, or anything else that developers produce,in this fashion. The trick is that you must modify the HTML to ensure that PageMill does not disturb the object's codes.

We have alluded to working in HTML mode earlier in this chapter. Now you will find out how this is done.

You can now use the HTML Source Code View and directly edit the HTML to ensure that non-supported HTML is included in the document but ignored by PageMill's WYSIWYG editor. You can also open an Object screen in the Inspector for Hidden Icons, such as the Unknown HTML object shown in Figure 9.6, and edit the HTML in the Inspector's window.

The Source Code View

A new feature of PageMill 2.0 is the ability to actually see the document source code of your page. Select HTML Source from the Edit menu (or press the key combination Command-H). PageMill opens a window displaying the HTML codes that underly your document. Figures 9.8 and 9.9 show you the PageMill interpretation and the HTML Source windows for the Earth&Ware site example I have used throughout the book.

Figure 9.8
This is what PageMill displays in the content area after you have completed your page.

You can drag and drop tables and other WYSIWYG page elements from the toolbar onto the HTML source page and the codes will be converted. Select HTML Source from the Edit menu again to return to the content area of PageMill (see Figure 9.10).

Throughout the book I have mentioned that the best way to learn tricks of great Web pages is to copy the source code of a page (not its actual graphics or text!). PageMill displays the WYSIWYG version of what you paste in the HTML Source window. I copied the codes for the Hayden Books Home page into PageMill (see Figure 9.11). Note that you cannot copy the actual graphics because the graphics are not actually pasted on the page but rather are located and displayed as needed by the browser. PageMill leaves boxes and filenames where the graphics should be.

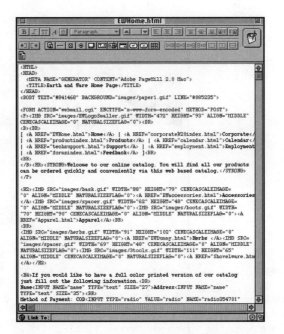

Figure 9.9
Selecting the HTML
Source command
displays its
underlying source
code.

Figure 9.10
Select the Source
HTML command
again to return to
the WYSIWYG
window.

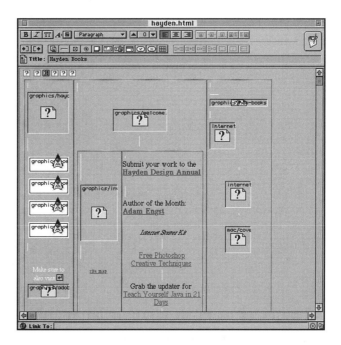

Figure 9.11
Copy the document source code for a page into PageMill to learn new HTML tricks.

In Figure 9.11, notice that there are several icons displayed on the WYSIWYG page representing different types of HTML problems, namely icons for the Unknown HTML, a Java Applet, a Comment icon, and links to external pages. PageMill 2.0 has ways to work with all of these alien elements.

Using HTML "Placeholders"

Earlier in the Chapter, I mentioned that there are tags from HTML version 3.2 and browser extensions that PageMill does not yet recognize. One of the earlier problems in PageMill was that the program would try to convert the unknown HTML and in the process change the code, thus messing up the function of the alien tags.

You can now insert a "Placeholder" object, which lets you tell PageMill to leave the enclosed HTML alone. Using placeholders lets you write custom HTML browsers can use but PageMill cannot interpret. Figure 9.12 shows a placeholder and how to edit its contents using the Placeholder screen of the Inspector.

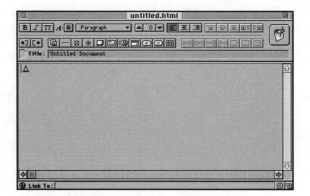

Figure 9.12
Insert a placeholder
to store HTML you
do not want
PageMill to
interpret.

Inserting and Editing a Placeholder

1 Select Insert Placeholder from the Edit menu.

2 Click to select the Placeholder icon with the Inspector open. The Inspector changes to the Placeholder Object screen (see Figure 9.13).

3 Click the box in the Inspector and type the HTML tags you want to add but want PageMill to ignore. Press Return.

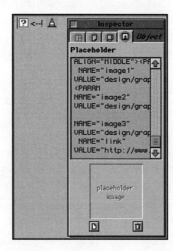

Figure 9.13
Use the Place-
holder screen in the
Inspector to edit
the contents of a
Placeholder.

Tip

Open the source code in SimpleText (the Apple text editor) or Notepad (the Windows' text editor) before you copy it into PageMill. Any tags you want PageMill to ignore should be surrounded by the following tags: <!--NOEDIT--> in front of the HTML and a closing <!--/NOEDIT--> in back of the code. When PageMill sees these comment elements, it replaces the contained HTML codes with a Placeholder and doesn't interpret those enclosed tags. You can also replace the Placeholder icon with a graphic representing what the HTML does to remind you what the Placeholder is hiding. To replace the Placeholder icon, type the following HTML:

```
<!--NOEDIT SRC="name of the graphic.gif" WIDTH=100
HEIGHT=50-->
<SPECIAL_COUNTER_TAG> (the name you want to appear in-
stead of the placeholder)
<!--/NOEDIT-->
```

Use placeholders to insert the text elements shown in Table 9.4 into your page to enhance text formatting (PageMill does not yet recognize these tags).

Table 9.4   Character Formatting Tags

<U> </U>	Underline text style
<Strike> </Strike>	Strike-through text style
<Big> </Big>	Places text in a large font
<Small> </Small>	Places text in a small font
	Places text in subscript style
	Places text in superscript style

Using Cascading Style Sheets with PageMill 2.0

A newly developing standard that is currently supported by Microsoft Internet Explorer 3.0 and will be supported by Netscape Navigator 4.0 are cascading style sheets. (See the W3 Committee Web site at `http://www.w3.org/put/WWW/TR/` `WD-css1.html` for information about this developing standard.) This is a way to tell the HTML you want standard values applied to attributes every place they are encountered. Create a style sheet in a separate document and link that document to your PageMill document as you would any other file. Files containing style sheets use the .sty extension.

Style Sheets are a set of new tags that present a series of statements or rules describing a document. You set up a style by typing

selector {property = value}

where *selector* is the tag element being lent a style, such as a header or paragraph, a list, and so forth; a *property* is something about the selector that varies, such as its alignment, text color, spacing, and so forth (you can think of the property as the attribute of the selector); and the *value* is the variable you select for the property, such as left, right, center, and so forth.

Therefore, you can set up a style sheet that states that each Level 1 Header will be red, Helvetica or Arial, 12 point type with 2 point leading, bold faced style by writing the following:

```
H1 {

    text color=red

    font-family=helvetica

    alt-font=arial

    font-size=12pt

    font-leading=2pt

    font-weight=bold

    }
```

In addition, you can use the <CLASS> attribute to add power to your style sheets by letting you define special styles to classes of tags. For example, you want to define some lists as being in a classification, called "key." By adding <LI CLASS=key> attribute to your HTML, every time the HTML sees this attribute it would apply the Li.key style to the list. This is a great way to set up paragraph styles for specialized formatting.

Right now, anything goes with how styles are applied to HTML, since each browser developer is working on their own system of applying styles. Therefore, you can also use a new tag called <STYLE></STYLE> to define the style of a paragraph as you go along. For example, our list above with the "key" classification would be manually formatted with a text color of lime green by adding the HTML <STYLE>LI {text-color=#00ff00"}</STYLE> to your document.

Remember that style sheets and their tags must be placed in placeholders in PageMill 2.0 because it cannot process these newfangled things, but your viewer's browser may be able to.

Working with Unrecognized HTML

Earlier in the chapter, I mentioned the "Huh?" icon PageMill uses whenever it encounters HTML it cannot understand. There are two reasons for PageMill to not be able to interpret HTML: either PageMill was typed incorrectly (if you are copying someone else's code), or it is not supported by PageMill. In either instance, PageMill 2.0 gives you a way to edit the unknown code to correct its errors or turn it into a placeholder by adding the NOEDIT tags before and after the code.

Editing Unknown HTML

1   Click to select the Non-Understood HTML icon with the Inspector open. The Inspector changes to the Unrecognized HTML Object screen (see Figure 9.14).

2   Click the box in the Inspector and type the HTML tags you want to add. Use the NOEDIT tags to change the Unrecognized HTML into a Placeholder. Press Return.

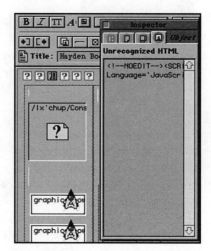

Figure 9.14
Use the Unrecog-
nized HTML screen
in the Inspector to
edit the contents of
a Question Mark
icon.

Adding Comments

Sometimes you want to add a notation to the page informing the Webmaster of a requirement for the page, documenting the use of a new HTML tag, or saying something you want hidden from the browser. You can use one of the invisible icons, called the Comments icon, to insert messages into the HTML source page the browser will not interpret but your editors and team can see.

Placing a Comment into PageMill

1   Select Insert Invisibles from the Edit menu and highlight Comments in its hierarchical menu. An invisible Comments icon is inserted on the page.

2   Click to select the Comments icon with the Inspector open. The Inspector changes to the Comments Object screen (see Figure 9.15).

3   Click the box in the Inspector and type the message. Press Return.

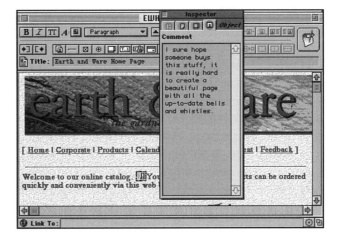

Figure 9.15
Use the Comment screen in the Inspector to edit the contents of a Comment icon.

Figure 9.16 displays how your comment is placed into the Source HTML. You can also see comments by clicking any Comments icons you encounter with the Inspector open. Notice that the message in the Source window is surrounded by "comment" tags (<-> <--/>).

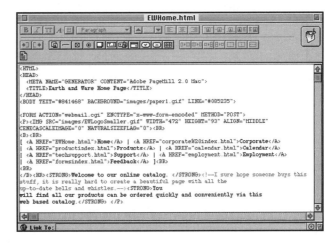

Figure 9.16
When you type a message in the Comment screen of the Inspector, the message is placed between Comment tags in the Source HTML.

Using Java Applets and JavaScript Macros

 Java is a portable programming language developed by Sun Microsystems. The usefulness of this language is that it can run on any computer with access to the Web. Suddenly, you can write programs and store them on the Web for use by anyone who has access to your site. True "groupware" is born. Java programs are fully compiled applications that contain only a little code, and so they are called *applets*. Java Applets perform a certain task, such as displaying an analog clock that tells time in an animated fashion. Netscape developed a scripting language (such as you use in Excel spreadsheets to write a macro that would run as a tiny program to do automatically what you regularly do manually) based on Java called JavaScript. You can write JavaScript macros directly in your HTML that cause the browser to perform some task as ordered by your HTML, such as increasing an incremental counter one unit.

PageMill does not recognize JavaScript, but can accept Java Applets as an object that you place like a picture on the page.

Placing Java Applets on a Page

PageMill accepts Java applets as objects to be placed on a page (although it cannot test or view them). All applets must have a .class suffix to be recognized. When you use the Place Object button on the toolbar to insert a Java Applet (see Figure 9.17), PageMill displays the Java Applet icon on the page.

Figure 9.17
You can place Java applets into your page, although PageMill cannot display them in WYSIWYG form or test their usefulness.

You can use the Inspector's Applet Object screen to give a name and value to the Applet to make the applets easier to track.

Identifying an Applet Using the Inspector

1   Click to select the Java Applet box with the Inspector open. The Inspector changes to the Applets Object screen (see Figure 9.18).

2   Click the Name box in the Inspector and type the Applet's name (you will find it in the HTML source code).

3   Click the Values box and type any associated object's name or other attribute's value. Press Return.

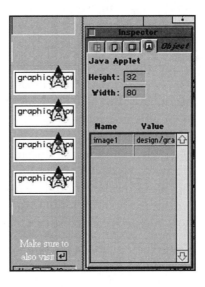

Figure 9.18
Use the Applet screen in the Inspector to name the Applet and identify its attributes.

As I stated earlier in the Chapter, PageMill cannot work with JavaScript macros as of yet. The following is an example of a piece of JavaScript from the Hayden Books Home page.

```
<SCRIPT LANGUAGE>='JavaScript';<!-- JavaScript Follows
function wordage (txt) {window.status=txt;
setTimeout("clear()",99000)}
function clear () {window.status= "";}
//JavaScript Ends --></SCRIPT>
```

When PageMill encounters a < SCRIPT LANGUAGE>=...> tag inside the <Head> </Head> tag, it must process any codes inside the script so as to find the closing </Script> tag. If PageMill tries to run the script (and it cannot), it may alter the code. To avoid this problem, you can turn the Java script into a placeholder by opening the HTML codes in a text editor and typing NOEDIT tags before and after the script, or you can turn the script into a comment by placing a Comment tag (<!--) on the line before the script begins and another Comment tag (-->) on the line after the script ends.

Using either method causes PageMill to ignore the script, although Java-enabled browsers do not see the comment or placeholder tags and will process the script as intended.

Summary

That's a quick and dirty lesson on HTML. Remember, you are using PageMill to create advanced Web page features, such as client-side active images, forms, tables, and so forth, without having to see the codes that produce the WYSIWYG page results. The only reason you should have for looking or working with HTML is to correct errors (in which case it is good to recognize tags and how they should be used) or to add HTML tags PageMill cannot process. With the Inspector and the HTML Source window, you do have access to what lies under the PageMill hood.

Chapter 10 takes an in-depth look at common gateway interfaces (CGIs) and how they work with your Web site.

Chapter 10

Common Gateway Interfaces

Let's face it, Web sites are just overgrown text files. They just don't do anything but sit there and let you jump around a lot. What if there was a way to make a Web page do something, like answer a question? There is a way. To make the information change on a page based on your responses and questions, you need to connect an outside program, such as a database, to the server where your page resides. The means to manage this connection is called a Common Gateway Interface (CGI).

We have discussed CGIs in terms of active image processing in Chapter 6 and in terms of forms processing in Chapter 8. Now, let's concentrate on CGIs themselves, how they work, what they do, how to set one up to run with PageMill documents, and where to find CGIs to run.

What Is a CGI?

As I said earlier, a Web page is just a collection of HTML codes that tell the browser what to retrieve and display on your computer monitor. The text and graphics only change if someone bothers to update the page with new information. It cannot change on its own. That is where scripts come in. Scripts are small executable files (programs) that link the Web server with the computer running the browser in a way that something can happen (for example, the computers can talk to one another to pass information back and forth). Scripts can speak HTML and the browser listens and responds. This is very powerful stuff. Suddenly, pages are no longer static, but can be customized by the script based on input by the viewer. Suddenly, pages are intelligent. Whenever you see a push button, an edit box, a checkbox, or radio buttons, the current time or date, or a people counter that changes, you know that a script is in use. (You can also see a directory name called cgi-bin in the URL of the Web page. We'll talk more about the cgi-bin directory later.)

A *CGI* is not a programming language but a set of conventions or rules for setting up two-way communications between the server's computer and the browser's computer. CGI scripts have been written for every computer platform (including Macintosh, Windows, and Unix) and can be written in almost any programming language. Web servers can pass information to CGIs (see Figure 10.1) as well as receive information from CGIs. CGIs can be launched by the Web server and can interact with applications other than the Web server (see Figure 10.2).

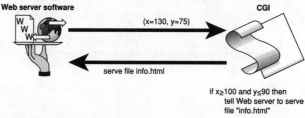

Web server software

(x=130, y=75)

CGI

serve file info.html

if x≥100 and y≤90 then
tell Web server to serve
file "info.html"

Figure 10.1
Web servers can send information to CGIs, and vice versa.

The Web server gives the CGI some information, which it passes through its set of rules, then sends some information back to the Web server instructing it as to what to do next.

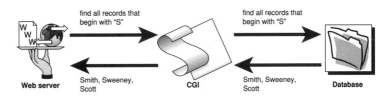

find all records that begin with "S"

find all records that begin with "S"

Web server

Smith, Sweeney, Scott

CGI

Smith, Sweeney, Scott

Database

Figure 10.2
CGIs enable Web servers to interact with other applications, such as databases.

The CGI can also act as an intermediary between the Web server and another application. The database doesn't know how to communicate with the Web server and vice versa. The CGI takes care of all of the communication.

CGI scripts extend the interactivity of your Web site by enabling you to add intelligence to your HTML via preprocessing so that each browser is given a personalized version of your Web page. CGI scripts also search databases; personalize email; provide fill-in form processing; process hot spots (although most of this is being pushed over to the client-side and handled by the browser); provide point-of-sale processing (setting up online stores that accept and process credit card accounts); and provide access counters or give the time of day or date. The excitement of Web pages is provided via CGI scripts. It is a CGI script that personalizes a response to a reader's completion of an order form with "Thanks, Joe for placing an order with WizzyWig. Your order is scheduled to ship next Wednesday." CGI scripts can create HTML text and pull in images on the fly, which are then returned and displayed on your reader's computer screen via his browser. CGIs are a standard within HTML Version 2.0, which means you can pull in CGI scripts from any type of server supporting HTML Version 2.0, be it a Unix, Windows NT, or Mac.

How CGIs Work

CGI scripts are files that reside on a special directory on the Web server computer called cgi-bin. When a reader clicks on a link that corresponds to a CGI script file, the server gets the file and exe-cutes it in real-time. The output is returned directly to the reader's browser. That seems simple enough. CGI scripts serve as mediators between the browser on the client side and the software on the server side. As intermediaries, CGI scripts must perform five functions:

1 Be able to accept information from the client browser.

2 Decide what to do with the information.

3 Be able to use the Web server's software resources to accomplish the job that is requested.

4 Be able to do something with the information returned by the Web server.

5 Be able to return something coherent back to the client's browser.

CGI scripts must follow two rules to make this happen: the script has to be able to write to an HTML file, and the script has to begin with an area, called a *header*, that tells the server how to handle the output of the script. You can't see these scripts like you can a Web page because the scripts do things when executed, but otherwise sit in a directory and wait for a call from the server. You can see the results of a CGI script.

There are three parts to a CGI:

■ A special URL the reader enters into their browser either directly or via a hidden hot link you placed on your page (remember the Inspector's Form mode screen from Chapter 8?).

■ CGI-compatible Web server software, which for Macs includes Quarterdeck/StarNine's WebStar or MacHTTP, InterCon's InterServer Publisher, or Tenon's MachTen; for Unix includes NCSA's HTTPd server or Apache; for Windows NT includes Microsoft's Windows NT 4.0 Server; and for Windows 95 might be Netscape's Fastrack Server 2.0.

■ The CGI application. CGIs can be purchased that perform specific tasks, such as forms processing, or you can write your own programs using practically any programming language, but most are written in a Unix scripting language, such as Sh or Perl, or some Mac or Windows equivalent, such as AppleScript or MacPerl on the Mac or Visual Basic on the Windows side. Scripts written in full-blown programming languages, such as C or C++ must be compiled to create executable code before they are usable. Most scripts, on the other hand, are interpreted (run line-by-line by the server).

What Do You Need to Know to Use CGI Scripts on Your Server?

If you want to use CGIs on your site, the first step is to find out more about the server where your page is eventually going to reside. You can start by asking the following two questions.

■ What type of computer does the Web server run on, and which server software does the machine use? This two-part question is important because you need to know what platform the CGI will eventually run on (you can't necessarily run a Windows CGI on a Unix machine).

■ Can you have CGIs running on the server? Many Web site administrators are wary of allowing users to put CGIs on the server because of the potential for a security breach.

After you find out what type of machine the CGI will run on, and get permission to place a CGI on that machine, there are a couple of Web sites that will help you with learning to write CGI scripts and containing archives of pre-written public-domain scripts.

Either way, the best place to start is at Yahoo, the index of Internet sites. Yahoo is arranged by topic, and there is a large list of links to sites with CGI information at:

```
http://www.yahoo.com/Computers_and_Internet/Internet/
World_Wide_Web/CGI_Common_Gateway_Interface/
```

Writing CGIs

When the Web was first developed it was necessary to write your own CGIs. If you could program applications on your computer, the transition to writing CGIs was fairly easy. Essentially, you would include information in your program enabling your application to communicate with the Web server software. If you weren't a programmer, you either learned the skills necessary to create your applications or just accepted the fact that you could only create HTML pages without cool stuff.

In the early days of the Web, an information provider needed two diverse skill sets to create a Web site: the ability to create good information systems and the ability to write computer code. This, of course, is a bad model. The idea that you needed two very different skill sets was ridiculous. The desire to overturn this model was part of what spurred the creation of PageMill. It also led to a growing community of programmers who began to create CGIs everyone could use on their Web sites without having to program the applications themselves.

The proliferation of available CGIs is almost at a point where building a Web site is like piecing together a puzzle. You can start with Web pages and add to them with CGIs. This is analogous to using QuarkXPress. Most designers know QuarkXPress extremely well and will use plug-ins such as color matching tables, text alignment tools, and so forth, to extend the functionality of the layout program. This way, they can add effects to their pieces without knowing the technical details of how the effects are created.

Dozens of CGIs are available to use with your Web site. But there is a chance you won't find one that does exactly what you want. Or, you might be one of the brave few—a real power user—who wants to get into Web publishing and write your own CGIs.

If you want to write your own CGIs, you need to know a few things first. If you already know how to program an application on your computer, check out the following online resources for writing CGIs:

- CGI Programmer's Reference found at `http://www.best.com/~heldund/cgi-faq/cgi-faq.text`

- Common Gateway Interfaces (CGI) found at `http://hoohoo.ncsa.uiuc.edu/cgi`

- Introduction to CGI Programming - A Tutorial found at `http://ute.usi.utah.edu/bin/cgi-programming/counter.pl/cgi-programming/index.html`

- Selena Sol's Public Domain CGI Script Archive and Resource Library at `http://www.eff.org/~erict/Scripts/`

■ Eric Lease Morgan's hypertext book *Teaching a New Dog Old Tricks* at `http://152.1.24.177/teaching/manuscript/default.html`.

These sites help you understand how to build code that accepts messages from the Web server and talks back to it.

Setting Up PageMill to Run a CGI Script

CGI scripts are linked to your Web page like any other hypertext link. The special nature of CGI scripts is where they are stored on the server, and what they do once the server locates the file.

There are several ways to run a CGI script:

1 Use a special attribute within an HTML Placeholder called #exec and pathname of the CGI to be run. (See Chapter 9 for a discussion of how to add Placeholders via the <!----> brackets, and how to edit Placeholders using the Inspector's Placeholder screen.)

2 Write a CGI script directly into the HTML, again using a Placeholder to contain the script and a <ISINDEX> </ISINDEX> tag in the Head area. This is called a Document-Based Query.

3 Create a Form using PageMill's Forms toolbar. PageMill automatically adds the <FORM ACTION> tag and the pathname of the CGI script to use with the form.

When you open the HTML Source window (see Chapter 9 for a discussion of using this window in PageMill) to view a link to a CGI script, you would see something like this:

```
<FORM METHOD="POST" ACTION="http://myorganization.com/
cgi-bin/cginame.cgi">
```

or

```
<!--#exec cgi=" http://myorganization.com/cgi-bin/
cginame.cgi"-->
```

Now we get to that cgi-bin thing.

The big issue with using CGI scripts is that they allow the world to access the Web server where your page resides. System administrators do not like this at all, because it poses a severe security threat to the computer maintaining the Web. The solution is to store all CGI scripts in a special directory called cgi-bin that is only accessible by users who have permission to access that directory, called *trusted users.*

The trick is to know what scripts are available and their names so that you can link to them from your Web page. You usually cannot go to the cgi-bin directory yourself and take a look, because this would violate security on the server. Instead, if you need a CGI script, speak to your Webmaster and get its full pathname so that you can enter it into PageMill. Then again, if you want to run a CGI script that is not resident in cgi-bin, ask the Webmaster if the ExecCGI program (on Unix servers) is running (again, highly unlikely because of security issues). ExecCGI lets files with .cgi extensions be run from any directory. Your Webmaster also may give you a cgi-bin in your assigned directory to let you run your own script from there (although this is highly unlikely, again because of security issues).

What About Windows and Mac Servers?

You can run scripts from Windows servers outside of secure directories by creating a .bat file that runs a batch file calling for the script. If your script is written in Perl, you must download a Perl interpreter, because Perl doesn't come with Windows NT or Netscape Navigator's server. You can get an Intel version of the Perl interpreter from `ftp://ftp.intergraph.com/put/win32/perl`.

 Note

It is not a smart idea to run a CGI script as a batch file because it lets anyone who has access to the server in whenever a batch file is run to make arbitrary commands anywhere on the system—a big security breach. The Webmaster will probably not allow you to create a .bat file, but rather have all CGI scripts be compiled as .EXE programs and use an EXE program to call the Perl script.

MacHTTP and its commercial successor WebStar work like a NSCA Unix server; in fact, MacHTTP is based upon HTTPd for Unix. Thus, you need to tell the server the absolute pathname of your cgi script for it to execute. The CGI scripts will be saved to a secure folder with limited access permissions, just as in the Unix server.

Running a Form Processing CGI: A Setup Example

In Chapter 8, we discussed how to create a form. In Figure 10.3, The HTML Source window of the forms.html file we created in Chapter 8 is displayed. Notice that the Head area of the document contains a tag called <FORM ACTION> that contains a URL naming the form processing CGI script you want to use and an attribute mentioning the method you want to use to run the CGI (GET or POST) (see Figure 10.4).

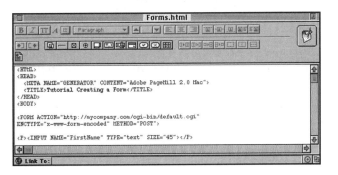

Figure 10.3
The URL of the CGI Script is invoked at the beginning of the Form using the <FORM ACTION> tag.

This is the information you placed in the Form screen of the Inspector, and is the same information you have to get from the Webmaster or system administrator, namely what is the pathname to the CGI script file. When you type the CGI pathname into the Form screen of the Inspector, PageMill inserts it into the HTML. When the browser first hits this line, it knows to execute that CGI to process the form. That is how PageMill runs form CGIs.

Figure 10.4:
In PageMill, the name you enter on the Form screen of the Inspector is the URL for the CGI used to process the form.

Configuring CGI Scripts

There are three things you have to do to get a CGI script to run on a server (given that you have permission to run the CGI in the first place). The trick is that you have to configure the CGI script you use to let it recognize where the files relating to your Web site are located on the Web server (if they have been moved). This means that you have to have access to your server and permission to modify a file.

1 Every CGI script must be configured to run on your local server. There is a .setup file that comes with many public-domain CGI scripts that centralizes server-specific variables and options so that you can update them in one place. If there is no .setup file, you will find the options and server-specific variables you have to set in the first lines of the main script.

You must always check the instructions that come with CGI scripts to see how they need to be configured (how to set up variables) to run properly. Each script has different instructions.

2 You also have to ensure that you have an interpreter on your server that can read the script, be it Perl, Sh, or Tcl (for Unix), Visual Basic (for Windows), or AppleScript or

MacPerl for Mac servers. You then have to make sure that the interpreter is referenced correctly on the first line of the script.

3 You need to ensure that the permissions are set correctly for each file in the script so that the Web server will run any applications, read any data, or setup fields and write to any supporting files that the script requires.

You can get the variables that the script requires by echoing the server's environment information into the HTML of your page. This process is called *Server-Side Includes* (SSI). You set up a special file on the server using either Unix, DOS, or AppleScript (depending upon the server's environment). Let's assume you are running on a Unix-based server because most people do. You set up a file called .htaccess in your public_html directory. In the .htaccess file you type:

Options Includes Indexes FollowSymLinks

AddType text/x-server-parsed-html .html

Then, in PageMill's HTML Source window you can add paragraphs that include the hidden comment <!--#echo var="*the name of the server environment variable*"--> and get information on the local date and time, the universal data and time, the date/time you last worked on the file, the e-mail address of the system administrator, and so forth.

Table 10.1 provides a list of NCSA server environment variables you can bring on to your page.

Table 10.1   Environment Variables for NCSA Servers

Variable Name	Description
SERVER_SOFTWARE	Type/Version of the server software
SERVER_NAME	Host address of the server
GATEWAY_INTERFACE	Name of the CGI script being used
SERVER_PROTOCOL	The software protocol and version number used by the server
SERVER_PORT	The Port Number (ususally 80)

continues

Table 10.1 Environment Variables for NCSA Servers Continued

Variable Name	Description
REQUEST_METHOD	GET or POST
HTTP-USER_AGENT	The type of browser making the request
HTTP_REFERRER	The originating URL of the user
QUERY_STRING	The data being requested by the user
REMOTE_HOST	The name of the requesting computer
REMOTE-ADDR	The IP Address of the user
REMOTE_USER	The identity of the user making the request
CONTENT_TYPE	MIME type of data
CONTENT_LENGTH	The size of the data being requested in bytes
DOCUMENT_NAME	Name of the current HTML File
DOCUMENT_URI	Path to the current HTML file
SCRIPT_NAME	Name of the currently running CGI script
DATE_LOCAL	The Local date and time
DATE_GMT	Universal date and time
LAST_MODIFIED	The date and time you last worked on the file
PATH	Current Unix path setting

 Note

If you are interested in writing your own Unix CGIs, there is a tutorial at `http://www.catt.ncsu.edu/~bex/tutor/cgi-bin.html`. This site is specifically advertised as being the place to come if you are a non-programmer, taking you through the details of CGIs from the very basics up through writing a simple script.

If your Web server runs under Windows NT and you're looking for a source for CGIs, check `http://rick.wzl.rwth—aachen.de/rick/ntweb/index.html`. This is an incredible site, filled with links to pre-built CGIs and tools that will help you develop your own CGIs.

Document- and Form-Based Queries

As mentioned earlier in the chapter, CGI scripts stand as the mediator between the browser and the Web server. The coin of the realm, per se, is the *query*. Queries are requests for information that fly back and forth between the browser and the server via the CGI script.

You can create Web pages that communicate with the server in one of two ways:

- Document-based queries
- Form-based queries

The request for information is what the CGI script does, but the Web page sets up the question. Document-based queries were the first types of interactive Web pages developed and supported by HTML Version 1.0. Form-based queries are newer types of information requests that were standardized in HTML Version 2.0 and further refined in HTML Version 3.0.

Document-based queries use a special tag called <ISINDEX> in the Head area of the document. All that this tag does is ask for a keyword from the user by displaying a text box. You cannot select your own prompt and you can't ask for more than one piece of information at a time. You also cannot select where the text box is placed on the page.

You can use Document-based queries to return pre-formatted HTML pages based on the information provided in the text box created by the <ISINDEX> tag. You write the script in a scripting language directly in the HTML Source window that returns the replay based on the response in the text box. The CGI script uses the data supplied by your reader and tests it against a set of arguments, and returns a response based on the results of the test. This is called using *parameters* (the stuff your reader types). For example, you can write a script that looks for any text in the text box created by ISINDEX and if there is some, returns a page saying, "Thank you for your response," you said, "*whatever was in the text box.*"

ISINDEX isn't used much any more because it is a clumsy way to look for information. Form-based queries are more powerful because you can ask for more information in more ways than you can with the ISINDEX tag and respond with more flexible HTML using many different scripts.

Form-Based CGI Scripts

The following paragraphs present descriptions of public-domain and commercial CGI scripts used for different purposes, yet all use Forms to format the data for processing.

 Note

CGI scripts are not transportable between computer platforms. You must use a script that is written in a language that can be understood by the Web server software. The language's interpreter must also be resident on the server computer and its location identified to the CGI script. Perl is becoming the most popular language for writing scripts because there are versions of Perl interpreters available for Unix, Windows, and Macintosh. You will find that today most public-domain CGIs are written in Perl, although scripts can be written in almost any programming language. Find out if you can run the CGI on your server before downloading it. Check its language first.

When you used PageMill to create fill-in forms in Chapter 8, the last step was pointing to a CGI in the Inspector. Chapter 8 talked about variables and how they were containers for the data the reader was going to input (either into the text areas we created or by choosing one of the radio buttons or checkboxes we provided).

It also talked about how the containers would then be sent to the server to be processed.

Well, imagine you are inside the server and this bundle of variables containing information has just arrived after a reader clicked a form's Submit button. What are you going to do with it? You can't just let it go out into cyberspace. That would defeat the purpose of asking for it in the first place. What you need to do is store the information somewhere such as

- ■ Text file
- ■ Database

Most CGI scripts make use of information hidden in your forms (not visible to the browsers but listing those environmental variables described earlier in the chapter). You can create hidden fields in PageMill to accommodate the needs of forms-based CGI scripts.

 ## Creating Hidden Fields

1. Open your Web form. (In this case, open the file Forms.html you created in Chapter 8.)

2. Click the mouse at the top of the page to set the cursor.

3. Select Insert Invisible on the Edit menu.

4. Select Hidden Field from its hierarchical menu.

   PageMill places an "H" token on the page to denote the hidden field (see Figure 10.5).

5. Select the Hidden Field icon with the Inspector open. The Inspector window changes to the Hidden Field screen.

6. In the Name text box, type the name of the FileMaker Pro field where special instructions are located. Enter what the name of the field was in FileMaker Pro. These must match.

7. In the Values text box, type the name of the FileMaker Pro database you want to write the data to. Your name must match the FileMaker Pro name exactly.

The result looks like the Inspector shown in Figure 10.6.

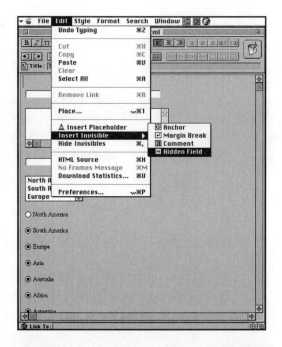

Figure 10.5
PageMill 2.0
supports the
insertion of hidden
fields in your Web
page.

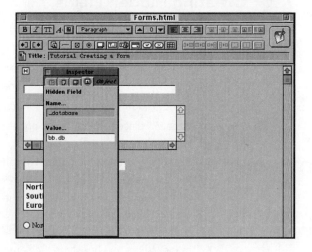

Figure 10.6
Use the Inspector's
Hidden Field screen
to tell the CGI what
to do with the data
in the Form.

Examples of CGIs

There are several ways to obtain CGI scripts that you need to process your documents and forms. The easiest way is to ask your System Administrator what is already available on the server to suit your needs (since most System Administrators do not like to add alien CGIs to their servers anyway and may not allow you to place your own on the system for security reasons). Also, if you are working with an Internet Service Provider, most ISPs do not let you add outside CGIs. Find out the pathnames of the specific types of CGIs you need and use the existing scripts.

If you are allowed to add CGIs, the Web is full of public domain CGI archives. You can download the scripts and their help files and follow the directions that come with the scripts as to how they should be installed. Note that you need access to the server via Telnet or a direct Unix connection to do this, because you have to change information used by the server to get it to recognize that the script is there. You can also ask the System Administrator to install the script (maybe it will get done in a timely fashion).

Lately, commercial vendors are selling CGIs. These scripts or programs need to be installed like any other program (or the public-domain software). Read the help files and follow the directions.

The following paragraphs provide a short overview of the types of CGI scripts available for three platforms: Unix, Windows, and Mac. This list is by no means exhaustive.

Forms and Guestbooks

As mentioned throughout this chapter, most CGIs process information via Web page forms because forms offer a flexible way to getting information from your reader and returning information back to the reader. There are specialized forms that collect information about readers of your site, called Guestbooks. You can then use the information to tailor the site to the interests of readers you are getting (or build a mailing list, or personalize the site for that reader, and so forth). Other forms take information and return data to your readers. Still other forms offer ways to email or fax information.

Note

As I keep saying, Perl has become the defacto scripting language because it is portable across platforms. Thus, many scripts that are written in Perl can be run on multiple platforms beyond the originating Unix, if the Windows or Mac server has Perl installed. Programs written in Visual Basic can only be run on Windows servers and programs written in AppleScript or Frontier can only be run on Mac servers.

Table 10.2   Form Processing Scripts

Scripts in Perl

Selena Sol's Guestbook 3.0 (Perl)

Guestbook.cgi (Perl) by Matt Wright

Poll it 1.0 (Perl) by Jason Berry

Scripts in C

Forms.acgi by Steve Johnson (`http://www.biola.edu/cgi-bin/forms/`) takes the data input from a form and puts it into an email message, and sends it to someone. Most of the configuration for Forms.acgi is done with hidden fields in your form, including names and addresses for both the sender and receiver and the subject line. This means that if you want a message to go to different people, you need to create separate fill-in forms for each.

NetForms by John O'Fallon, Maxxum Development (`http://www.maxum.com/NetForms`) (Commercial $199). NetForms runs native on Power Macs. In addition to taking the data from a form and dumping it into a text file (the text is tab delimited, so you can easily import it into a database), you also can have it formatted as HTML. This way, you can have user-input information posted at your Web site and create bulletin-board style discussion areas on your Web site. You can also embed hot links into the text file pointing to other related forms or hidden fields pointing to other CGIs that can further process the data. This forms-processing CGI is useful for collecting information that records user feedback, registers products online, reports problems and tracks information collection, and takes online orders. In fact, any information sucked up into a text file and analyzed off-line can be collected via NetForms.

Scripts Written in AppleScript/Frontier

Email CGI by Eric Lease Morgan (`http://www.lib.ncsu.edu/staff/ morgan/email-cgi.html`): Email.acgi is an AppleScript-based program that does the same thing as Forms.acgi: It takes information from a form and drops it into an email. Email.acgi, like ROFM.cgi, needs a few commercial AppleScript Scripting Additions (Parse CGI and TCP Scripting Additions) to work.

 Note

> In addition to a Web server, you also need to be running a Simple Mail Transfer Protocol (SMTP) server to use these CGIs. This is because the CGI creates a mail message and sends it through your Internet email server. Again, if you are running Delphic's NetAlly, you probably won't need another application because SMTP is part of the package. If you are running any other server, check out the Apple Internet Mail Server (AIMS), available from Apple's Web site at `http://www.apple.com`.

ROFM by Russell Owens at `http://rowen.astro.washington.edu/`: If you have information in Claris' FileMaker Pro database program, you can use ROFM CGI to serve as the intermediary between the data and your server.

Interaction/IP written by Terje Norderlaug and available from the Media Design inProgress site (`http://www.ifi.uio.no/~terjen/ interaction/index.html`): Interaction/IP performs the same text dump functions and bulletin board support functions as NetForms. The benefit of Interaction/IP is that it supports numerous plug-ins and tool scripts, such as a tool creating a collaborative calculator for joint math problem solving over the Web.

Counters

Not long ago, it became incredibly popular to have a counter on your Web site's home page. There's no point to this other than to let people know how popular your site is or to show off your Web know-how (counters require CGIs).

Muhammad Muquit wrote an elegant counter called Count in Perl (available at `http://warm.semcor.com/~muquit/`) that keeps a raw count of hits on your site and displays the number in an elegant GIF file of a digital clock.

You can also hire a company called Internet Audit (`http://www.internet-audit.com`) that links to your site and records all the information about your visitors for you. An inline GIF file linked to their home page uses a unique personal code that activates recording software. You can get the results by clicking another GIF connected to a statistics script.

Analog by Stephen Turner written in Perl can be downloaded from `ftp://ftp.statslab.cam.ac.uk/put/users/sret1/analog` records usage statistics for a Web site.

Logger.cgi by Rod Clark, available through the CGI Collection, is a program written in Perl that keeps a log of every person who "hits" your page.

You can also purchase a commercial counter program for $695 from Interse called Market Focus (`http://www.interse.com`). The program analyzes the use of Web sites or pages and downloads the results to a Word 6.0 document.

ServerStat runs on the Macintosh and processes your log and creates an HTML page giving you the vital statistics of your Web site. ServerStat charts connections by the day and hour and tells you how many connections were made from various domains (such as education, commercial, or government). ServerStat is at `http://165.247.199.177/ss.html`.

Count WWWebula is a C-based shareware package from Kagi Software available at `http://198.207.242.3/`. The counter displayed on your Web page is a GIF image when you are using a

CGI, rather than just a number. A few GIFs come with the package, plus there is a way to have your own GIFs displayed as the numbers. The coolest is an odometer graphic.

NetCloak, from Maxum Development is listed here as a counter CGI, but providing a quick way to display a counter is only a small part of what NetCloak can do. In reality, NetCloak provides about 30 new HTML commands giving you control over what information is displayed on your Web site.

You might be saying, "HTML? I thought the whole point was that I didn't have to write HTML?" This is true, but remember that PageMill does enable you to put HTML commands into your document by assigning text the raw HTML attribute. If you plan to use NetCloak, you need to format the commands as raw HTML. See Chapter 11 for how to work with raw HTML.

Besides displaying a counter, NetCloak can have items randomly displayed. It can change the look of your page depending on any number of qualities of the browser software (for example, you can display information to clients viewing from educational sites differently from those viewing from commercial sites). NetCloak can even change the information on your page depending on the date or time of day.

NetCloak is made by the same people who make NetForms: Maxum Development. You can download a sample copy of NetCloak from `http://www.maxum.com`.

Active Images

It is easy to create client-side and server-side active images using PageMill. For those server-side active images to work, however, you need to have a CGI on the server that can process the information that comes in when the mouse is clicked.

If you have created active images, talk to the Webmaster so that he knows that he'll need to either have a CGI installed that can interpret the map file output by PageMill, or set up his server software to handle imagemaps.

Unix and Windows servers based on NCSA's HTTPd server software use a built-in active image processing CGI called Imagemap. A similar CGI script is available for the Macintosh called ImageMap.acgi.

ImageMap.acgi comes from Lutz Wiemann. Lutz's CGI is fast, somewhat easy to use, and free. You can download ImageMap at `http://weyl.zib-berlin.de/imagemap/Mac-ImageMap.html`.

You've already seen how to use PageMill to create the map file that contains the coordinates for the active images (see Chapter 6). What ImageMap.acgi does is provide the server with the intelligence to read that map file and tell the server what URLs to serve when a particular coordinate is clicked. This is a prime example of CGIs extending the functionality of the Web server. The server only wants to serve files, not figure out what a set of coordinates means, so it passes that information to the CGI and lets the CGI figure out what it means.

MapServe is another CGI for the Mac that works similarly to ImageMap.acgi. The basic concept is the same. The Web server software hands off the coordinates returned when a viewer clicks a hot spot on a map to the CGI, the CGI converts that to a URL based on information it has read from a map file, which then hands it back to the Server. MapServe can be downloaded from `http://www.spub.ksu.edu/other/machttp_tools/mapserve`.

NetAlly is the Macintosh server software from Delphic Software. Delphic has a vision of a single software package that can handle just about any Internet server requirement that you need. Part of this is built-in support for active images.

If you are using NetAlly you won't need another application to turn the coordinates into a URL; the server will have built-in capability. You still will need to produce the map file, and create a link to it in the Inspector, but you won't need to install another application.

Animations

You can create moving pictures on your Web page without having to use video or movie files. Animated GIFs can be created just like cartoons used to be: by drawing a sequence of pictures, each one slightly different, and displaying them rapidly one after another.

There are three ways to receive moving pictures on your Web page: Client-Pull animations, Server-Push animations, and Animated GIFs.

Client-Pull Animations

Client-Pull refers to the fact that the browser requests an object from the server (meaning that the animation is initiated by the browser). The browser requests the next page automatically through a command embedded in the HTML. You can embed scripts that create random backgrounds or replace images randomly using Client-Pull techniques. The secret to Client-Pull is the <META> tag in the Head area of the page (see Chapter 9 for a discussion of the parts of an HTML document). You provide an attribute/value pair called HTTP-EQUIV="Refresh" which causes the server to automatically replace the page with another within a specified time period. The limitation of Client-Pull animation is that the entire page is replaced each pass. A more sophisticated way to animate an image is via Server-Push animation.

 Note

The <META> tag is supported only by Netscape Navigator browsers.

Server-Push Animation

The benefit of Server-Push animation is that it is triggered on the server-side by a CGI, and so is able to affect individual elements on your page. The CGI sends a series of individual GIF images to the browser during a set time frame. An example of a Server-Push Animation CGI is RandPic 1.0 by Robert Niles available via the CGI Collection. This random image generator uses SSI that you must configure (see discussion of SSI earlier in the chapter). Robert Niles also wrote RandImg in Perl that does the same thing without SSI.

Animated GIFs

Netscape Navigator uses a feature of GIFs called *GIF animation* that incorporates all of the animation frames into one file that downloads as a piece. This is a more efficient use of the server and saves storage space as well. GIF animation uses a special format for images called GIF89a. Shareware for the Mac called GifBuilder assists you in creating GIF animations by collecting the frames and providing you with options for the number of repetitions, image transparency, and so forth. You place Animated GIFs as one file in PageMill using the Place Object command, just as you would any other GIF image.

For More Information

For more information about working with Client-Pull, Server-Push, and animated GIFs via CGIs, surf Meng Weng Wong's Perl page at `http://www.seas.upenn.edu/!mengwong/perlhtml.html`.

Online Stores

If you are creating your Web site to sell items, you can use a stand-alone CGI program serving as a product catalog. Another CGI is used to process the orders. You can generate dynamic catalog pages and take electronic orders. Catalog and order processors create dynamic HTML documents personalizing the use of your catalog for each browser. There is one such program suite, iCat's Electronic Commerce Suite 2.0 available at iCat's site (`http://www.icat.com`). The two parts of the suite are: iCat Commerce Publisher for building and maintaining online catalogs and iCat Commerce Exchange for processing electronic orders (including credit cards). The Publisher lets you build a database of products on either a Mac or Windows platform. It then creates dynamic HTML documents based on a reader's queries. The Publisher comes with many pre-defined templates where you can add product information and objects (including such things as images, movies, video, audio, PDFs, or animated GIFs). The Exchange portion of the suite uses Secure Sockets Layer standard to provide encryption for credit card transactions.

Database Processing

When you collect information, such as the stuff you got from your forms and CGI scripts, you need to put it somewhere. The somewhere is called a *database*. Database CGIs take the information from a browser's form, place it in a semi-permanent repository and then is able to retrieve parts of the information, based on options selected by the user, and redisplay them on a page. Typically, there are several pieces of script and HTML required to handle database management:

■ The data repository—typically a commercial relational database of some sort

■ A CGI script that writes to the database

■ A CGI script that takes information from the database

■ A page to display the retrieved information

It is the CGI script that retrieves the data that does most of the work. CGI scripts can also connect to Structured Query Language (SQL)-based database management systems via embedded SQL queries. Microsoft markets a SQL server that can be linked to the Web via a CGI script, called Microsoft SQL and runs on a PC with Windows NT. Unix can use the shareware mSQL server available for $129 from `http://hughes.com.au/product/w3-msql/`.

Other database CGI scripts and SQL server software are available as follows.

Tango by EveryWare software (`http://www.everyware.com`) for the Mac. The Macintosh does not come bundled with a relational database, such as Access. There is only one serious structured query language (SQL)-based relational database available for the Mac, namely EveryWare Development's Butler SQL 2.02. Butler SQL is a database server supporting both AppleTalk and TCP/IP network protocols (a great cross-platform Internet database server). Butler also supports queries from any Open Database Connectivity (ODBC)-capable client (providing your Mac with connections to Windows and Unix-based database servers). You cannot, however, query the database from your Web page unless you also have EveryWare's Tango 1.5.

Tango is data capture taken to the next level. It is a complete CGI enabling you to tie Butler to your Web site. By using Tango, you can make queries to any ODBC-compatible SQL database, including, but not exclusive of Butler and those running on Windows and Unix platforms. Tango includes a query-definition editor so you can define HTML snippets—letting Tango capture both the query request and the results in a single file. Tango then uses these snippets to build HTML pages on the fly. Suddenly, you can publish an entire site from within the database. You can also edit individual forms and update your database through your Web page. You do need to know HTML to make use of Tango and Butler because the CGI is not particularly user-friendly (unlike PageMill).

Just like the FileMaker CGI, you need to have a Butler database before you can use Tango.

 Note

EveryWare Development, the makers of Tango and Butler, has several examples of what can be done with the tools on their Web site. One example includes a slick online store using a shopping cart metaphor that enables users to click through several pages and pick up products as they go.

NetLink 4D by ACI US manufactures one of the major relational database environments for Macintosh: Fourth Dimension (or 4D). The 4D environment is a complete programming language programmers use to develop applications.

Some developers, however, have created externals for 4D. These externals are little pieces of software enabling 4D programmers to create complex applications without having to rewrite code.

ForeSight Technologies has created a 4D external enabling a 4D database to interact with a Macintosh Web server. The software, called NetLink 4D, gives you all the capabilities of having a database integrated into your Web site (enabling users to input data, do finds, and assemble dynamic pages to be published on your site), plus the serious data crunching power of a 4D database.

Apple has a powerful document search engine working over local networks called AppleSearch. Robin Martheus, a programmer at Apple, has released a CGI enabling you to search through AppleSearch archives over the Web.

Using the CGI requires you to have the AppleSearch application either on the same Macintosh as the Web server, or on a Macintosh accessible over your network. AppleSearch.acgi has the same problem with custom configuration that Forms.acgi has: you have to poke around in the resource with ResEdit.

 Note

This CGI is free, but AppleSearch is not. AppleSearch does come bundled with the Apple Internet Server Solution; Download the latest version of AppleSearch.acgi from `http://kamaaina.apple.com`.

TR-WWW (found at `http://www.monash.edu.au/informatics/tr-www.html`) is another solution for providing searching capabilities on your Web site. TR-WWW is a stand-alone application that searches all documents you have placed in a particular folder. The advantages of TR-WWW over AppleSearch.acgi are that you don't need another application running in addition to the CGI, and you don't need to prepare the documents to be searched the way that you do with AppleSearch.

The downside is that TR-WWW needs some configuration that is not very intuitive. It has a dreaded configuration file—a long text file with strange codes that tell TR-WWW how to behave. You also need to create your own form (not so with AppleSearch), but that's easy to do with PageMill.

For More Information

For more information about Perl CGI scripts, surf Selena Sol's Pubic Domain CGI Script Archive and Resource Library at `http://www.eff.org/~erict/Scripts`.

Another source for Perl and C scripts is Matt's Script Archive at `http://www.worldwidemart.com/Scripts/`.

More CGI scripts for Unix servers are available at The CGI Collection at `http://www.selah.net/cgo.html`.

Check out Jon Weiderspan's CGI Applications Directory at `http://www.comvista.com/net/www/cgi.html` for more CGI scripts and a good tutorial on writing CGI scripts for the Mac.

Summary

CGIs take your Web site to the next level. For a long time, implementing CGIs on your Web site meant you needed to be a programmer and code them yourself. Today, there are CGIs available enabling you to interface with databases, and allow readers to search through archives of information; you don't have to program a single line of code. If you want to create your own CGIs, though, there are a number of tutorials that help you get started.

The next chapter summarizes all of the nitty gritty of Web publishing you have learned in chapters 4 through 10. Chapter 11 provides guidelines on how to put it all together.

Chapter 11

Putting It All Together

By now, you should feel pretty comfortable using PageMill to design and create Web pages with stylized text, fill-in forms, graphics, animations, tables, frames, active images, and hypertext links. But remember, thousands of Web pages look terrible because the author understood only the technical details. The Web author needs to know the technical details of presenting a Web page and she needs to think about how viewers will use it. Many of these pages might have great information, but if they are unusable, the information might as well not be presented.

This chapter provides useful information on how to avoid some of the pitfalls many first-time Web designers encounter. This chapter also discusses how you can use PageMill's features to create powerful, well-designed pages.

Human Interface Design

Apple Computer, Inc. has an entire department devoted to developing guidelines for building human interfaces. You can peruse their work in *Inside Macintosh: Guide to Human Interface.* When publishing on the Web, you are responsible for creating a human interface, and that is not an easy job. Human interface design is the study of how people learn by using information. This is a complex subject that incorporates research from architecture about the aesthetics of design, environmental engineering about how people find their way around places, commercial art research into successful communications using images and words, and educational research about how people learn. The goal is to produce a front-end to technology (such as computer operating systems or databases) that assists readers in collecting the data they need in the most efficient and pleasant way possible.

Interface (how people connect with or work with things) is a crucial element to every electronic item. An example of bad human interface is my new clock radio. I went from a simple clock with two knobs in the back and a couple of bells to a fancy electronic whiz-bang one. The new clock has 15 buttons, 6 of which can change function. I'm expected to understand intuitively the difference between a Sleep button and a Snooze button (I think I snooze on weekends and sleep on weekdays). The manual, which is the size of a small novel, is confusing. I need to use my clock radio, and there aren't any other clock radios immediately available to me, so I have to figure it out. The bottom line is that people need to understand intuitively what things mean or the most high-tech, neat-o feature will have no purpose because it will not be used. Most people don't program their VCRs because they don't know how. People don't read manuals until they are desperate, and even then, they want to get the information they need and get back to work.

The design of a Web page must follow the same logic. Each image, animation, hypertext link, text block, splash banner, and so forth, must have a purpose that is intuitively understood. People need to *want* to click a hotspot to see what is behind it. Moving pictures, three-dimensional logos, and sound effects are worthless if they take so long to download that the viewer doesn't stay on your page to enjoy them. In this day of MTV videos and video games, people have very short attention spans. Web pages must work like a combination of magazine page and video game: present combinations of graphics and text that lead easily to information but entertain and operate fast at the same time.

If you present the viewer with a confusing interface on your Web page, much like my new clock radio's feature set, it is very likely that he is going to click past your page.

Good user interfaces provide a friendly, well-thought-out, and easy-to-use way of navigating through information. The Macintosh Finder is an example of good user interface. New users can sit down at a Macintosh and start creating folders, opening files, and using applications in a matter of minutes. Notice that Windows 95 has been called "very Mac-like" by the press—a situation where imitation is the sincerest form of flattery.

This ability to "get to work without a fuss" is what you should strive for with your Web page. You want every new user to navigate through the information on your page intuitively, find what he or she wants, and have an enjoyable experience.

What Is the Internet?

You hear the term "Internet" and "intranet" bandied about a lot these days. The Internet is a conglomeration of computers linked by a myriad of networks into a baffling, decentralized global network. The "intranet" is a corporation's version of the Internet—an internal Internet for that firm. The Internet is the invention of the Defense Department and its affiliated labs and universities. It is old and complicated; the network is based on 1960s software technology, namely Unix. In 1991, The National Science Foundation lifted its restrictions on commercial use of the Net, and "Net surfing" tools proliferated. That same year, for example, Gopher, a search engine

continues

for usenets was published by Paul Lindner and Mark McCahill of the University of Minnesota, and Tim Berners-Lee at the University of Illinois' National Center for Supercomputing Applications developed the graphical entry-way to Internet, called HyperText Transfer Protocol (HTTP) —and euphemistically the World Wide Web (WWW).

The World Wide Web is a front-end, a human interface design, not a place or network. Berners-Lee's invention provided a way to intuitively navigate through gallons of data via pictures and hypertext. The invention of the Web (the http you see in URLs when you surf the Web indicates that you are using this method to communicate on the Internet) is a way to move around the Internet by exchanging documents via hyperlinks (internal and external computer addresses included with the documents). It was revolutionary.

By 1992, there were one million host computers connected to the Internet. The public's interest in using these networks to communicate was astounding.

Browsers and the Web

The Web is a way of looking at the Internet. This vast network consists of computers that manage data and the communications links via software called *servers*. Web servers receive requests for information, go out and find it in their databases, and return the proper "pages" of data to the requesting computer. The operating systems that run the servers' computers are all different. The operating system is the "brains" of the computer, and it "speaks" to itself in many different ways, called *languages* (mostly variations on Unix, such as SCO, Xenix, SunOS, AIX, A/UX, and so forth; but also Windows variations and Macintosh). The wonder of early efforts to share information was cutting through this "Tower of Babel" to share information between dissimilar computer environments. HTTP was developed as a way to find information and retrieve it over telephone lines in a coherent fashion. The revolutionary portion of HTTP is the separation of collecting data from displaying the data. You hear the term *bandwidth* a lot when talking about the Internet. This is the capacity of telephone lines and direct connections between computers to handle the electronic pulses required to transmit different types of information (text, pictures, sounds, animations, and so forth).

The more bytes it takes to store information, the more bandwidth needed. Graphics need bytes to describe the lines of which they are composed, the colors of the lines, and how to draw the lines. Sound and animation need even more storage area, or bandwidth—too much to actually be sent over a telephone line and be coherent on the other side. By lowering the amount of data crossing the telecommunications links, HTTP found a way to communicate with pictures and sounds without needing to actually transmit all of the information.

On your computer, a *browser* translates what is sent over the wires into the pictures and words you see onscreen as a Web page.

How did browsers come to be? Early users of the Internet, prior to the advent of HTTP, had to be Unix gurus to understand Unix communications protocols because in order to communicate with another computer using the Internet, you still had to deal with the server software to query and receive information. Data coming across the Internet was in textual form because nothing stood between you and the server except Unix. Of course the question of how to increase the amount of data that crossed a limited amount of bandwidth could not go unchallenged. Computer science students began to write programs that resided on local computers (termed *clients*) that could understand the HTTP protocol. These browsers served as intermediaries between the server and the user. Now that there was a way to send virtually unlimited amounts of data over limited resources, a way to send how the data should be displayed on the other side was needed. Print shops already were accepting print jobs on tape from their clients. The digital version of a print job used tags that told the printers how to output data, (ways to tell your computer that a stream of data is a paragraph, or a list, or a citation, for example). The tagging method is called Standard Generalized Markup Language (SGML). Computer scientists looked at SGML and simplified it considerably. The simplified version of the markup tags was to travel with the data and be interpreted by the retrieving software—the browser. Hypertext (such as Apple's HyperCard) supplied ways to connect disparate pieces of data that resided on separate computers using more tags. Together, the hypertext and display tags that tell the computer how to interpret Internet documents came to be called HyperText Markup Language (HTML). It became the standard way to tag pages of information that traveled over the Internet via the WWW.

Network Publishing Grows Up

By 1994, commercial online services also made the WWW available to their subscribers by building gateways and browsers from their proprietary sites. Currently, America Online, CompuServe, and Prodigy all have gateways to the Web. With commercial access providers becoming more ubiquitous and prices for access becoming cheaper, millions of regular folks are exploring what used to be the sole providence of scientists and students. Meanwhile, the growth in users and resulting marketing possibilities of the Internet made commercial tools for browsing the Web a possibility.

Today, 90 percent of all Internet users use Netscape Navigator 3.0 and Microsoft Internet Explorer 3.0 as browsers. These browsers are growing in capabilities of what they can interpret and display. So the problem of displaying retrieved information was solved.

Meanwhile, more and more businesses and organizations saw the possibilities inherent in a network of millions of connected computers. The ease of use of the publishing and serving side of the Internet equation began to be addressed. Inevitably individuals and companies wanted to use the Web for commercial purposes, transferring what had been published on paper and broadcast on television and radio on to this new medium. The fact that users could be led between pieces of information via hypertext links made the concept of Web sites (collections of documents, called pages, interconnected via hypertext links).These people were not computer wizards, but commercial artists and marketing folks. They needed tools to match the ease of use of the browsers used to display the results of their endeavors. A few adventurous vendors began to write desktop publishing (DTP)-based layout tools to overlay the HTML spoken by the Web. So were PageMill and its related cousins born.

Web Publishing for the Masses

We are now in the second generation of Web generation tools offering more than just an overlay to HTML, but also providing tools to build upon this code to create highly professional graphic pages. The tools to create electronically published documents lags behind the theories and rules developed to govern proper design.

People could use intuitive page layout tools that translated mouse movements into HTML, but it didn't mean that what was produced was good design. It didn't mean that it followed the Human Interface Engineering practices already developed for computer programming and commercial print art. So, similar to what happened in the earlier desktop publishing revolution, Sturgeon's Law ("99 percent of everything is junk") began to happen on the Web—bad design proliferated.

As the Web became more public, researchers in businesses and universities began to apply the same human interface design theories used to upgrade print and broadcast journalism to network journalism. They developed usability engineering guidelines for Web sites. (Usability engineering studies show how computer users search and use information on computers.) This book shares the results of these studies on how to create great Web sites with you and applies this information to using PageMill 2.0's powerful features so that you can publish the most informative and useful pages you can without having to be a HTML programmer.

 Note

The Web community debates whether it's better to create pages utilizing Netscape extensions (termed the HTML Version 3.2 standard) or to design pages for the agreed upon HTML 2.0 standard. Many Web pages state: "This page looks best when viewed with Netscape 3.0 or Microsoft Internet Explorer 3.0" and often provide a link for the Net surfer to download one of those upgraded browsers. Some people in the Web community want to define a set of standards so that one or two companies can't dictate de-facto standards. Some say that waiting for standards slows innovation, and the market should decide whether their extensions are accepted as the standard. Ultimately, the market will decide, although the debate continues.

The Evolution of Web Site Design

PageMill is a tool for creating Web pages. But a Web page doesn't work without links to other pages. A collection of Web pages and links to outside servers constitutes a Web site. Most Web publishers are creating sites and not pages. The following sections provide insight into how to design a great site consisting of beautiful Web pages.

Ongoing Discussions about Web Site Design

According to Web page designer David Siegel, we are now in the third generation of Web site design. David is interested in the aesthetics of Web page design. Other master Web publishers, such as Jakob Nielsen at Sun Microsystems, are interested in the human interface engineering of a page. Although there is little agreement about how to deliver a beautifully designed and commercially successful Web site, every master designer agrees that the purpose of Web pages is to pull readers into the site, grab their attention, and present information that is timely, original, and custom-tailored to user preferences in a computer-savvy responsive fashion.

First-Generation Web Site Design

The first generation Web page, circa 1993 to '94, was text-based because early browsers such as Mosaic were used on black and white dumb terminals or low-resolution color display-based personal computers. Because modems were slow (2400 baud or so) and monitors could not display much color, pages were linear, running top-to-bottom and left-to-right. The metaphor for first-generation pages was the word processor—heavy reliance on bullets, line feeds, and minimal use of graphics such as icons pointing to hypertext links within paragraphs. The object of these pages was to display as much information as you could, almost to prove to your readers that your content was the most useful on the Web. Figure 11.1 from The Dilbert Zone (`http://www.unitedmedia.com/comics/dilbert/`) illustrates a first-generation page.

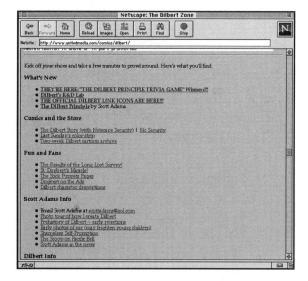

Figure 11.1
First-generation
Web pages
presented gobs of
information in a
linear fashion.

Second-Generation Web Site Design

Second generation Web pages, circa 1995, continued with the concept of content-filled sites but replaced the linear, text-driven pages with graphics and icons pointing to pages filled with information. Web pages were still designed in a linear fashion. The metaphor for second generation Web pages and their sites (see Figure 11.2, Travelocity at `http://www.travelocity.com/`) is the corporate organizational chart with its hierarchical structure and top-down management style. Meaning, you go from a subject to its contents and are not allowed to browse haphazardly through a site to tangential ideas and subjects while navigating. You would click an image of a newspaper, for example, to get a corporate newsletter, but you could not link to someone else's write-up on that site.

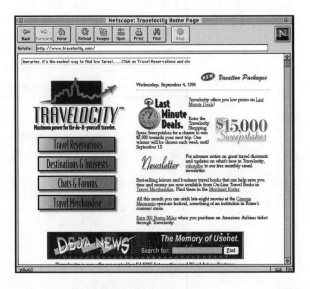

Figure 11.2
Second-generation Web pages relied on graphics as icons, still linearly, to lead readers to different information pages.

These sites were early examples of translating corporate documents, such as annual reports, to the electronic medium. Second-generation sites used graphics like they are used on paper: to add information to what is in text, or as a table of contents to lead to a new subject, not to present information as a stand-alone object. Because images were used as stepping-stones, soon too many pictures cluttered pages because there was a lot of data to point out and direct the reader to. The trouble with graphics-heavy sites is that they are slow to browse because graphics take so much time to download and they do not serve to increase a reader's understanding of a site, but merely to point to more information—like a billboard announces a product, and a series of billboards strings along a reader without getting to the point of the advertisement.

Third-Generation Web Site Design

As multimedia techniques began to be applied to electronic publishing (such as the ability to animate a picture or add sounds to text), designers were given the tools to increase the amount of information provided by fewer images. Now, an active image provided a theme for the site, as well as a doorway to more information. Also, hotspots provided tangential connections that suddenly made two-dimensional electronic publishing (the act of simply using a picture as a button to lead to more text) into three-dimensional publishing, where the user decides what data to connect together based on the dense communication possibilities of animations and increased hypertext links (see Figure 11.3, the University of Illinois School of Art and Design at `http://www.art. uiuc.edu/dialect/hi5link.html`). As a site using images as heavy content containers, the University of Illinois site is a good example of third-generation Web design. The opening page pulls you into its world by providing several avenues of entry, each with different themes and activities to keep you interested. The pictures are in intuitive because they provide you with instant information about what their links contain, yet offer additional advertisements about the quality of design offered by the school of art, enticements to see more art, and information about the state of commercial art in the electronic age.

Figure 11.3
Third-generation
Web pages are
graphics-intense but
non-linear, letting
the reader enter the
site from different
avenues.

A Scientific Approach to Web Site Design

On the one hand you have commercial artists who are now composing electronic designs and are interested in the overall aesthetics and communication opportunities inherent in multimedia. On the other hand you have journalists and computer scientists who are interested in the content of a site and those things, such as bandwidth, that hold back the flow of information to viewers. There is a conflict inherent in this tug-of-war between artists and scientists; between those who want to exploit new media, such as Shockwave, to enhance the information content of images, and those who see the purpose of the Web as a free-flowing information sea where no technology should stand in the way of a user gaining the data he or she seeks.

Jakob Nielsen at Sun Microsystems representing the scientific "User Engineering" approach, summarizes the less is more philosophy in the "Top Ten Mistakes in Web Design" in the Sun on the Net site `http://www.sun.com/960416/columns/alertbox/index.html` (paraphrased from the "Alert Box" for May 1996):

- **Keep the page structure simple.** Avoid using gimmicks, such as multiple URLs on a page (frames) if it detracts from the presentation of information. Too many frames, for example, makes it too hard to figure out where the data is going to appear when you click a hotspot.

- **Keep the technology appropriate.** Don't use gratuitous bleeding-edge technology. Mainstream users are not attracted to sites because they are beta-test beds for new animation techniques or virtual reality but because the site offers customer service and content. Use technology appropriately. Virtual reality (VRML) and QuickTime VR are useful for games sites, pages where you want to show information in 3D, and so forth. In addition, too much multimedia uses excessive bandwidth, slowing down the access time needed to get information.

- **Keep the images from interrupting the message.** Avoid using page elements that move incessantly because they overpower peripheral vision. As Mr. Nielsen says, "A Web page should not emulate Times Square in New York City in its constant attack on the human senses: give your user some peace and quiet to actually read the text!"

- **Keep URLs humanly readable.** Today's browsers lack sufficient support for easy Web navigation (such as easy ways to return to a previous thought, easily edited bookmarks, and so forth). Often, readers use the URL (Universal Reference Location) to identify where they are because the browser doesn't give them a clue. Users also need to type URLs if they don't have bookmarks at a site. Minimize the risk of typos by using short names, lowercase characters, and avoid using special characters.

- **Keep your Web pages in the family.** Avoid creating orphan Web pages that lack a reference back to the home page. Users often bookmark internal pages directly. Give them a method to link to your home page, as well as a sense of the structure of your site.

- **Use a single screen full of information.** Avoid having the reader scroll down past a screen. Studies show only 10 percent of users actually scroll to critical content. Use active images and hypertext links to move your readers to information. Provide navigation options at the top of your page. Adobe Corporation's site (`http//:www.adobe.com`) is a great example of a well-designed navigable Web site.

- **Provide navigation support.** Don't assume your readers understand how you designed your site to be read. Provide a strong sense of structure and place to the site. Including a site map tells readers where they are and where they want to go to get the information they are seeking. Provide a good search feature to allow readers to browse your site's database (if one exists).

- **Be consistent in your link colors.** Do not stray from the established standards for link colors. Most browsers rely on links to pages not yet seen by users to be displayed in blue and links to previously seen pages to be displayed in purple or red. Assist your reader in understanding link colors and their significance.

■ **Update your site often.** Maintain the information on the Web site so that it is always current. Eliminate outdated pages and build new links. Readers will return to your site if they know you keep its content up-to-date.

■ **Keep download times short.** Be responsive to the typical user's technology—a 14.4Kbps modem. Size graphics to fit in a typical user's window (a maximum of 465 to 532 pixels wide or the default Netscape screen). Optimize graphics files for Web display and limit their size to 20K per graphic. Usability studies show that readers lose interest in a site if they have to wait longer than 10-15 seconds for the site to display. Because bandwidth congestion is getting worse as more users enter the Internet, keep the size of your pages in mind as you create your site design.

For More Information

For more information on designing great Web sites, check out the following Web sites:

■ `http://webreference.com`: a searchable index of page layout and design documents.

■ `http://www.sun.com/960416/columns/alertbox/index.html`: Jakob Nielsen's Alert Box articles, published by Sun Microsystems, provide helpful hints on human interface engineering issues.

■ `http://info.med.yale.edu/caim/StyleManual_Top.HTML`: Patrick J. Lynch's Web Style Manual is a technical reference document for designing Web pages using HTML 3.0 standards.

■ `http://www.killersites.com`: David Siegel and his company Studio Verso's Web site of up-to-date information on how to design third-generation Web sites is a companion to the book *Creating Killer Web Sites* by David Siegel and published by Hayden Books in July 1996.

So, What Does This Mean for Me?

We have looked at two applications of usability engineering, David Siegel's artist-based approach and Jakob Nielsen's computer science-based approach. Both philosophies work with the premise that the goal of good Web page design is to keep your audience at your site.

Let's study the Web site we started in Chapter 4 to apply these gentleman's ideas to our model Web site. Start by looking at the first page: the *home* page. This is the entrance to your site—the first text and images viewers see when they hit your URL. The best way to think about the design of your site is to consider the purpose of each page. You want to accomplish the following with your home page:

- Let people know where they are
- Let people know what type of information they will find
- Provide links to the rest of your site.

There are, however, at least two other considerations: getting attention and establishing your Web site style. These are a little more difficult to accomplish than the basic goals mentioned here. Look at how a home page can be created when you start with these goals in mind. Take a look at the home page shown in Figure 11.4.

Figure 11.4
An example of a poorly executed home page.

Pretty bad, huh? What makes this site unusable? The site does let people know where they are: The WidgetWare Home Page. The designer accomplished the first goal.

Unfortunately, the page doesn't do as well with the second goal; that is, the designer doesn't let people know what type of information they can find. There are links to other parts of the site, but why would you want to browse a catalog if you had no idea what type of products you were browsing? Occasionally, you can rely on the company name to let people what they will find on your site, but if you had never heard of StarNine before, would you intuitively know what products they sell?

The designer did, however, score well on the third goal, providing links. Assuming there are no pages other than the Catalog, Price List, and Mailing List, this page is a good jump point for the rest of the site.

A few of the basic considerations, however, are wrong here. We obviously did not obey an important rule of Web site design: **Format your links in a consistent way** (Figure 11.5 displays how our list of subjects ought to be presented).

Figure 11.5
Consistently format
your links.

The page shown in Figure 11.4 displays three links, each formatted a different way. The best way to organize a list of links is to use a list. Start by phrasing each one of your links similarly and remove any "click here" phrases. Your hyperlinks should be fully integrated into your text. If, for example, you are creating a link to the Apple Web site, make the words "Apple Web site" the link, like this:

You can get great Macintosh information from the <u>Apple Web site</u>.

The preceding statement flows better than

You can get great Macintosh information from the Apple Web site, which you can get to <u>by clicking here</u>.

Other than making the text on your site easier to read (by making the sentences shorter and more concise), phrasing your links in as shown in the first example enables people to scan your site quickly to see what links are available.

The type of list you should use depends on the type of information you are incorporating with your links. If, for example, you are giving pointers to pages with self-explanatory names, you can use a bulleted list:

- Add your name to our *mailing list*

- Browse our *catalog*

- Check out our *price list*

If you have a description that accompanies the pointers to each page, you can use a definition list, such as this:

- Mailing List

  You can add your name to our mailing list and receive regular updates on our current products, plus news about new product releases.

- Catalog

  You can browse through an online catalog of products, including information on ordering. The catalog also can help you determine if a part is in stock or needs to be ordered.

- Price List

  The online price list reflects the current price of all items, including sales tax for customers within the State of California.

Using Active Images

You learned how to create active images in Chapter 5. Active images are extremely useful ways to quickly point your reader to areas in your site as well as to set up the aesthetic theme of your site. Using an active image enables the viewer—when he or she first connects to your site—to learn immediately what information is available on your site and to understand the theme of the site. A good example of the use of an active image that accomplishes both high-level goals is at Nancy McNelly's Mayan archeology site (`http://www.he.net/~nmcnelly`) (see Figure 11.6). This active image consists of Mayan glyphs that are beautiful and informative. They say "click me" without speaking.

PageMill has several tools to help you work with active images. See Chapter 6 for details on how to create active images.

Figure 11.6
An active image not only points to areas within your site, but quickly advertises who you are.

 Note

Many people browse the Web with Images Off to save download time. Therefore, if you create an active image, you should provide some text links as well so that users will be able to move around your site.

Using Links Wisely

Too many fonts is to desktop publishing what too many links is to Web publishing. Fonts on the Web are controlled almost entirely by the browser, so misusing them is hard to do. Hypertext is the real power of Web publishing.

Note

> The capability to link documents together was one of the main
> goals of the development team that created the HyperText
> Markup Language (HTML). The CERN scientists who developed
> HTML wanted the technology to have the capability to reference
> one paper to another and a link taking the reader to that paper.

When you do want to incorporate links into the body of a paragraph, make sure the links are meaningful. In WidgetWare (see Figure 11.4), one of the hypertext links is the word **started**. At first glance, the viewer has no idea what **started** links to. Is it a detailed story about the genesis of the company? Is it a definition of the word started? Who knows? The point of a link is to provide an entry to more information on a particular topic. Make it clear what viewers find when they follow a particular link; otherwise, there is no compelling reason for them to follow it.

Grouping Links

All hypertext links on your Web site connect to URLs. URLs can point to anything on the Internet, such as other Web pages, gopher sites, FTP sites, or email addresses. There is a tendency when you build links to group items according to the resources from which they originated. Grouping together all files available via FTP (the protocol used to upload or download files much as HTTP is the protocol used to link sites) is an example. What does FTP have to do with the contents of your site, the purpose for which you spent all this money to create this multimedia extravaganza? The reader doesn't care how he or she gets the data (whether downloadable files or another Web page; although ultimately you should provide information about the format of the data so that users can choose how they want to retrieve it) but does care about what the information is about. People get on the Internet to get information, not to use FTP. Therefore, you should group information by topic, such as "Catalog" (shown in the illustration of our re-edited home page in Figure 11.4), not by resource. Creating a bibliography and linking to the Web sites of individual books is another useful way to group links. The point is that you should provide as many entry ways as possible to information via different groupings of links (an active image with different hotspots for visual learners, a text list for the more analog learners who don't like to spend the time to see pictures, animated buttons with sounds for audio learners, and so forth) all pointing to the same data.

Generating Themes and Web Design

Your site should apply a common type of art: a style such as art deco, retro-1950s, retro-1970s, cartoons, childhood, painterly, and so forth to all images, buttons, banners, and headings. The use of themes immediately gives the reader an overall impression of what the Web site is all about. Combine your theme with a metaphor—a storefront for a catalog store with pictures of merchandise in windows, each leading to different areas of the store; a montage of changing photographs or illustrations (see Chapter 9 for how to use the <META> tag to refresh images with new images), each leading to different jobs that the firm can accomplish for a design studio's site; and so forth. Colors, textures, lighting, and graphic styles can be combined with actual pictures to create a general mood. Use bright, primary colors, such as a background of yellow and red buttons, for example, if you are presenting big or flashy information. Macromedia's Web page does just the opposite. It uses subtle pastel shades and shadows to advertise Shockwave by blasting the Shockwave logo on top of the subtlety. Figure 11.7 shows you the Shockwave page of the Macromedia Web site (`http://www.macromedia.com/shockwave/`).

The use of a metaphor (in Macromedia's case they chose the juxtaposition of antique telephone and communications equipment photos with bright electronic symbols) provides an appealing and interesting background from which to collect information, as well as furthers the goal of the site, in this case advertising Macromedia's multimedia authoring software suites (see Figure 11.8).

Figure 11.7
Using a pastel color
theme advances
the goal of the
site—advertising
Shockwave.

Figure 11.8
Macromedia uses
the metaphor of
antique communica-
tions juxtaposed
with modern
electronics to
advertise their
software suites.

Signing Your Name

When you enter a store, it's helpful to know where to ask questions or who to talk to when there is a problem. The same thing
goes for Web sites—especially commercial Web sites. You also
want to take credit for the design of a beautiful and useful Web
site.

Understanding this concept, the creators of HTML utilized a convenient way for you to accomplish this: the Address format, which is a feature found in PageMill. Typically, text at the bottom of a page (usually found below a horizontal rule) includes information about the person or organization responsible for that page.

Signing Your Name

1   If you haven't already done so, create a horizontal rule to separate the body of your Web page from the bottom, and press Return.

2   Type **Copyright 1995 Webs-R-US** and press Return.

3   Type your email address in the format **yourname@yourhost.domain** (ixchup@ix.netcom.com, for example) and press Return.

4   Type **Last Updated, October 30, 1996**, and press Return twice.

5   Highlight the text.

6   Select Address from the Format menu. The text now appears italicized (see Figure 11.9).

Figure 11.9
Example of Web page company information formatted as an Address.

Logical versus Physical Tags

What's the difference between the Address attribute and the Italics attribute? The answer is somewhat cryptic, but it has to do with *logical* and *physical* tags in HTML. A physical tag makes text bold or italic. It affects the physical look of words. A logical tag is a little different. It is used when you want to classify text as having a specific purpose, such as an address or as a citation from another work. Using Netscape, the Address attribute and the Italics attribute will look the same onscreen. However, that is not true of all browsers. The reason to use logical attributes for an item such as an address is to create consistency from page to page (see Chapter 4 for an additional discussion of logical and physical tags).

You also should make your email address a hypertext link to your email. PageMill supports the mailto value for attributes, making it easy to send text messages from your page to your email.

Creating a mailto: Link

1   Highlight your email address.

2   Click in the Link Location bar.

3   Type the URL: **mailto:yourname@yourhost.domain**, press Return.

The text now appears underlined in blue because it is a special type of hypertext link. The PageMill Preview mode is not a mail-capable browser, so you can't test this functionality from PageMill. You can, however, test this functionality from your browser.

If you want to send a feedback form to your email as plain text, open the HTML Source window (select HTML Source from the Edit menu) and edit the <FORM ACTION> tag to read as follows:

```
<FORM ACTION="mailto:yourname@yourhost.domain"
METHOD="POST" ENCTYPE="multipart/formdata">
```

Note that this only works if your viewers are using Netscape Navigator as their browser.

Creating a Clean, Concise, and Consistent Design

You should present a unified look to your Web site. To create a site looking like more than just text on a page, you need to establish and follow a plan.

Multimedia designers look at projects as a long process.

1   Evaluate the purpose of the project. Will it educate, entertain, or distract?

2   Decide the style of the project. Will it be new wave, traditional, or retro?

3 Evaluate what resources are available to you, such as images, movies, and content.

The intended audience also will help determine many of these factors. The multimedia team moves forward only after a concrete plan is created and a commitment to a defined purpose and style is made. You need to follow a similar process with your Web site to ensure it is successful and usable.

The most important thing to do when designing a Web site is to spend time away from the computer before you begin. Do some research and determine who your audience is and what they want. This could be as simple as determining that your audience is your customers and what they want is more information on your product. Or, it could be more complex. Your audience, for example, might be 8th-grade boys who simply want to be entertained. Either way, you need to determine what your audience wants to look at and whether they are reacting positively or negatively.

The ideal situation would be to do a six-month research project with random groups of people in your demographic target audience. That probably won't happen, but you can talk to people in your target audience and find out how they feel about the information available to them.

Another option is to begin building your site using your best ideas. Find a discussion group on the Internet or online service dealing with your topic, announce your new Web site, and invite people to check it out and provide feedback. You will be amazed at the response you receive. Finally, based on the feedback you receive, you can begin creating your site and growing it into a full-fledged Web site functioning exactly as you envisioned.

Web Site Interaction

Web sites are interactive media. The process of following hypertext links is an interactive process. Filling forms is especially interactive. And, just like interaction with people, most viewers become frustrated if your Web site is not responsive to their requests and actions.

Of course, a number of factors, over which you have no control, go into the responsiveness of your Web site. You can't mandate that people use a fast modem, nor can you quit other applications running at the same time as their browser. And you definitely can't make them upgrade to a faster computer.

You can do the following performance optimization tricks to your Web site:

■ Make sure all your links lead to where you are pointing. Nothing is more frustrating for a viewer than clicking a link and receiving an error message stating that the server could not find a file. Servers are extremely picky when it comes to filenames. One typo in the URL, and your file will never be found. Test all your links.

■ Make sure your images are interlaced and have a small byte size for fast downloading. Limit the color palette to the 216 colors viewable by VGA monitors for all photographs (run the image through Adobe Photoshop to reduce its color palette). Make the images transparent to further reduce their size.

■ Update your site often, presenting new information, new technologies, new ways of presenting old information. Give the reader some reason to return to the site, even if it is just to see what's new.

■ Maintain your site. Checks link to outside pages to ensure that they are still viable. Make sure that your own links are good by using a Web site management package, such as Adobe SiteMill (described in Chapter 12), that lets you maintain the links between images and pages using a graphical-user-interface (GUI)- based filing system. If you move files out of their initial locations, reconnect the links and reload the site to your server (see Chapter 12 for instructions on uploading your site to the server).

If you are also the Webmaster and have access to the server where your site is stored, you can optimize the performance of the server. You also can play with the settings and preferences on your server software. WebSTAR, for example, enables you to control several aspects of its performance with the WebSTAR administration application. It can optimize performance by determining the number of connections WebSTAR can handle simultaneously. Adjusting these settings involves some trial and error, but you can experiment to see where you can adjust the settings to get the maximum amount of performance.

Summary

As you can see, designing a Web site is not a matter of slapping some images down and adding text. It takes the same careful planning that any other publishing effort takes. In addition, using technology wisely enhances the readability of your site, while throwing in animations or sounds haphazardly distracts from the legibility of your pages.

Know your audience and use your media tools based on their needs. Eight-year old boys may like video game metaphors, but businessmen probably would do better with a more linear, information-rich approach.

Remember the bandwidth issue: every addition of color, movement, sound, and so forth adds to the size of a file, and hence to the time it takes to download to the browser. Make your files as small as possible and use clever ways to limit the time it takes to download files (using an image more than once, for example, so that it downloads once and the browser's cache installs the subsequent uses of the picture, or use linked thumbnails and let the user decide if they want the whole image or sound file).

A lot goes into making your Web site a usable resource. Most importantly, you must create an interface viewers enjoy using, and one that helps them get to the information they want. When you do that, you can think about adding more media and more cool features.

Chapter 12 instructs you how to upload your site to the server. It discusses the various options for running a site and introduces the server technologies available today.

Chapter 12

Getting Online

OK, you created the coolest Web page. You loaded it up with animated GIFs, forms, imagemaps, links to other sites, fabulous virtual reality trips, and so forth. You have probably noticed that although PageMill 2.0 lets you create fabulous Web pages and sites, you cannot run them because PageMill is *not* a browser or a server. Now, how do you get your Web site to run? You must upload the Web site, including all of the folders, image files, HTML files, and so forth, on to a Web server so that folks can dial into the server using their telephones or dedicated local area network lines and download your Web site with their browsers.

This chapter describes how to get onto a server and manage your Web site once you have access to a server.

Gaining Access to the Web

The Web is one method of accessing the information of a huge network called the Internet. The Internet communicates through special networking rules called TCP/IP (Transmission Control Protocol/Internet Protocol).TCP/IP is the network standard used on most Unix Computers and has become the de facto standard for large networks running different types of computers. The IP portion of TCP/IP lets multiple processes communicate with each other over a network using packet-switching technology. The goal of TCP/IP is reliability no matter how congested the transmission traffic gets. The IP enables multiple networks to connect to form internetworks by routing data via datagrams (packets of information routed over a common network) between networks. The TCP portion of the network standard manages how dissimilar computers speak to one another. So, together, TCP/IP provides communications between networks and operates on a variety of computer platforms, from Macintosh computers, DOS-based personal computers using Windows 3.1, Windows 95, and Windows NT systems to IBM mainframes and RISC processor-based Unix workstations. TCP/IP uses two types of network protocols to connect to the physical LAN media: the X.25 packet protocol for wide area networks and the IEEE 802 specifications (such as Ethernet and Token-Ring) for local area networks.

TCP/IP is the glue that holds together different local area networks running on many types of computer platforms and includes two important functions to you as a Web publisher: FTP (file-transfer protocol) and telnet (remote terminal emulation).

Most computers using TCP/IP are permanently connected to some sort of high-speed network (such as Ethernet, ISDN, or T1 lines). You also can dial into a TCP/IP network using a modem. If the modem is used to connect with the network, two types of protocols assist the connection: SLIP (serial line Internet protocol) or PPP (point-to-point protocol). Either way, you call into a central computer whose software controls the flow of talk between computers but provides the files and directories that can be accessed via the Net. This software is called a *server*, a term that describes both the hardware on which the software runs, such as an Intel Pentium personal computer or a Power Mac, and the software managing the process, such as Microsoft Windows NT 4.0, Netscape Enterprise Server, Netscape Fastrack Server 2.0 for Windows operating systems, HTTPd or Apache for Unix operating systems, or StarNine's WebStar server for the MacOS. If your computer is connected to a high-speed network, you have direct access to the server. Today, however, most people who use the Web use an intermediary service accessed via a modem; it is this Internet service provider's hardware and software that connects with the Web server.

You can gain access to a server in several ways:

■ By joining a commercial online service that provides *gateways* or a door to the Web. America Online, CompuServe, and Prodigy are the three main commercial online services with access to the Web. You can publish your Web pages using their servers for free or for an additional fee (each provider offers a different service).

■ Use an Internet service provider (ISP). For a monthly fee, you can use the ISP's server as the intermediary between you and the Web. Many ISPs offer personal home page space (about 1 to 2MB) for free or they offer Web site space leases for an additional fee.

■ Use a corporate server. If your company lets you have access to its server, and its server has access to the Internet via leased T1 lines, and if you have permission of the system administrator, you can publish your Web page there. You can also use remote access software, such as Apple Remote Access to dial into a network and on to the Internet.

Commercial Online Services

Commercial online services, such as America Online (AOL) or CompuServe offer space for personal home pages. AOL and CompuServe used to be closed systems offering their users forums and chat areas separate from the Internet. Today, both services, as well as Prodigy, offer gateways to the Internet. You need to set up an account on one of these services. AOL and CompuServe supply free access software through attachments to computer magazines, through the mail, in stores; any way they can. Part of the access software is a browser for connecting to the Web.

AOL is offering either Microsoft Internet Explorer or Netscape Navigator with the newest version of its proprietary client software. You can connect to the Web from anywhere within AOL by clicking one of its numerous links. The browser is invoked and the server dialed when you make this connection. AOL provides two options for publishing Web pages: "My Home Page" for beginners and "My Place" for Webmasters. My Home Page is a template where you fill in the blanks to create a single page. You cannot add anything to the format provided by AOL, and you are allowed up to five free screen names of up to 2MB each per account.

You can upload graphics to your page using AOL's proprietary file transfer program. Modifying the page can be costly because you can only make changes to the page while online. For serious Web page builders, such as yourself, AOL offers the more advanced area called "My Place." You can create your Web site using PageMill (or any other HTML editor) and upload it to the area. You use an online utility to manage your files, and you need to know Unix to work with subdirectories to the directories created by AOL's program. My Place is an anonymous FTP site where files or directories you create become accessible to anyone who knows your screen names, although you do have a private directory.

CompuServe uses a less-integrated system to access the Web. You must set up a separate PPP connection and launch individual Internet applications (a Web browser, telnet software for communicating with the server, Usenet newsgroup software, file transfer protocol (FTP) software, and so forth). CompuServe provides Web site space in an area called "Our World." You can build very creative Web sites offline and upload your files to CompuServe's server. You are allocated 1MB of hard disk space at no extra charge, but no additional space is available. You cannot import HTML pages from outside the program.

Internet Service Providers

ISPs offer cheaper access to the Web, but for the lower price, you must be able to configure your own TCP/IP software and PPP or SLIP connection. Most ISPs offer 2MB of space (or more) for personal home pages.

With the introduction of MacPPP and MacTCP client software came the hordes of telephone and cable TV companies, small-scale network providers, and former video stores offering dial-up Internet access. There is a price war coming because the big telephone companies (MCI, AT&T, Sprint, and the Baby Bells) all want to get into the ISP business. So, you should start to see more user-friendly software and support, as well as flat fee service from ISPs. There are also national ISPs, such as Netcom and EarthLink, that offer local telephone access to their extremely large networks.

 Tip

Make sure that your ISP offers a local *point-of-presence* (POP) so that you do not have to pay long distance telephone rates on top of the monthly Internet access rate for your browsing and site managing. If you live near a metropolitan area, there should be a local telephone number available.

Corporate Servers

Many large companies and most universities offer access to the Internet over very fast leased telephone lines (called T1 lines). You can connect to the Internet from your desk using your organization's local area network and server. The downside of this free access is that you must go through your computer operations or MIS department to gain access and permission to maintain a Web site. Often you are limited in the access you are accorded to the server (you may, for example, not have access to CGIs for imagemaps or forms except for what is provided on the server and you must access the server by the rules of the computer department).

Uploading Your Page

After you have determined where you want to publish your Web site, you need to upload it to the Web server. This is a two-step process: setting up a folder or directory to store your Web site files, and actually uploading the files.

The following paragraphs assume that you will be communicating with a Unix server because this is the most ubiquitous server system, with Windows NT servers coming in a close second. Setting up the Unix server for your Web site entails working with Telnet, or similar terminal emulation software, to communicate with the Unix operating system and to work with the FTP server to send folders and documents to the correct directories. Assuming you are installing your Web site on an ISP's Unix-based system, use Fetch (`http://www.dartmouth.edu/pages/softdev/fetch.html`) or a similar FTP utility to manage the task. You must speak to the ISP (or the system administrator of your organization) to set up an account with a user-ID and password prior to uploading. Find out how to get an account and what the rules for working with your server are before you start.

Note that many ISPs do not allow you to upload files but rather make you use their proprietary HTML editors to build home pages. Find out if you can upload home pages prior to beginning the uploading process. You might find you can bypass the Telnet session because your provider has pre-selected a remote directory for your use.

Mac

Uploading Your Web Site to Unix-based Servers

1   Launch a Telnet terminal emulator program, such as NCSA Telnet and log into your ISP's host system. You should be at the root directory (the lowest directory on the server).

2   Type the following: **mkdir public_html** (No period). This creates a special directory named public_html in your shell account's home directory.

3 Type the following: **ls -ld public_html** (No period). This displays the directory called public_html so that you are sure you created it, and it has the permissions set up the way you want. The permissions are a string of characters: **drwx——**.

4 Type the following: **chmod o+rx public_html** (No period). This adds public permissions to the directory so that users can see your Web page.

5 Type the following: **ls -ld public_html** to display the public_html directory once again, checking that it displays the new public permission flags: rx rather than wx.

6 Type the following: **cd public_html** to change the working directory to the new directory.

7 Launch Fetch and in the New Connection dialog box type the host directory name (such as ftp.apple.info), your user name, a password, and the name of the directory (in this case public_html) you want to access (see Figure 12.1).

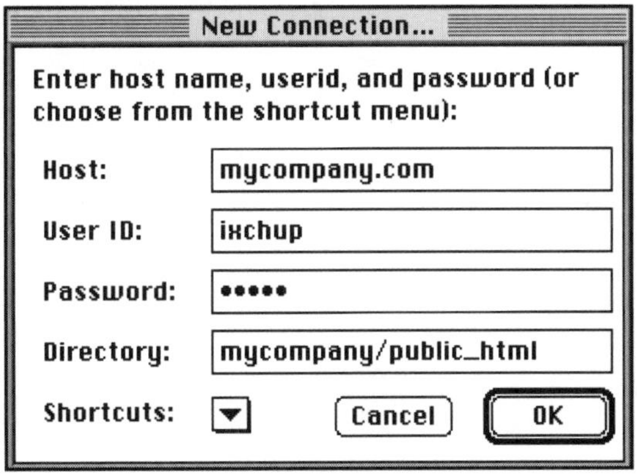

Figure 12.1
Enter the host name, your name, password, and the remote directory name you want to access in the New Connection dialog box.

```
╔═══════════════════════════════════════╗
║  ▤▤▤▤▤  New Connection...  ▤▤▤▤▤       ║
║                                        ║
║  Enter host name, userid, and password (or
║  choose from the shortcut menu):       ║
║                                        ║
║  Host:      │mycompany.com         │   ║
║                                        ║
║  User ID:   │ixchup                │   ║
║                                        ║
║  Password:  │•••••                 │   ║
║                                        ║
║  Directory: │mycompany/public_html │   ║
║                                        ║
║  Shortcuts: ▼    [ Cancel ]  [[ OK ]]  ║
╚═══════════════════════════════════════╝
```

8 Fetch connects you to the ftp or http server you identified and displays the Fetch dialog box. Select the Put File button or choose Put Files and Folders from the Remote menu (see Figure 12.2).

9 In the resulting Put Files dialog box, find the resources folder where you saved your Web pages, attendant images, and so forth in the top list box. Select the page files you want to copy to remote directory public_html. Hold down the Shift key to select more than one file at a time. Start with the graphics files. Make sure you are sending the files in Raw Data format so that Fetch does not convert the files. Click Done (see Figure 12.3).

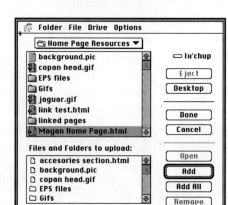

Figure 12.2
Choose Put Files
and Folders from
the Remote menu.

Figure 12.3
Select your page
resources from
your hard disk on
the top list box and
use the Add or Add
All buttons to select
files and folders to
upload.

10 Next, locate the text files you want to transfer from your re-sources folder. Add them to the Files and Folders To Upload list box and click Done. Make sure that Text format is selected in the Choose Formats for Uploaded Files dialog box.

11 Check to see if the files were properly uploaded by opening the remote directory public_html in your Fetch dialog box window.

12 If satisfied, select Quit from the File menu.

13 Return to your telnet session and type: **ls -l** to list the home page files. Make sure that the permission flags for the files end with **r—-** to indicate read-only.

14 Log off the Telnet and FTP sessions.

Uploading Your Site Using PageMill 2.0 for Windows

One of the nice features of PageMill 2.0 for Windows is that it includes an FTP uploader. Now, when you are finished testing your site to make sure that all of the links work as planned, you can click a button and automatically be connected to your server. The Upload Wizard walks you through the setup of your FTP session and manages the upload process.

Windows

Using PageMill's Upload Feature

1   Select Upload the Page from the File menu (if your site does not use frames) or Upload Everything from the Frameset pop-up menu on the File menu (if your site uses frames).

2   In the resulting Uploading dialog box, make sure that the Site mapping name (the file that contains the FTP settings for your site) is correct. You assign a name when you first upload the site. If you want to edit the settings file, click Edit.

3   In the resulting dialog box (see Figure 12.4), enter the information in the following table.

Site Mapping Name	Type a name that will identify the settings file for the specific site.
Hostname	This is the URL for the remote server. Use the first portion of your site's URL (for example, *www.yourcompanyname.com*)
Remote folder	this is the rest of the URL for the remote server. Use the rest of the address in your site's URL up to the name of your default file (for example, if your URL is *www.yourcompanyname.com/~your name*, type "*/~yourname/*")
Local folder	Type the pathname for your local directory or click Browse to let Windows Finder locate the site's directory.
Authentication	Enter your UserID as assigned by your ISP and your password. Note that the password does not display on the screen.

Upload Basis   PageMill can detect which files were changed since your last upload and upload only those files. Select a radio button to pick one of three options: Previous Log File, Remote File Status, or Always.

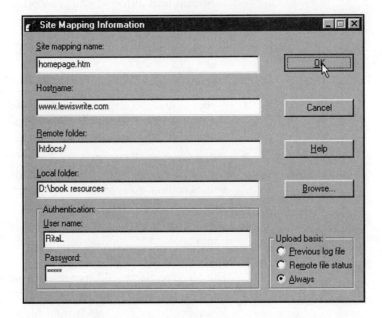

Figure 12.4
The Site Mapping Information dialog box displays your FTP Settings file name. If correct, click OK to begin the session.

Selecting Previous Log File tells PageMill to use its log file from your last session to compare file modification dates. If the current files' dates are newer than the log's recorded dates, those files are uploaded. Older dated files are ignored.

Selecting Remote File Status tells PageMill to look at the file names and if they are different to upload the new names. Then, PageMill checks the size of files with the same name and their modification dates and uploads only those files that have different sizes or dates.

PageMill will automatically upload everything if there have been any changes to the remote server or the remote path between the log file and the current site settings since the last upload session.

If you are happy with your FTP settings, click OK to return to the Upload dialog box. Click Upload to begin the FTP session.

4 If you are not already logged on to the Internet, the Internet Dialup Wizard's dialog box is displayed. Type your password and click Connect (see Figure 12.5).

Figure 12.5
Use the FTP Settings dialog box to set up your upload session addresses.

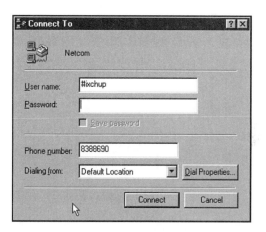

5 Windows dials into your ISP and then returns command back to the Upload dialog box (see Figure 12.6).

Figure 12.6
The Upload dialog box displays the amount of time, the size of the files being uploaded, and their status as the process is performed.

6 The Upload dialog box displays the status of the FTP session. When the upload is complete, the box will disappear. If there is a problem with the session, the dialog box will display any error messages.

When you have completed uploading your page files, you can check to see if your site is really live by opening your browser and selecting the URL for your new site. The URL should be formatted as follows:

```
http://your ISP's site name/~your shell account log-in
name/
```

My home page is located at `http://www.lewiswrite.com/` `index.html/` for example.

You can register your own domain name (remember those virtual servers on many Web servers?). Ask your system administrator or ISP for instructions and fees for registration. The domain names must be registered with InterNIC (`http://www.internic.net`), because all domain names must be unique. InterNIC researches the availability of names and sells them on a first-come, first-served basis. Think of several domain names because someone may have already registered your pet name.

Managing Your Site

Running a Web server does not mean managing how the files in your Web site are linked and arranged. Because your Web site is filled with different types of files—images, sound files, videos, virtual reality files, PDFs, and so on, you need a way to maintain the timeliness of your site's contents: both the accuracy of its links to outside sites and the contents of its pages. Renaming files or moving files to another directory changes all of the links to those files throughout the site. Site management software lets you view a map of your site and maintain links.

The following section describes Adobe SiteMill 2.0 (the companion piece to PageMill), although their are many others available, such as NetObjects Fusion for Mac and Windows or Microsoft FrontPage for Mac and Windows. All three packages let you manage filenames, links, and file relationships by dragging and dropping icons in a model of your site.

SiteMill

One of the frustrating things about Web publishing is that you must be careful not to move images files or HTML files after they are created or you create absolute havoc with your site's functions. PageMill cannot present a bird's-eye view of your files and their interconnections because it is too close to the files (displaying actual pages and letting you simulate a browser). You need a program that lets you move around files and rename them while it maintains and manages the interconnections between files. That is where SiteMill and its ilk come in. SiteMill lets you maintain hypertext links in real-time (while the site is live) because it automatically tracks all of your site's files and assists you in updating these files.

SiteMill basically does three things: maintains incoming links between objects and pages, maintains outgoing links between pages, and maintains remote links between your Web site and other sites.

When you first open SiteMill it asks you to identify the site you want analyzed. Open the folder containing the site and click the In The *foldername* button (see Figure 12.7). SiteMill analyzes the folders and files within your selected local resource folder (see Figure 12.8) and displays a hierarchical map of the structure of your site (see Figure 12.9).

Figure 12.7
Use the Select Site dialog box to identify the local resource folder where your site is stored.

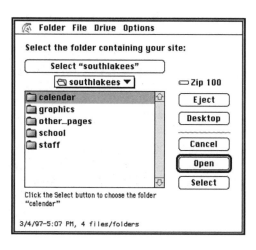

Figure 12.8
SiteMill runs a scan of the resource folder to check all links and associated files.

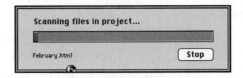

Figure 12.9 displays the SiteMill Site View window you use to view the folders and files in your Web site. The window resembles a Finder window in its use of arrow tabs, folders, and file icons. You drag and drop files between folders to organize your files and maintain links.

Figure 12.9
The Error window and Site View window displays a hierarchical picture of your site.

One of the most powerful features of SiteMill is its capability to analyze all of the links within your site and display any broken connections in an Error window. You can then use drag and drop to repair the links.

Repairing a Broken Link

1. Select a file indicating a broken link (its name shows up in the Error window).

2. Drag the file on to its twin in the Error window.

3. SiteMill displays an alert box informing you of the number of files that will be changed by your actions. Click OK to accept the changes (see Figure 12.10).

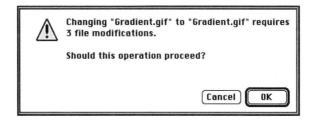

Figure 12.10
An alert box tells you how many files will change by replacing the file.

4   In the SiteView window, click the outgoing links pop-up menu next to the file you corrected. It should display no missing files (see Figure 12.11).

Figure 12.11
Use the Incoming and Outgoing pop-up menus to view links to files and objects.

You can also add links to live sites. SiteMill 2.0 is tightly integrated with PageMill 2.0. When you click an underlined Title bar in SiteMill or a file icon, PageMill opens that page. Use the Page icon to create links in the same manner as you ordinarily do, by dragging and dropping the icon onto selected text or an image(see Chapter 5 for a discussion of links). You can also replace links from within SiteMill using the Replace Links command.

Replacing a Link

1   Open SiteMill and load the site you want to analyze. (In this case, I am using my business site.)

2   Select Replace Links from the Site menu.

3   In the resulting Replace Links dialog box, drag and drop the linked page you want to change on to the Find every link to text box. Next, drag and drop the linked page you want to replace the original link with on to the And REPLACE with a link to text box (see Figure 12.12). Click Replace All.

continues

Figure 12.12
Drag and drop pages onto the Replace Links dialog box to universally replace faulty links in your site.

4   SiteMill displays an alert box informing you that this change is non-reversable. If you are sure you want to swap links, click OK.

5   SiteMill scans the site and performs the replacements. Select the Outgoing pop-up menu next to the new link to see if the old link has been replaced (see Figure 12.13).

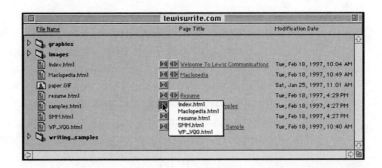

Figure 12.13
The Outgoing Links pop-up menu shows the newly linked page (in this case "Maclopedia.html."

You can also create new links by dragging the destination file onto the source page. SiteMill inserts the page title on the source page for the linked file.

SiteMill makes it very easy to delete files that have no links. Highlight the file you want to delete and select Delete Selected from the Site menu. SiteMill puts the file in the Trash.

You can rename folders or files and have SiteMill track all associated links and update them with the new name. Select the file or folder you want to rename. Type a new name (make sure that it has no spaces by using the underscore key where spaces should be and remember to include the file type in the suffix of a file name) (see Figure 12.14).

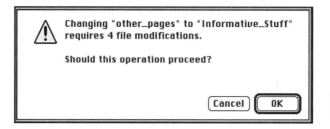

Figure 12.14
Highlight a name
and type a new one.

SiteMill alerts you of the effect of your action. If you are sure you want to perform the rename, click OK (see Figure 12.15). SiteMill scans the site and replaces all of the former named folder paths with the new folder name (or filenames if that is what you renamed).

> ⚠ Changing "other_pages" to "Informative_Stuff" requires 4 file modifications.
>
> Should this operation proceed?
>
> [Cancel] [**OK**]

Figure 12.15
SiteMill displays an
alert box informing
you of the effects
of your action.

Use drag and drop to move files between folders and SiteMill updates the associated links.

Use SiteMill to organize your resources into folders prior to uploading. Then, when you add or delete files, or replace files and links, you can use SiteMill to ensure that all of your links remain unbroken and files are where they belong. You can use SiteMill to open live HTML files in PageMill to perform maintenance and updates without disturbing links.

The beta version of SiteMill 2 offered a glimpse of a new feature, the ability to upload the site directly from SiteMill to the remote server. Although the beta did not have this feature activated, it seems to work exactly like the FTP upload application in PageMill for Windows. Use the Preferences dialog box to create the FTP settings for your site. The Upload command on the Site menu will begin the upload process.

Summary

After you upload your Web site using the FTP server and Telnet you will appreciate how little you have to work with Unix these days. Use a site management package, such as SiteMill, to make updating your site easier and more flexible.

One rule of thumb in Web publishing is that readers will not return to your site if they sense that it is not routinely updated with new information. Information is everything on the Web. Keep changing the site to keep it fresh, which means keep your links accurate using the maintenance package and you will have a successful Web site.

Chapter 13 describes how to work with the server-side of Web management. Tools such as SiteMill assist you in maintaining your site on the client side. After you upload the site to the remote server you need other tools to ensure that it operates correctly. Maintaining the Web server is beyond the scope of this book, but the next chapter introduces the concept as it pertains to your responsibilities as a Web publisher.

Chapter 13

Future Trends

"We're not in Kansas anymore, Toto!
— H.L Baum's *Wizard of Oz*

The first version of this book finished with a quote from the movie *Toy Story*—"To infinity and beyond!" Well, in the past year, we have passed infinity. Things on the technology side of the World Wide Web are developing so fast that they get outmoded before they become accepted.

Witness HTML 3.0, a passing standard that everyone is basing their Web publishing software on, including PageMill 2.0. While Adobe was developing PageMill 2.0, Microsoft upped the ante by introducing style sheets and real fonts to the Web. We jumped to Version 3.2 of HTML, yet no one has agreed upon 3.0 and all those Netscape extensions, such as tables, frames, blink, and so forth.

How do you keep up with the information overload?

Well, you don't.

When you are designing your Web page, keep in mind that your reader wants information. Your job is to provide the most efficient means of giving this to him or her. This may mean you don't have to include virtual reality players, animations, sound effects, and other multimedia tricks in your site if your goal is to present a catalog of environmentally sound household products.

Right now, we are poised on the edge of a vast technology divide. We know how to do cool stuff, but it takes lots of powerful computers and modems to receive this stuff and lots of money to manage the transmission of it. You have to decide what your budget will be, what the goal of your site is, and then design your Web page for your readers.

The following pages present an overview of the current developments on the "bleeding edge" of the Web. These are in use now, but think before you decide to use them. Look at active image technology. When the first edition of this book was published two years ago, you needed lots of help on the server's end to use graphic hotspots. Today, PageMill 2.0 builds client-side maps on the fly. So just wait and some of these very expensive, cool items may become ordinary enough to actually use.

Component Software and the Web

The newest trend in programming, called *component-based programming*, is extending its reaches to the World Wide Web. Currently, a battle is raging for the right to be the ultimate standard for how components work on the Web. Components are small programs that can be fit together to form a modular, customized application in real-time (as you need them). The beauty of components is that they can be written in cross-platform languages and rapidly compiled to work on many platforms. For example, if you want a spell checker for your spreadsheet, use a component and you don't have to purchase a large program such as Microsoft Excel to gain that function.

Component-based programming has come to the Web in the form of a fight for acceptance as standards between Sun's Java programming language, Apple/IBM's OpenDoc technology, and Microsoft's technology (formerly called OLE). Basically, Netscape

Navigator has chosen to use Java applets and its own JavaScript to provide extensions to basic browser functions.

Recently, Netscape announced it will include OpenDoc support for Navigator on the Macintosh. Microsoft has built Internet Explorer from ActiveX technologies but plans to support Netscape Navigator's JavaScript and supports Sun's Java via ActiveX controls. Confusing, isn't it? Wait, it gets better.

Basically, the battle is over two models of how Web browsers will grow, and hence, how Web pages will be enhanced using component software. Microsoft depends on the Distributed Component Object Model (DCOM) whereas Netscape, Apple, IBM, and Sun have agreed upon the Object Management Group's Common Object Request Broker Architecture (COBRA). These competing models make you decide which browser to use, but you must publish your Web pages for both Internet Explorer and Netscape Navigator (as well as other browsers of lesser capability, such as Unix's Lynx and NCSA's Mosaic). Luckily, the technologies do the same thing, enabling you to view objects placed into HTML, such as GIF animations, Virtual Reality, and Shockwave objects (such as FreeHand illustrations or Director animations). The difference is in how they do it.

All About Plugins

Netscape Navigator began enhancing the capabilities of its browser in 1994 through inline plugins and browser- and file-specific software (called helpers), which display or play foreign files referenced in HTML. Plugins are platform-specific; you have to know which computer operating system the plugin will operate with because not all of them work on every operating system. The benefit of using plugins is that Web designers can control where their data appears on the page and how it relates to other HTML text and graphics on the page (because the foreign file object is embedded in the HTML). The plugin recognizes the data by its file extension. (Refer to Chapter 9 for a discussion of using the correct file extensions when naming your files).

The problem is that you must have the plugin, or access to a player that works on your computer, in order to enjoy the enhanced visuals

continues

and sound produced by the embedded object. Plugins are on the wane, being replaced by Java applets, JavaScript, OpenDoc, and ActiveX. These are programming technologies, not just single-function applications. They extend the functionality of the Web server as well as the client's browser because they are written onto the Web page and call on external programs to operate as needed. Their goal is to integrate the computer operating system with the browser more completely so you can use Internet-based data with more local applications.

Java and JavaScript

The hottest thing to hit the Web is the programming language Java, which Sun Microsystems introduced to make programs portable. This is important because the nature of the Web is that you don't know anything about what your reader is using to access your site. Netscape created a lighter version of Java, which lets users customize their browser and create a more interactive environment on the Web. This capability is called *Web-delivered scripting*, which enables you to execute programs within a browser. The scripting language based on Java is called JavaScript. Both Java (as in the Java applets I have mentioned throughout this book) and JavaScript (covered briefly in Chapter 9 in terms of how to get them to run on PageMill) are supported by PageMill 2.0.

Having the ability to create dynamic interactive features that play on anyone's computer, are relatively easy to create, and are virus-free and relatively tamper-proof is very powerful. Java is used to write fully compiled programs that do things you can add to your Web pages, such as a visitor counter or an analog clock. JavaScript is useful for writing small instruction sets in your HTML used for processing simple user actions, such as how HTML-based documents are displayed (scrolling title bars, flashing buttons, scrolling scrollbar messages, and so forth).

Java applets are small independent programs written in the Java programming language and are pre-compiled. These small programs can be used to create a word processing program that operates over the Web or bounce pretty balls across your screen. Java applets are programs requiring browsers to understand the language because the beauty of the language is that it is interpreted in real time. There are two browsers that understand Java—Sun's HotJava browser and Netscape Navigator 2.0 or higher. Microsoft has invented a competitor called ActiveX that is supported by its browser Internet Explorer.

PageMill accepts Java applets but not ActiveX objects (see the following section for a discussion of ActiveX controls and documents). You have to follow the instructions in the applet to properly install it. This also entails possibly editing PageMill's HTML source code (see Chapter 9) because most applets require you to set parameters, such as how many balls to bounce and what color to make them. Some Java applets are included on the CD-ROM that accompanies this book. As with most shareware, please honor the requests of the programmer before publishing his or her work. To find more Java applets, visit the Gamelan Web site at `http://www.gamelan.com`.

An example of Java applets that add background music to your Web page is shown in Figure 13.1. These music snippets were built using Java and can be embedded in your Web page using the <Applet></Applet> tag.

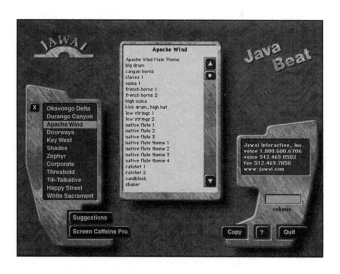

Figure 13.1
Jawai offers a CD-ROM of Java applets providing background music for your Web pages, called Java Beat.

Java and JavaScript provide Web pages with the capability to interact with the user. The fact that you can perform all kinds of calculations and display the results on a reader's computer enables you to suddenly personalize your Web pages. You can add, for example, a JavaScript to calculate how many days until your reader's birthday and give them the result. Now all you have to do is learn how to write JavaScript-based macros (scripts) and add them to your PageMill-generated HTML source code.

Cool.

ActiveX

ActiveX is a set of technologies that lets you create more interactive Web pages. ActiveX is a subset for networking of Microsoft's OLE technology that lets you open external programs and create active documents within another document.

ActiveX provides both client and server technologies as follows:

- **ActiveX Controls.** Interactive objects you embed in your HTML that provide interactive and user-controllable functions.

- **ActiveX Documents.** Lets you view non-HTML documents through a Web browser.

- **Active Scripting.** Lets you integrate the functions of several ActiveX Controls and/or Java applets from the browser or server.

- **Java Virtual Machine.** Lets any ActiveX-supported browser run Java applets and integrate Java applets into ActiveX controls.

- **ActiveX Server Framework.** Provides Web server functions such as security, database access, and others to Web pages.

ActiveX Controls (formerly called OLE custom controls) are small applications that run inside a container, such as Web browser. Because ActiveX Controls must be recompiled for each computer system, they are not currently compatible with any operating system except Windows. Metroworks is working on a Macintosh version using Bristol and Mainsoft to support ActiveX on Unix platforms.

One of the benefits of ActiveX is that it is a subset of OLE. After ActiveX Controls are downloaded into Internet Explorer 3.0 or Netscape Navigator with ScriptActive, the Controls can be shared among any OLE-aware application, such as Microsoft Excel or Word, just like any other OLE object. ActiveX Documents contain code that launches applications identified as the originating programs for Web page objects, such as Shockwave Director files or Adobe Portable Document Files (PDFs) so that more types of files can be viewed and manipulated within Internet Explorer.

ActiveX Documents, built into future versions of Internet Explorer, will let users interact with local and networked data almost transparently. Although ActiveX Controls are more flexible than plugins because they use the Windows Registry system for identification of file extensions, this limits ActiveX to Windows environments. Netscape Navigator plugins and Java applets use the MIME (Multipurpose Internet Mail Extension) system, which is less flexible than Windows Registry but is available on all platforms. Remember, ActiveX is machine-dependent. Java applets are machine-independent and download as needed via software interpreters. Future versions of Netscape will use Just-In-Time compilers to speed up the performance of Java applet downloading processes.

ActiveX Controls can also function as servers. The DCOM standard enables client and server controls to communicate with each other and distribute the workload across multiple networks. In addition, VBScript (Visual Basic Script) enables you to write ActiveX scripts to provide controls on your Web pages automated from within the browser.

Many vendors have developed ActiveX Controls Macromedia. Shockwave, for example, is both a plugin for Netscape Navigator and an ActiveX control. If you use the Microsoft Internet Explorer as your browser to visit a Web site where an ActiveX Shockwave is used, the control will be downloaded and installed automatically. Netcompass offers a plugin called ScriptActive to provide ActiveX control for Netscape Navigator for Windows users.

OpenDoc

OpenDoc is a component-based programming tool similar to ActiveX but available for most computer platforms. OpenDoc was developed by Apple but now is supported by CI Labs, a non-profit association with over 2,000 members, including IBM. OpenDoc applications are automatically OLE applications because OpenDoc is based on ComponentGlue technology, so that it writes directly to published OLE specifications. Functionally, OpenDoc is a superset of OLE but is easier to program than ActiveX Documents or Controls. OpenDoc applications are called LiveObjects and can provide the same capability as ActiveX Documents to provide live links and views of the Internet in any document that is OpenDoc-savvy, such as ClarisWorks 4.0. OpenDoc is based on the Common Object Broker Request Architecture (COBRA) for distributing objects over multiple platforms, and so it's much more compatible today with Windows, Macintosh, OS/2, and Unix systems than is ActiveX.

OpenDoc and Java are complementary technologies. An OpenDoc component (called a LiveObject) can be written to understand how to execute Java applets, so you can embed Java applets in any OpenDoc-savvy application, not just in your Internet browser.

Apple recently introduced an OpenDoc-based browser system called Cyberdog. Cyberdog lets users integrate live Internet data into their desktop applications by embedding Cyberdog components (such as a Web browser) into any OpenDoc-compatible application. Cyberdog is a combination of a browser and an HTML authoring tool—you can use it to embed live Internet data into OpenDoc documents. When you dial into the Web from the application, its Internet data is automatically updated. Check out the CyberPound Site about Cyberdog at `http://www.microserve.com/~dhughes/` for more information about Cyberdog.

For More Information...

For more information about component-based software, surf the following Web sites:

- **ActiveX**. `http://www.microsoft.com/activex/` Or `http://www.activex.org/`.

- **OpenDoc**. `http://opendoc.apple.com/dev/dev.html` Or `http://applenet.apple.com/`

You can learn more about JavaScript at the following sites:

- **Netscape's Official JavaScript Reference Guide.** (`http//home.netscape.com/eng/mozilla/2.0/handbook/javascript/index.html`)

- **Tecfa's JavaScript Manual**. A JavaScript tutorial. (`http://tecfa.unige.ch/guides/java/tecfaman/java-1.html`)

- **JavaScript 411**. A JavaScript FAQ, tutorial, and more. (`http://www.freqgrafx.com/411`)

- **JavaScript 411's Snippet Page**. Provides advanced JavaScript code. (`http://freqgrafx.com/411/library.html`)

- **Example Site.** Provides examples of JavaScript macros, including a temperature converter, a metric converter, a calendar greeting program, and a loan interest calculator. (`http://www.cis.syr.edu/~bhu/javascript.d/`)

Multimedia Tools

The buzz in the news is about multimedia on the Web. We are standing on the edge of the ability to broadcast on-demand video and audio over the Web, such as a live event (the Presidential debates?), while they are in progress. In addition, working in three dimensions in real-time motion (called virtual reality) opens up new vistas.

We are not quite there yet. The problem is bandwidth and browser compatibility. These are huge programs—thousands of kilobytes. Even on the speediest of telecommunications lines, these communications get bogged down when transmitting over today's fastest connections (a 128-Kbps ISDN Internet connection).

PageMill 2.0 lets you import sound and movie file data types as objects into your Web pages today. The paragraphs below cover the different aspects of multimedia and how to use them with PageMill. The question of whether you want to spend what it takes on hardware to broadcast what most users cannot afford to see is dubious today, but who knows about tomorrow...

Databases for Multimedia

More and more Web sites serve as front-ends for very large relational databases. Databases keep tabs on content of sites, track copyright information during the production of a site, create templates for Web pages, and manage transmission traffic. Multimedia databases, such as Illustra Information Technologies, automatically open information sent via email and store images, captions, and text in separate fields. Because of the growing size and number of HTML pages, Java code snippets, and audio/video files that make up a site, you need databases to manage the storage and use of multimedia items.

There are four types of databases available for managing Web sites: traditional relational databases, such as Oracle and FileMaker Pro; object-oriented databases, such as ObjectDesign's ObjectStore; relational-object hybrid databases, such as Illustra; and specialty databases, such as Cinebase.

The biggest players are the traditional SQL-based relational database companies: Oracle, Informix, Sybase, Computer Associates, and IBM. Webmasters use these monster databases to manage huge transaction loads, such as customer orders and inventory management. You can't store images, sounds, or video on SQL databases because the software handles text, images, and video as one large object (called a BLOB—binary large object), which is difficult to search and retrieve.

Oracle now supports multimedia storage via its new Universal Server Enterprise Edition that includes Oracle Spatial Data option for storage and retrieval of images, the ConText Option for full text retrieval through SQL, and the Oracle Video Option that serves video files to multiple clients via switched Ethernet and fiber optic cable systems. IBM also has multimedia extensions for its DB/2 relational database that supports text, audio, video, image, and fingerprint data.

Object-oriented databases are useful for storing images, video , and audio because they use an object model rather than a tabular model in the design of the database. An object, as in PageMill, can be anything, whereas in relational databases if it cannot fit in a field, it can't be easily managed. There are many small companies producing these more graphic-oriented databases, such as Objectivity, ObjectDesign, and Versant Object Technology. Computer Associates is set to release Jasmine, a joint-development venture with Fujitsu using Fujitsu's ODB-II technology that defines images in terms of its parts. Because component relationship information is stored with the data, you can easily call up images by selecting a single part.

Hybrid mixtures of object-oriented and relational databases use the benefits of tabular data and object-based data. The hybrid system is scaleable for large amounts of data and uses SQL; yet it can handle complex relationships, new media types, and formats. You can extend the database's capabilities by adding plugins, in Illustra (the most popular product in this category) called DataBlades, that handle complex data, such as searching using a visual keyword or Web page authoring. You can create HTML page templates with embedded SQL statements that do not require a CGI script to perform a search and build a resulting Web page on the fly. Informix recently bought Illustra and plans to speed its performance and add streaming capabilities for displaying video and audio files. Its new Universal Server will incorporate Illustra's hybrid systems with Informix' Dynamic Scaleable Architecture.

Specialty databases are built for single purposes, such as Media-On-Demand, an asset and workflow management program built by Bulldog Group. Media-On-Demand uses Illustra but tailored it for use by commercial art production departments to provide database storage along side Web authoring capabilities using video, audio, and text objects. A companion database is being designed that will manage transactions over the Web. Cinebase is used for archiving large amounts of video materials.

A new development are Web servers that function as relational databases. The DynaWeb server from Electronic Book Technologies (EBT) manages large libraries of multi-page manuals for storage and retrieval. EBT is also developing DynaBase, a combination Web development and content-management system that would run on Windows NT, Solaris, and Silicon Graphic's IRIX systems. DynaBase produces Web pages on the fly based on the results of database searches by browsers.

Audio Broadcasting

One of the exciting new technologies coming out of multimedia developer's workshops is the capability for the browser to play sound data as it is received. This technology is based on a data-type called MIME (Multipurpose Internet Mail Extensions) where the computer sends the data packet first so that the browser can interpret information as it comes screaming down the wire. The benefits of this system are that users do not have to store large chunks of data to enjoy the music, and servers do not have to take up large chunks of storage space processing the sounds. Live audio data is highly compressed (typically 44:1), meaning that an hour's worth of music can be saved in a 3.6MB file. There are competing ways to do this that are battling it out.

The problem today is that telecommunications lines are not screaming, but sputtering—there is no such thing as a continuous, error-free flow of data. So you have to install a plugin in your browser that buffers (saves in memory) some of the information so that lost or delayed data can be accommodated. You hear this as a long pause before the music starts. In addition, data does not usually flow at a continuous rate, always 28.8K baud, but slows down if the host or client computer is occupied with other matters while surfing (such as printing or traffic surges on the server-side of things). You will hear the problem of bandwidth shortage very soon.

Live music requires two pieces of software: server software and player software. Typically, the server software you buy and the player software is offered free for downloading. PageMill supports files (plays their contents) that you place on a page if you put a copy of the plugin in the PageMill Plugins folder and restart your computer prior to placing the file. Today, Netscape's Web page (`http://home.netscape.com/comprod/products/navigator/`) offers the following plugin players for Macs and/or Windows 3.1/ NT/95.

 Note

> Your player plugin only supports the data type it was written for. There are two types of music systems on the computer: MIDI (Musical Instrument Digital Interface) and digital audio. Digital audio files are recorded audio waveforms stored as data (bits and bytes). The most common general audio format on the Macintosh is AIFF (Audio Interchange File Format) and on the PC, the most common digital audio format is Microsoft's Wave (.WAV). The Internet also supports Sun Microsystems' uLaw format. In addition, the Web supports MPEG (Motion Picture Expert's Group) compression format for video and audio as well. You can only hear audio that your browser and computer supports. Be careful when embedding digital audio files in PageMill; check that they are in a format your listeners can accept. MIDI is just the opposite of digital audio in that what is stored is information about the music that the player software uses to produce the sounds. The player is usually a sound synthesizer or sound card in the user's computer.

■ **Crescendo Plus** by LiveUpdate. Crescendo is a MIDI player that uses QuickTime's built-in MIDI synthesizer to play the music. Crescendo downloads the MIDI sound file and plays it as a continuous sound loop (you cannot stop it from playing until you leave the page). You place a MIDI object in your PageMill document and Macs and Windows 3.1/NT/95 systems with Crescendo automatically play the file. Figure 13.2 illustrates the control panel for Crescendo.

Figure 13.2
Crescendo plays
background music
on a continuous
loop until you turn it
off using the control
panel.

■ **InterVU** MPEG Player by Intervu, Inc. InterVU provides streaming MPEG audio-video downloads for Netscape Navigator 2.0 or better browsers. You can play any MPEG file without requiring decoders. The InterVU plugin is available for Macs and Windows NT/95 systems.

■ **Koan** by Sseyo. Koan plays MIDI music formatted in Koan Music on all types of Windows systems. The music is generated locally in real-time by the PC's sound card.

■ **MacZilla** by Knowledge Engineering. MacZilla supports just about any audio format from QuickTime, MIDI background sound, WAV, AU, and AIFF audio, MPEG and AVI video on a Macintosh.

■ **MidPlug** by Yamaha. MidPlug plays MIDI background music on PowerMacs and Windows 3.1/95 systems. You may require external MIDI playback equipment to hear the music on your computer that is downloaded with MidPlug.

■ **RealAudio** by Progressive Networks. RealAudio is the grandmaster plugin (the first and probably the best) for playing live, on-demand real-time audio over 14.4Kbps or faster connections to the Internet. RealAudio players and creation software (server-side) are available for Macs and all Windows 3.1/95/NT systems.

■ **StreamWorks** by Xing Technology. A high-end counterpart to RealAudio. StreamWorks' plugin supports high-speed digital Internet connections not supported by RealAudio, including 44.1kHz CD-quality stereo sound transmitted over 128Kbps ISDN line. There is no server software available for the Mac to create StreamWorks files, but you can play these files or place them in PageMill on the Mac or any Windows system.

Digital Video

There are two video compression formats vying for power on the Web: QuickTime and MPEG. Digital video does not have the picture quality of broadcast video because personal computers (both Macs and Intels) cannot support the bandwidth required to transmit all of the data involved. Digital video is also called *animation* because the picture is sent one by one in a single pass without interlacing and at half the number of frames per second as broadcast video (digital video is transmitted at 15 frames per second, typically).

The pictures on the screen are small (typically 160 by 120 pixels) to also save bandwidth. There are three ways to compress digital video for the Web: Cinepak, TrueMotion-S, and Indeo. Digital video files are saved as .mov, .moov, .qt, .avi, .mpeg, and .mpg files. QuickTime (.qt and .moov/.mov) is the most common file format for combined audio/video files. AVI is Microsoft's file format for Windows. You can convert your QuickTime files to AVI files using shareware on both Mac and Windows platforms. MPEG is a new medium that is just beginning to provide combined audio and video in a single file. With the advent of cable modems, you will see more live broadcasts using MPEG compression technology.

You place a movie file into PageMill just as you would any other object. Because the files are large, you may want to create a link using an anchor (see Chapter 5 for a discussion of using anchors) between the .mov file and your page so that when the reader clicks a thumbnail still shot from the movie, he or she is jumped to the file. The viewer then decides, based on which plugin they have installed, whether to download the movie and play it off-line or play it in real-time. The newest type of plugin lets you preview the movie clips by streaming the clips while they are downloading.

Netscape supports the following plugins for viewing and creating digital video animations:

- ■ **Action** by Open2U. This Windows 95/NT plugin lets you embed MPEG movies with synchronized sound into your pages and play them back offline.

■ **CineWeb** by Digigami. Plays standard movie and audio files (AVI, MOV, MPG, WAV, MID, and MP2) on Windows systems. You can create standard movies using Weblisher and MegaPEG, also by Digigami.

■ **CoolFusion** by Iterated Data Systems. The CoolFusion plugin plays streaming Video for Windows (AVI) files. Using CoolFusion, you can preview AVI video in real time as it downloads on Windows 95 systems.

■ **InterVU** by InterVu, Inc. InterVu is an MPEG player that lets you play audio and video MPEG files without decoders or video servers. Videos are transmitted in streams so that they can be previewed as they download on Macs and Windows NT/95 systems.

■ **MovieStar** by Intelligence at Large. This plugin plays QuickTime movies. If the QuickTime files have been optimized with MovieStar Maker, users of the plugin can preview the films as they are downloading on Macs and Windows 95 systems.

■ **QuickTime for Netscape** by Apple Computer. The Netscape Navigator comes with a QuickTime viewer plugin that previews streaming downloads of QuickTime files. You have to prepare standard Macintosh QuickTime movies before they are useable on the Web by moving the meta data located at the end of the file to the beginning. The QuickTime Web page at `http://quicktime.apple.com/` tells you how to do this. PageMill treats QuickTime movies as objects and will play them back if the QuickTime plugin is placed in its Plugins folder.

■ **ViewMovie** by Ivan Cavero Belaunde. This shareware plugin lets Macs view QuickTime movies, whether linked with anchors or embedded as active images directly on the page, as they download.

Animation

There are four popular ways to provide animation on Web pages: server-push (described in Chapter 9), animated GIFs (GIF files composed of multiple frames), a Java animation applet, and Macromedia Shockwave.

Server-push uses commands embedded in the HTML that create an open connection between the server and the browser. A CGI script is used to push images to the Web page until the script stops the pushing or the user pushes a Stop button. (See Chapter 9 for a discussion of how to edit your Web page in PageMill to include a server-push animation.) You cannot control image speed: you can produce montages of photographs, or cool moving pictures. For more information about server-push animation, check out Meng Weng Wong's Web site at `http://www.seas.upenn.edu/~mengwong/perlhtml.html`.

The GIF89 format and programs, such as GIF Construction Set on Windows machines or GIFBuilder for Macintosh, assists you in implementing the building of GIF frames. The GIF89 format lets you take all of the separate drawings you pushed on the Web page using a server-push CGI script and consolidate it into one file that downloads as a single unit. These files are more compact than server-push animations and take the load off of the server.

As I described in the paragraphs on Java, you can use Java applets to provide sound- and motion-interactive animations on your Web page. You can get pre-built applets from shareware or you can write your own Java applets. Check out Sun Microsystems's Web site at `http://java.sun.com/` for examples of applets and a discussion of writing Java programs.

Macromedia, Inc. has lead the way in the production of animated presentations. The Director program is unique in the way it stores animated sequences because it tracks the paths objects take along with transformations in an object's appearance rather than simply recording frames per second transmissions. This makes Director files smaller and more compressed than typical animated film files. You can insert Director files in your Web page using PageMill if you have the Shockwave plugin installed. Shockwave plays both audio and video and is used to animate logos and banners because the animations should be kept short to save bandwidth. You use Macromedia's AfterBurner program to convert and compress Director files before inserting them into your Page. Shockwave is available for Macs and all Windows systems. Contact the Macromedia Web site at `http://www.macromedia.com` for information about the various Shockwave products for viewing other Macromedia graphic package outputs over the Web, such as FreeHand.

Narrative Communications (`http://www.narrative.com`) has developed a product that supports streaming animation and audio called Enliven. Enliven is a server-based technology for streaming 2-D animation sequences for Windows 95 and Windows NT servers. Enliven competes against RealAudio and Shockwave to provide fast downloading and real-time playing of animations with sounds. The technology is comprised of a viewer, a server, and a post-production authoring package called Producer that converts Macromedia Director applications into Enliven-compatible files. The viewer is a Netscape plugin.

3-D Images and Virtual Reality

There is currently a competition on whose 3-D animation standard will become Virtual Reality Markup Language (VRML) 2.0. Two proposals have been submitted to the VRML Architecture Group: Moving Worlds from Silicon Graphics, Sony, WorldMaker, and Apple, among others; and Active VRML from Microsoft. Both proposals build on existing .WRL (World) format files, adding innovations such as timed events, 2-D and 3-D animation, user interaction with objects (avatars), sound effects, collision detection, and automatic frame generation.

You can create the illusion of three dimensions on the two-dimensional computer screen using a new markup language derived from HTML called Virtual Reality Markup Language (VRML). You need a VRML browser, such as Netscape's Live3D, to view the results. QuickTime VR lets you create panoramic shots, turn them into a QuickTime movie, and view them as QuickTime videos without VRML on Macs. You place QuickTime VR files in PageMill the same way you would QuickTime files. You need to have the QuickTime VR plugin installed in the PageMill Plugin folder to view the results in PageMill's Preview window.

For more information about VRML, surf the following sites: `http://www.sdsc.edu/vrml` or `http://www.w3.org/hypertext/WWW/MarkUp/VRML`

Helper Applications

A helper application is basically a program that cooperates with Netscape and other browsers to perform functions, such as displaying the contents of files, which the browser cannot do.

If you surf the Web, you know that there isn't really just one application that you use. The browser software (such as Netscape or Internet Explorer) is your chief tool for clicking through the Web and reading pages, but the Web is a multimedia environment complete with sounds, images, and movies. In general, there are way more types of data on the Web than Web browser software can display. One example of this is JPEG images.

Currently, only the Netscape Navigator can display JPEG images inside its main window. Other browsers use what is called a helper application to display JPEG images. On the Macintosh, the helper application to view JPEG images is called JPEG View. If the reader of your page is using a browser that does not support direct JPEG image viewing and comes across a JPEG image, that image is handed off to the helper application, which displays it in a separate window. Other helper applications are listed in Table 13.1.

Table 13.1   Helper Applications for Macs and Windows

Purpose	Macintosh	Windows
VRML viewing	Whurlwind (requires Quick-Draw 3D plugin), WebSpace for Power Macs (`http//www.sgi.comm/Products/WebFORCE`	Live3D by Netscape (formerly Paper Software's WebFX); Microsoft Direct3D for

continues

Table 13.1 Helper Applications for Macs and Windows Continued

Purpose	Macintosh	Windows
	`/WebSpace/`), WebFX for viewing 3-D spaces in Internet Chat Rooms (`www.paperinc.com`), Virtus browser (`www.virtus.com`), WorldView browser(`www.webmaster.com:80/vrml/`)	use with Internet Explorer
Movie viewing	Shockwave Director Internet Player, Apple MoviePlayer	AVI video player for Windows; MPEGPLAY Ver 1.61 for Unix and win3;VT motion scale -able MPEG player; MPEG players for windows
MPEG animation viewing	Sparkle	Ghostscript; lview 3.1
QuickTime VR movie viewing	Apple QuickTime VR Player	—
MPEG audio playback	MPEG/CD Player	—
AIFF or AU audio playback	SoundMachine	WHAM 1.33 audio player

Wanted: More and More Bandwidth

Multimedia transmissions over networks take a lot of bandwidth. Even with compression, multimedia downloads are slow. On the other hand, MIDI and VRML do not have great bandwidth requirements but require extensive prepatory work. There are limited applications available to perform this work and so are of limited usefulness today. Useful media types, such as audio, video, and animation, need broader bandwidth, called fat pipes in Internet jargon, to be efficient.

ISDN has slightly sped up performance by providing speeds five times greater than the fastest modems. That is only half the necessary performance jump necessary to truly provide real-time multimedia on the Web. The next bandwidth jump will use a new technology called Asymmetrical Digital Subscriber Loop (ADSL), video cable modems, and spread-spectrum radio signals. This is just on the end-user side. The backbones of the Internet also need to speed up. Currently, the backbone can handle transmissions at 45Mbps. Work is starting to extend that performance to 155Mbps. It is already assumed that this increase in bandwidth will not be enough to support all of the data being transmitted.

Electronic Publishing

It is one thing to use PageMill to send pictures and text over telephone wires to remote computers where a browser interprets arcane codes to display a replica of what was broadcast. It is quite another thing to be able to reproduce published documents with their complex layouts, colors, and art on a remote computer. The remote computer may not have the fonts installed that were used to produce the document nor the software used to layout the document. What is needed is a way to make documents electronically portable.

The Web is a great way to share work among organizations, if this problem of fonts and layout is solved. Adobe Systems has one solution called the portable digital file (PDF). Adobe invented PostScript, the printing description language. Encapsulated PostScript (EPS) was developed as a way to print vector-based objects using PostScript. PDFs use PostScript to print documents to a file with their fonts and images embedded. PDFs need a reader that is able to translate the Postscript and display the file. Adobe Acrobat, among several competing software applications, is able to create and display PDFs.

The newest version of Adobe Acrobat, code-named Amber and in public beta testing as Acrobat 3.0, is able to transmit PDFs over the Internet containing hypertext links, animations, movies, and so forth that are readable by a PDF plugin to Netscape Navigator or Internet Explorer directly on the Web. Now you can use the Web to electronically distribute documents with all of their layout, plus multimedia features, intact.

PageMill 2.0 treats PDFs as objects you can place on a page or link to selected text. The program knows that any file with the extension .PDF is a portable digital file. Users click the PDF icon or hyperlink to download the document to their computers for viewing. You can view the document as it is downloaded and print selected pages or save the entire document on your computer.

For more information about PDFs and Adobe Acrobat, surf the Adobe Acrobat site at `http://www.adobe.com/acrobat`.

Summary

Having finished reading and learning with this book, you are now ready to be a full-fledged Web publisher. You have the tools to create Web pages using PageMill, plus some knowledge of what PageMill is doing with HTML so that you can fully use its capabilities. You do have to learn some illustration and photo-rendering software so that you can create beautiful, yet economically sized images and animations to use on your page, but you have the ability to publish and manage a Web site.

The challenge is to keep up with the changes happening to the Web. PageMill 2.0 provides you with a learning curve, from formatting text to creating CGIs and Java applets. You have also learned where you can go on the Web to retrieve pre-built objects to use on your pages.

You have learned that producing a Web site takes planning. Web pages must be designed in the same manner as commercial artists design paper magazine pages, yet Web pages are interactive and animated, so you have to understand computers, too. This book has provided insights into the worlds of the artists and the scientist. Use PageMill to bridge the gap.

Appendix A

Toolbar Summary

This appendix provides a detailed view of the PageMill 2.0 toolbar buttons and their keyboard equivalents. The HTML produced by each button is also listed. Icons are provided as a visual reference. These keyboard shortcuts do not appear in the menus. Many other keyboard shortcuts are displayed in the various menus on the menu bar.

Toolbar Buttons and Commands

Button	Action	HTML Equivalent	PageMill
	Left Align Text	ALIGN=left	Command Left Arrow
	Center Align Text	<CENTER> </CENTER>	Command Right Arrow
	Switches between top, middle, and bottom alignment	ALIGN=top or ALIGN=middle	
	Insert Horizontal Rule	<HR>	Command 2
	Place Object	<IMG SRC=" path/ filename"WIDTH= "XX" HEIGHT="XX" NATURALSIZEFLAG= "X"ALIGN=bottom>	Command 1
	Insert Checkbox	<INPUT TYPE="check-box" NAME="checkbox" VALUE="checkbox">	Command 3
	Insert Radio Button	<INPUT TYPE="radio" VALUE="radio"Button NAME="radio30327" CHECKED="true">	Command 4
	Insert Multi-line Text Field	<TEXTAREA> NAME= "name COLS="12" ROWS="1" </TEXT-AREA>	Command 5
	Insert Single-line Text Field	INPUT NAME="name" TYPE="text" SIZE="30">	Command 6

Button	Action	HTML Equivalent	PageMill
	Insert Password Field	\<INPUT NAME= "name" TYPE= "password"SIZE="30">	Command 7
	Insert Popup	\<SELECT> \<OPTION- SELECTED item one \<OPTION>item two \<OPTION>item three \</SELECT>	Command 8
	Insert Submit Button	\<INPUT NAME= "name"TYPE="submit" VALUE="Submit">	Command 9
	Insert Reset Button	\<INPUT NAME= "name"TYPE="reset" VALUE="Reset">	Command 0
	Toggle between Preview/Edit mode		Command Spacebar

Note

Command-C or Command-Enter places the cursor in the link location bar.

Appendix B

Glossary

A

Absolute Pathname: A detailed and explicit way of locating a file or device on a network by starting with the name of the computer on which the object or file resides, and then listing any intermediate folders or directories, thus ending with the name of the file or object. For example, <`http://upubs-71.uchicago.edu/wwwbook/appendixes/glossary.html`>.

Acrobat: Portable document software developed by Adobe Systems, Inc. It enables a user to save a file as read-only and enables any number of users to view the file with the free reader utility. Acrobat 3.0 (code-named Amber) enables you to open and read portable digital files (PDFs) on the Web via a Netscape Navigator or Internet Explorer plug-in.

Active Image: A graphic image that has been "mapped" so that every pixel in the image potentially corresponds to a URL. Regions of an active image, called "hotspots," can be drawn that, when the user clicks within the x,y coordinates that define that region (a square, circle, or polygon, for instance), the URL corresponding to that region appears onscreen. See *imagemap*.

Address: The location of a computer, file, or other object on a network (as in FTP address).

.AIFF (Audio Interchange File Format): An audio format standard first developed for Amiga computers and now widely accepted for Intel-based systems.

America Online: Commercial online service.

Anchor: A hypertext link created in an HTML document. For example, `<A HREF="http://www.mycomputer.com/files/doc.html">Clickable text goes here</A>`. In PageMill 2.0, an anchor is an icon that indicates a hypertext link within a page.

Animated GIF: A method of providing moving images on a Web page. Animated GIFs are based on the GIF89 file format that enables you to include multiple pictures in a single file. You can place animated GIF files (designated by the .GIF extension) in your PageMill document by using the Place Object command.

Anonymous FTP: FTP (File Transfer Protocol) is a common way to connect to a network, access directories, or obtain files. It uses TCP/IP commands and usually requires a username and a password. Anonymous FTP enables users to log in to remote FTP sites as guests without requiring a password.

AppleScript: 1) An Apple system extension. 2) Apple's scripting language, which creates an interface between Apple Events and scriptable programs. Distributed with System 7.5.

Applet: Program written in an independent language, for example, Java, that executes within an HTML document displayed by a World Wide Web browser without requiring the application and/or language that created it.

Aretha: The current freeware release of the Frontier scripting tool by Dave Winer. Frontier is a scripting environment that enables you to control scriptable Macintosh applications.

ARPAnet: The original name for the Internet, which was developed in 1969 by the Advanced Research Projects Agency of the U.S. Department of Defense (ARPA).

ASCII: American Standard Code for Information Interchange. Pronounced "ask-ee." Computers don't know what letters or numbers are; they recognize only bits of information—zeros and ones. ASCII is binary code that represents characters. It enables computers to display, transmit, and print textual information.

Attribute: A qualifying property of an HTML tag. Attributes are set using the toolbar or using the Format and Style menu commands in PageMill.

.AU (Audio File): A type of sound file format used by Sun OS-based systems (Unix) and widely used on the Web because of its portability between operating systems.

.AVI (Audio-Video file): A combined video/audio compressed file format used by Microsoft Windows-based systems.

B

Bandwidth: The capacity of a computer channel or data transmission cable, often expressed in bits or bytes per second.

Bin: Abbreviation for binary. Binary means "made up of two parts." All input to a computer is binary, made up of combinations of 0 and 1 data bits. Binary is also a techie term for a computer program. "bin" is often used in "cgi-bin," a commonly used name for a folder/directory where binary files such as CGIs are stored.

BinHex: A method of encoding files from 8-bit to 7-bit format while preserving file attributes.

Bitmap: A binary representation of a graphical object created by translating the object into pixels. Pixels are computerized dots, each of which represents a binary bit of information. In a black-and-white bitmap, for instance, white is on and black is off.

Blocks: One part of a GIF file, either a header or an image. A GIF file usually consists of two blocks—a header and an image. However, the structure defined by the GIF 89a specification supports GIF files that contain multiple images and several additional optional block types.

Bookmark: A record of the URL of a Web page you have visited.

Boolean Queries: Feature of a Wide Area Information Server (WAIS) that provides a search for two related keywords joined by the Boolean operators *and, or,* or *not* that appear in a search string.

Browser: A program designed to read HTML files and retrieve and display information on the World Wide Web. Also called a client. *Graphical browsers* have the capacity to display images, colors, and other graphic elements. *Non-graphical browsers* display textual information but not graphics. (See *Netscape Navigator* and *Mosaic.*)

C

Cache: A part of computer memory that can be reserved for storing/processing a specific type of data.

Cell: The smallest modifiable part of a table. Cells change their size based on their contents, but can only be manually resized in combination with the rest of the cells in a row or column.

CERN: The European Laboratory for Particle Physics, where the World Wide Web was created.

Certificate: Document issued by a certifying agency that attests that the owner of the key to a Web page has proven authentic identity.

Certificate Information: Information on a Web page that tells you about a page's origin as well as its security status.

CGI: Common Gateway Interface. A standard interface between a Web server and an external (or "gateway") program such as a Web browser. A program that handles a request for information and returns information or performs a search or other routine. Can be written in a number of programs.

Cgi-bin: The secure directory containing all bundled CGI programs on Unix Web servers.

Character Styles: HTML tags used to add emphasis to specific words, rather than paragraphs, such as <B> </B> for bold, <I> </I> for italic, and so on.

Clickable Image: See *imagemap.*

Client: A synonym for browser. A program that reads and navigates through the Web and retrieves files. (See *browser.*)

Client Pull: One way of creating dynamic documents in which data on a Web server is reloaded after a specified amount of time by "pulling" the data from the server to your browser.

Client-Side Image: A method of processing mouse clicks and associated hyperlinks by embedding the hotspot coordinates and URLs directly in the Web page or in a file linked to the Web page using the <USEMAP> tag. Client-side imaging is processed on the user's own computer by the browser, rather than by doing the processing on the Web server's remote computer, and thus works faster and better than a server-side imagemap. (See *imagemap*.)

Client/Server: An arrangement of computers in which desktop computer systems, called clients, make use of data management services provided by another computer, called the server. The Web browser installed on the desktop computer acts as the client to the centralized computer at your Internet Access Provider's site, which in turn is hooked to thousands and thousands of other servers at remote sites.

Cobweb Site: A Web site that has not been updated for a substantial length of time and whose contents are obviously out of date. It is considered bad form to let your site become a "cobweb site."

Color Palette: A color palette directly relates to the pixel depth. A pixel depth of 8-bit color results in a 256 color palette. This defines the full range of colors that an image can be comprised of.

Comment Blocks: Comment blocks are primarily useful for placing author and copyright information or comments about the images. They are not visible when viewed through a Web browser.

Common Ground: Portable document software developed by Common Ground Software. It enables a user to save a file as read-only and to enable any number of users to view the file with the free reader utility. Users cannot change text.

Compression: A scheme that makes files smaller, usually by finding a pattern and substituting shorthand for the pattern.

Continuous Document Streaming: Instead of waiting for a document to be assembled *in toto* on your computer before it is displayed, the data is sent to your screen much more quickly and appears in stages.

.CPT: A filename extension that denotes a file created by the shareware program CompactPro.

Cyberspace: A term originally used in the novel *Neuromancer* by William Gibson to describe a computer network of the future that can be connected directly to peoples' minds. Now represents the Internet and/or the Web.

D

Digital Signature: A way for a certifying agency to sign an X.509 or other type of security certificate.

Disk Cache: A part of a computer's disk space set aside for storing/processing information.

Dithering: Dithering an image converts it to fewer colors while maintaining as close of a match as possible. It enables you to simulate intermediate color shades with clouds of points. It should be used with continuous-tone images. With dithering, the color table should be chosen so that the image isn't dithered a second time on the target machine.

Division: A significant section of a long HTML document, such as an appendix or glossary, and designated in HTML 3.0 by the <DIV CLASS=*name*> element.

DNS: Can stand for 1) Domain Name System; 2) Domain Name Service; 3) Domain Name Server. (See *domain name system or service* and *domain name.*)

Document Information: A window that displays general information, such as location and security status, about the Web page onscreen.

Domain Name: A textual alias for an IP address based on the domain name system. Components of a domain name are separated by a period. For example, an IP address for a computer might be 197.99.87.99; it might then have several aliases, one of which is www.mycomputer.com.

Domain Name Server: A computer that keeps track of addresses in a given organization or domain and routes requests to specific addresses.

Domain Name System or Service: A way of distributing information worldwide across the Internet so that no one computer, person, or organization has to keep track of everyone in the world. Instead, computers are assigned standard types of names depending on their domain, and domain name servers share information about their specific area with other computers. Computers in educational institutions are given names ending in the suffix .EDU, governmental offices have the suffix .GOV, commercial ones end in .COM, and so on.

Download: The act of copying a file from the Internet to your computer.

DPI (Dots Per Inch): The term used to measure the resolution of graphical images. Images on the Web need be only 72 dpi because that is all most computer monitors can translate anyway. The higher the dpi of the image, the slower the transfer rate.

E

Easter Egg: A hidden message, graphic, or other feature built into a program that users discover by typing or choosing undocumented commands.

Encoding: A way of translating Mac files that enables them to be served from a non-Macintosh platform.

EPS: Encapsulated PostScript. (See *PostScript.*)

Ethernet: A high-speed coaxial cable local area network that uses a bus topology (physical layout). Ethernet LANs are extensively used as the physical transmission medium for the Web.

External Image: An image that is not an inline image and thus part of an HTML document, but that resides in a separate file and is accessed by means of a hypertext link.

F

FAQs: Frequently Asked Questions. FAQs are often seen as sections of Web sites or as updated files posted to newsgroups or servers. They answer the most common questions on a certain topic. It's considered poor form to ask a question that's covered in a FAQ.

Firewall: A security system that restricts traffic between a secure network and the outside world. The secure host machine is the only computer in an organization actually connected to the Internet. Everyone in the organization must go through the host machine to connect to the Internet, and vice versa.

Fixed-Width Fonts: Fonts that have distorted letters so that they are all of the same width.

Flame: A "heated" message from a fellow surfer in regard to a breach of "netiquette."

Font: A set of characters that, together, make up a typeface such as Times or Helvetica.

Fonts: Netscape Preferences: General dialog box that enables the user to change the font used to display text.

Frame: A frame is 1) one sequence in an animated GIF consisting of the image and all associated blocks or 2) a segment of a Web page, separated by rules and treated as a separate entity by the browser. You can scroll separately in different frames even though they appear on the same "page."

Frame Offset: GIF Animations enable you to place each frame or image at specific X and Y coordinates relative to the primary frame. This enables you to animate small sections of an image while retaining a background image.

Frame Relay: High-speed packet switching protocol suited for data image transfer. Used with WANs (Wide Area Networks). Not the most efficient way of transmitting real-time voice and video.

Freeware: Software created by independent technoids and available to users free of charge by downloading it from the Internet or from local areas. (See *Shareware.*)

Frontier: A scripting environment for the Macintosh.

FTP: File Transfer Protocol; a method for transferring files to and from remote computers on the Internet. (See *Anonymous FTP.*)

G

GIF: Graphics Interchange Format; a file format commonly used with graphics or photos displayed on Web documents. It is the most supported and popular graphics format on the Web. Originally popularized by CompuServe.

GIF89a: An extension of the GIF standards that enables transparency of selected colors.

GIF Animation: Combining several GIFs into one image through scripting. When viewed through a Web Browser, the image flips through the various frames, creating animation.

Global History File: File that includes a record of all the Web sites you've visited since the last time the Global History File was updated.

Gopher: A text-only, menu-driven Internet information system developed at the University of Minnesota that preceded the Web. It's still very common, and most Web browsers can connect to Gopher servers.

Graphical User Interface: A browser program, such as Netscape, that provides a way for an individual user to graphically view the masses of information on the Internet with inline or external images, sounds, buttons, icons, and so on.

.GZ: Filename extension for a file compressed with the application Gnu Zip.

H

Helper Application: Programs that cooperate with Netscape and other browsers to perform functions, such as displaying the contents of files, that the browser cannot do. Browser plug-ins have made helper applications less critical, because plug-ins enable direct viewing of files on the Web.

History: A Netscape command (under the Window menu) that brings up a window containing many (not all) of the Web pages you have visited in the current session.

Hit Counter: A script on a Web server that calculates each "hit" or visit to a Web page every time a connection is made, and displays the current total on the page to the current user.

Home Page: The welcome page of a Web site; the place where visitors are supposed to start when finding out about a particular site.

HotJava: Dynamic Web browser developed by Sun Microsystems, Inc. that uses Sun's Java programming language. HotJava can execute "applets" or programs written in Java that can be included in HTML documents.

HREF Link: See *anchor* or *hypertext link*.

HTML: HyperText Markup Language; the set of commands used to mark up documents with standard elements so they can be displayed and read on the World Wide Web by different browsers on different computers. A subset of SGML (Standard Generalized Markup Language).

HTML Cookie: (Also called the HTML tag.) The tag "set" that makes up a complete HTML markup command. In <B>Attention!</B>, for example, the <B> </B> is the cookie.

HTTP: HyperText Transfer Protocol, the protocol used by Web servers to communicate with Web clients.

Hypertext Links: Also called an anchor. A hypertext link in an HTML document, usually distinguished by underlined or high-lighted text that, when selected, takes the user to another file or Web page. The hypertext link is added to the document by using the HTML tag, <A HREF> </A>.

I

IETF: Internet Engineering Task Force, the community of Internet users that determines how the Internet will evolve and operate. Most of its technical operations are conducted in workgroups. Maintains two types of Internet documents, Internet-Drafts and Requests for Comments (RFCs).

Imagemap: 1) The CGI program provided by HTTPd-based servers that processes active image hotspots during server-side imaging. 2) The name of the file that contains the mouse click coordinates and associated URLs for an active image. Imagemap files usually use the .map extension. 3) An older term for an active image that is going out of use with the advent of client-side imaging.

Index: A service on the Internet, such as Yahoo, that arranges information to help you select what you want to read (see `http://yahoo.com`).

Inline Image: A photo or graphic image that can be displayed in the window of a Web browser along with HTML text (as opposed to an external image, which must be downloaded and viewed with a separate program).

Interframe Delay: When creating animated GIFs, the interframe delay is the delay between the current frame and the following frame's renderings. It is specified in hundredths of seconds (100 means 1 second, for example).

Interlacing: A process that loads a GIF file in sections when viewed through a browser. By loading in different lines of an image rather than from the first line to the last, it becomes recognizable more quickly. The browser displays a low-resolution version first, a better version, and then a full-blown version.

Interlaced graphics are best used for large static images that take a long time to load. This way the user can see the image building while waiting for the entire image file to download. It's better that just staring a blank spot.

Internet: An international network of networks, originally started for military purposes, that connects about 40 million higher education, government, military, and commercial users.

Internet Explorer: Microsoft's fast, easy-to-use Web browser. Internet Explorer runs on Windows and Macintosh systems and is a direct competitor to Netscape Navigator.

IP: Internet Protocol. The set of standards by which information is transmitted on the Internet.

ISDN: Integrated Services Digital Network. A set of standards for transmitting voice, data, and video data simultaneously. A reasonably inexpensive way of getting higher bandwidth through a digital connection.

ISO: International Standards Organization. A group that defines computing and communications standards.

J

Java: Computer language developed by Sun Microsystems that enables the creation of "applets" or "live objects" that execute in response to mouse clicks and produce sound, video, or other effects within Netscape 2.0 or other Web browsers.

JPEG: Joint Photographic Experts Group; a graphic image compression format.

K

Keyword: Word(s) used in a search query.

Knowbot: A type of artificial intelligence software that roams the Web looking for information. You can use a knowbot such as KIS (Knowbot Information Service) to find a specific individual's location on the Internet, the name of a Web server, or other information.

L

LAN: Local Area Network; a network usually associated with a single office, building, or organization.

Launch: To start up an application.

Live Object: 1) A clickable element in an HTML document that responds to a user's mouse clicks by producing animation, sound, or other "live" effects within a Web browser window. 2) The new name for OpenDoc containers that can be embedded on a Web page to process Java applets.

Link Location Bar: A text-entry window that contains the URL of the site onscreen, or a site, file, or object you want to go to.

M

MacBinary: A standard for storing resources in a Macintosh file's data fork. Also, the name of an application that both decodes and encodes MacBinary files.

MacTCP: Apple Computer software that enables a Macintosh to interact with other computers via TCP/IP.

Memory Cache: A part of a computer's RAM (Random Access Memory, the memory used to run applications) set aside to process/store information.

MIME: Multipurpose Internet Mail Extensions, a standard used for transmitting varying file formats across computing platforms.

Modem: Short for MOdulator/DEModulator. A device that connects a computer to a phone line. It converts the computer's digital signals to analog audio frequencies so they can be transmitted over phone lines.

Mosaic: A graphical information browser for the World Wide Web developed at NCSA. (See *NCSA*.) Its user-friendly interface was instrumental in the Web's popularity.

MPEG: Moving Pictures Experts Group; a movie file format commonly used on the Web.

N-O

NCSA: National Center for Supercomputing Applications at the University of Illinois at Urbana-Champaign. An interdisciplinary group consisting of scientists, artists, engineers, educators, and others involved in computational science. The place where NCSA Mosaic was born.

Netiquette: A set of rules of behavior on the Internet that cautions against using abusive or offensive language in electronic communications, invading privacy, sending out "chain letters" or unsolicited requests for business, and so on.

Netscape Navigator: A fast, easy-to-use graphical information browser for the World Wide Web that was developed by some of the same people who created Mosaic. Created by Netscape Communications Corporation.

Newbie: A newcomer, someone just getting started on the Internet.

News Server: A machine that collects postings, sorts them, and passes them along to other servers required to use Usenet. Also called a NNTP (Net News Transfer Protocol) server.

NNTP Server: See *News Server.*

NSFNet: National Science Foundation Network, which linked researchers with high-speed supercomputer centers. For a while, this was the "backbone" of the Internet.

P

Parser: A module or routine within a program that reads or "parses" computer code and processes it to make it usable or readable.

PDF: Portable Document Format in which documents created with Adobe Acrobat portable document software are presented. Acrobat documents end with the suffix .PDF.

Perl (Practical Extraction and Report Language): A cross-platform computer language whose features make it very useful for writing CGI scripts that will run on various servers.

Photoshop: Common parlance for Adobe Photoshop, image editing software that allows a number of sophisticated graphics functions such as retouching and editing of images on personal computers.

ph Server: Served database of email addresses and other personal information about users on a particular network, often maintained by educational institutions.

PICT: A graphics file defined with the Mac's QuickDraw screen description language.

Pixel Depth: Refers to the number of colors that comprise an image. It is calculated by taking two to the xth power with x being the bit number. For example 256 colors would be 8-bit color (2^8). Because most users have only 256 pixels of color, it is always a good idea to limit images to 8-bit color.

Plain Text Blocks: Plain text blocks specify text to be overlaid on an image. The position and color of the text can be controlled.

Plug-in: Plug-ins are software components that extend your browser's capabilities—giving you, for example, the ability to play audio samples or view video movies from within the browser. Generally, plug-in installation requires you to save the plug-in to your hard drive, then double-click the saved file to start the installation. You tell your browser which type of plug-in you have installed, and it knows from then on what to do when it comes across this type of file.

Pop-up Menu: Generally, this describes any menu that "pops up" on your Macintosh screen; Netscape's main pop-up menu appears when you click and hold the mouse button over a Web page.

PostScript: A page description/programming language developed by Adobe Systems, Inc. It describes a page in a way that is device-independent so that the quality of the output depends on the resolution of the device on which it is printed.

Private Key: A Web user's personal key, which is never distributed on the Internet, used in public/private key transactions. A key is a very complicated encrypted series of numbers that would take so long to decode that it's essentially unbreakable. Enables a user to read encrypted messages while others cannot.

Progressive JPEG Image: A JPEG image that, like an interlaced GIF image, loads gradually onto your computer and appears onscreen before it is fully loaded, so you can identify an image sooner.

Proportional Fonts: Fonts that vary in width from character to character.

Protocol: A specific method of communication or "conversation" for exchanging information on the Internet. SMTP, FTP, HTTP, and NNTP are all protocols.

Proxy: A software application that is allowed to pass information through a firewall. A firewall is a security system in which one computer, a secure host machine, is the only one in an organization that is actually connected to the Internet. Everyone in the organization must go through the host machine to connect to the Internet, and vice versa.

Public Key: Widely distributed key used in public/private key transactions. A key is a very complicated encrypted series of numbers that would take so long to decode that it's essentially unbreakable. The benefit of a public key is that it is widely available. The fact that a public key is widely available does not lessen security because the public key works only with a private key. (See *Private Key*.)

Q-R

QuickTime: A method developed by Apple Computer for storing movie and audio files in digital format.

QuickTime VR: Hot new format that allows visual representations of scenes wherein you can pan around a full 360 degrees by clicking-and-dragging.

Quote: A button in the Message Composition dialog box that enables you to import the contents of the current page into the text-entry field.

Relevance Feedback: Feature of a Wide Area Information Server (WAIS) that ranks answers judged to be most relevant to your query by putting them highest on a list and scoring them on a scale of 1,000.

RFC: Request for Comments, the agreed-upon designation by which all methods of communicating over the Internet, such as the various versions of HTML, are developed and defined.

Robot: A program such as InfoSeek or Aliweb that searches huge numbers of files automatically when given search criteria (also called a worm).

S

Script Editor: Application that comes with the full AppleScript 1.1 implementation that enables you to build AppleScripts.

Search Engine: A program used by a search service, such as InfoSeek, that takes you through the Internet to find what you want to read. Also called Web "crawlers," "spiders," wanderers," or "worms"; they automatically journey across cyberspace, visiting huge numbers of Web sites and recording titles and some of the contents of individual documents. When you send a search request to a service with such an engine, your request is checked against the index that the engine has already compiled.

Server Push: One way of creating dynamic documents whose contents are refreshed periodically by "pushing" data to your browser.

Server-Side Imaging: An older method of processing active images that uses software located on the server, typically Imagemap CGI on HTTPd-based servers, to process mouse click coordinates and their associated URLs to retrieve the linked page.

SGML: Standard Generalized Markup Language, an agreed-upon international standard for specifying and marking up documents. HTML is a subset of SGML.

Shareware: Software created by independent technoids and available for downloading to anyone for a trial time. At the end of that time, users are asked to pay a fee if they decide to keep the software. (See *Freeware.*)

S-HTTP: Secure HyperText Transfer Protocol, a security standard established by EIT/Terisa Systems.

Signature File: A text file appended to the bottom of your email messages and news postings. Commonly called .sig files. Best kept to about four lines.

Silicon Graphics, Inc. (SGI): Silicon Graphics, Inc., a manufacturer of computer hardware and software, including the Indy workstation. Actively exploring virtual reality applications on the Web. (See *VRML.*)

.SIT: Filename extension that denotes a file created by one of the StuffIt software programs, such as StuffIt Expander. Denotes a "stuffed" or "archived" file.

SLIP: Serial Line Internet Protocol. A way of using TCP/IP over a serial line, such as a dial-up modem. A very common way of connecting to the Internet from home. Often referred to as a point-to-point connection. Also lovingly referred to as "slirp."

SMTP: Simple Mail Transfer Protocol. A set of standard procedures for transferring mail.

Spider: See *Search Engine.*

StuffIt Expander: Freeware published by Aladdin Systems that decodes and decompresses encoded files that have also been compressed.

Sun: Sun Microsystems, Inc., a company that makes high-performance workstations and servers using its SPARC architecture. Its Solaris operating system is based on Unix.

Symmetrical Cryptography: A coding scheme that uses a single key to encode and decode messages. Some schemes, such as public key cryptography, require both a public and private key to decode messages. (See *Public Key* and *Private Key.*)

Style Sheet: A text file that defines the stylistic elements of a series of HTML files. Style Sheets are not supported by PageMill, except as objects that can be placed in HTML Placeholders. Style Sheet files, designated by the .sty extension, are a part of HTML Version 3.2 and provide the benefit of allowing organizations to impose a "house style" on Web pages that can be changed on all pages by editing a single .sty file.

T

TCP/IP: Transmission Control Protocol/Internet Protocol, a packet-based communication protocol that forms the foundation of the Internet.

Telnet: An application developed at the University of Illinois that acts as a sort of intermediary application to other programs running on remote computers on the Internet.

TIFF: Tagged Image File Format, a format for storing computerized image files.

Title Bar: Appears at the top of the screen; gives you the title of the document currently displayed.

Transparency: Defined in the GIF89a standards, transparency allows you to take an image and define one color as being transparent. This is useful in Web sites by allowing the background color or image to show through.

Transparent GIF: A GIF image that appears to float directly atop a Web page without its own background or border. A specific number in the GIF color palette (#89) is assigned to be the same color as the background of the page, giving the image a transparent appearance.

U-W

Unix: A multi-user/multitasking operating system developed by AT&T and written in the C programming language (also developed by AT&T). Its TCP/IP protocols are integral to the Internet.

URL: Uniform Resource Locator. A standard address for a file or location on the Internet. URLs always begin with an Internet protocol (FTP, Gopher, HTTP), an Internet host name, folders, and the destination file or object.

Usenet Newsgroups: A global computer network run by the community of Internet users that can be accessed either from within or outside the Internet. (Usenet is short for User's Network.) A tremendously popular means of sharing information over the Internet. Usenet is older and more extensive than the Web.

VRML: Virtual Reality Modeling Language (VRML; sometimes pronounced "vur-mole"). It has been proposed as a standard way of describing virtual reality experiences accessed via the Internet and integrated with the hypertextual power of the Web.

WAIS: Wide Area Information Server. WAIS was developed as a way of allowing big businesses to search for electronic information quickly and easily from a large number of sources by using English-language queries.

WAN: Wide Area Network. A communications system that spans great distances, as opposed to a LAN.

.WAV: A format for storing audio files that is native to Microsoft Windows-based systems and is not as portable as .AU formatted files.

Web Crawler: See *Search Engine.*

Web Project: A term used to describe a collection of Web pages that are in development. Web projects are independent of the Web servers that serve them.

Web Server: A computer set up to exchange information with another computer over the Internet using one or more standard protocols, such as HTTP, FTP, Gopher, and so on.

Web Site: A collection of Web pages residing on a Web server. Web sites are usually synonymous with a URL. One server can host several Web sites by providing URLs that define a path to the Web site. Some types of computers can support multiple unique URLs on a single server.

Webmaster: Someone who both creates Web pages and manages a Web server.

Web Publisher: A person who creates Web pages.

What's Cool: A page on Netscape's Web site that lists "cool" sites you might want to visit.

What's New: A page on Netscape's Web site that lists pages that have recently come online.

World Wide Web (Web): A subset of the Internet that enables hypertextual navigation and multimedia presentation of information globally.

Worm: See *Search Engine.*

X-Z

.ZIP: Filename extension for a file created by PKZip, the standard compression software used in the world of DOS and Windows.

INDEX

Symbols

(pound sign), numbered lists, 94
/ (backslash) (URLs), 126
@ (at sign) (addresses), 125
3-D images, 346-347
4-bit color graphics, downloading, 59
6-bit color graphics, downloading, 59

A

<A> tags, 234
absolute pathnames, 126-127, 379
accessing
    corporate servers, 315
    ISPs, 315
    online services, 313-314
    WWW, 312-315
Acrobat (portable document software),
    349, 379
Action (video player), 343
Action field, 221
active images, 137-139, 141-142, 277-278,
    302, 379
    colors, changing, 150-151
    coordinates, 154
    creating, 147, 148-153
    defining region of, 147
    mapping, 139-141
    pixels, 146-151
    preparing Web sites, 144-146
    URLs, 141
    workings of, 142-146
    see also imagemaps
active links, 82
Active Links menu commands,
    Custom, 83
active maps, *see* active images
ActiveX, 334-335, 337
adding
    borders, tables, 178, 180
    cells, tables, 182-183
    objects, tables, 185
    targets, frames, 192-194
    text, tables, 171
    see also inserting
Address format, 306
address restrictions, URLs, 125
<Address> tags, 234

addresses
  defined, 380
  domain names, 384
  URLs, 124-126
adjusting cell width, 174-176
  Inspector, 175
  mouse, 175
  No Wrap, 176
  see also editing
Adobe Acrobat sites, 350
Adobe Illustrator, 226
Adobe Photoshop, 226
Adobe SiteMill
  links
      repairing, 324
      replacing, 325-326
  sites, managing, 323-328
AIFF (Audio Interchange File Format)
  defined, 380
  file extensions, 231, 341
Align Center buttons (toolbars), 230
Align objects, 172
aligning
  cell content, 176
  form elements, 205
  text to images, 106-107
alignment, paragraph formatting, 85-86
Allow Multiple Selections boxes, 214
Alternate Label dialog boxes, 108
America Online, 14, 380
America Online (AOL), 313-314
American Standard Code for
  Information Interchange, *see* ASCII
Analog counter, 276
anchor icons, 151, 230
anchors
  creating links, 129-131
  defined, 380
  naming, 130

animated GIFs, 280, 345
  defined, 380, 387
  frame offset, 386
  interframe delay, 389
animations, 278-280, 345-346
  Client-Pull, 279
  Server-Push, 279
anonymous FTP, defined, 380
anti-aliasing, *see* halo effect
AOL (America Online), 313-314
Apache, 313
Apache Unix server, 156
appearance, design
  data collection, 53
  file preparation, 57-59
  interrelationships of pages, 53-54
  links, 54-56
  Web sites, 44, 51-63
Apple Color Wheel dialog boxes, 177
Apple Color Wheel windows, 77
Apple Computer, Inc., Web sites, 48
Apple Desktop Patterns Control
  Panels, 34
Apple Internet Server Solution, 283
AppleScript
  defined, 380
  Script Editor, 395
AppleScript/Frontier, CGI scripts, 275
AppleSearch, 283
AppleSearch.acgi, 283
Applet Object screen, 255
<APPLET> tags, 231
applets
  defined, 380
  Java, 254-256
      animation, 345
      identifying, 255
      placing, 254-256

applications
    CGI part, 260
    helper, 347-349
    launching, 390
applying tag pairs to format items, 229
Aretha (Frontier freeware release), 380
ARPAnet, defined, 380
ASCII (American Standard Code for InformationInterchange)
    character set, Latin-1, 239-240
    characters, adding special, 238-240
    code set, 238
assessing imagemap files, 153-154
at sign (@), in addresses, 125
attributes
    Cell Padding, 181
    HTML tags, defined, 381
    ISMAP, 156
    <IMG> tags, 140
    MAP NAME, 156
    modifying, tags, 229-230
    Table, 170, 177
    Table Cell, 170, 174
    USEMAP, 139
.AU (audio file)
    defined, 381
    file extensions, 231
audience of Web site, content design, 47-48
audio
    file formats
        QuickTime, 394
        .WAV, 398
    broadcasting, 340-342
    files (.AU), defined, 381
Audio Interchange File Format, *see* AIFF
audio/video file, *see* .AVI
autoscrolling, 131

.AVI (audio/video file)
    defined, 381
    file extensions, 231
    file formats, 343

B

<B> tags, 234
backend program, part of form, 198
background colors, cells
    adding, 176-177
    changing, 174
Background Image dialog boxes, 75
background images, download time, decreasing, 59
Background menus, 177
Background menu commands, Custom, 177
background patterns, inserting, 75
backgrounds
    colors
        editing, 78-82
        default, 78
        multiple, 76
    images
        deleting, 82
        editing, 79-82
backslash (/), in URLs, 126
bandwidth, 289
    defined, 381
    multimedia transmission, 348-349
<Base> tags, 234
<Basefont> tags, 234
.bat file extensions, 264
batch files, running, CGI scripts, 264
<Big> tags, 249
binary, defined, 381
BinHex encoding, defined, 381

bitmaps
    defined, 381
    images, 147
<Blink> tags, 234, 241
block-level, Body elements, 232
<Blockquote> tags, 234
blocks, GIF files, defined, 381
Body, HTML documents, 232-240
<Body> tags, 234-235
Body elements
    block-level, 232
    text-level, 232
    see also Content Tags
body text, colors, editing, 76-78
Body text menu commands, Custom, 77
Bold buttons, toolbars, 70
Bold commands (Style menu), 70
bold text
    Bold physical style, 89
    Strong logical style, 88
bookmarks, defined, 381
Boolean queries, defined, 381
borders, tables
    adding, 180
    changing, 180
    deleting, 180
    images, editing, 112-120

 tags, 93, 232, 235
Browser-safe Palettes, Web sites, 59
browsers
    component-based programming
        ActiveX, 334-335
        features, 330-337
        Java, 332-334
        OpenDoc, 336-337
    Cyberdog, 336
    defined, 382
    helper applications, 347-349
    history, 13-14
    HotJava, 388

HTML tag support, 241-243
Internet Explorer, defined, 389
Mosaic, 391
Netscape Navigator, 392
    dragging links, 133
plugins, 331-332
text enhancement, 20-22
browsers (Web), 288-289
building CGIs, 223
Bullet List commands
    (Format menu), 92
Bulleted List commands (List menu),
    92, 95
bulleted lists, 91
    converting to numbered, 95
    creating, 91-93
    defined, 91
Butler SQL, 281
buttons, defined, 3
Button radio buttons, Object mode
    screen, 114
buttons
    Align Center, 230
    alignment, 172
    Bold, toolbars, 70
    Center Align Text, toolbars, 70, 86,
        183, 352
    Circle hotspot, 149
    Delete Row, 182
    Edit Mode, 24, 72
    Find Next, Find and Replace dialog
        boxes, 117
    form elements, 199, 201-207
    Horizontal Rules, toolbars, 72
    Indent Left, toolbars, 86
    Indent Right, toolbars, 86
    Insert Check Boxes, 205, 217, 352
    Insert Columns, 183
    Insert Horizontal Rules, toolbars,
        97, 352
    Insert Multi-line, 352

Insert Password Field, 201, 210
Insert Popup, 206, 353
Insert Radio Buttons, 203, 204,
    215, 352
Insert Reset, 353
Insert Rows, 182
Insert Single-lines, 352
Insert Submit, 353
Insert Tables, 166, 168
Insert Text Areas, 210
Insert Text Fields, 201, 202, 209
Join Cells, 183
Left Align Text, 71, 352
Middle Align Object, toolbars, 106
Object, 159
Place Object
    inserting images, 104-105
    toolbar, 71
Pointer toosl, 149
Polygon hotspots, 149
Preview, 72
Preview/Edit modes, 24, 353
Quote, Message Composition
    dialog boxes, 394
radio
    cloning, 203-204
    offering options with, 215-216
    working with, 203-205
Rectangle hotspots, 149
Remove Columns, 183
renaming, 220
Replace, Find and Replace dialog
    boxes, 117
Replace All, Find and Replace
    dialog boxes, 117
Replace and Find, Find and
    Replace dialog boxes, 117
Reset, 201, 220-223
Row, 182
Split Cells, 184
styles, 171

Submit, 201, 220-223, 271
Tables, 169, 182
Target, 192
Top Align Object, toolbars, 106
types, 201
see also icons

C

C language, CGI scripts, 274-275
C scripts
    Forms.acgi, 274
    NetForms, 274
cache, defined, 382
cascading, style sheets, creating, 250-251
case sensitivity, 228
catalog sites (Web), 50
cell contents
    aligning, 176
    selecting, 170
cell padding
    attribute, 181
    defined, 178
Cell Padding text boxes, 178, 181
cell spacing, defined, 178
Cell Spacing text boxes, 181
cells
    adding, 182-183
    background colors
        adding, 176-177
        changing, 174
    copying, 171
    defined, 165
    deleting, 182-183
    formatting
        Inspector, 174-177
        toolbars, 171-174
    joining, 183-184
    moving, 170-171

selecting, 170, 170-171
splitting, 183-184
width
    adjusting, 174-177
    Inspector, 175
    mouse, 175
    No Wrap, 176
Center Align buttons, 183, 352
center alignment, paragraphs, 85
<center> tags, 235
Center Text alignment buttons,
    toolbars, 70
CERN (European Laboratory for
    Particle Physics), 382
certificate information, defined, 382
CGIs (Common Gateway Interfaces)
    building, 223
    database, 281-283
    defined, 382
    forms, running, 265
    information, sending, 221
    parts
        applications, 260
        URL, 260
        Web servers, 260
    programs, 50
    Programmer's Reference, Web
        sites, 262
    ROFM, 223
    scripts, 259-260
    Unix CGIs, 268
    writing, 261-263
CGI scripts
    AppleScript/Frontier, 275
    C language, 274-275
    configuring, 266-269
    examples, 273
    form processing, 274
    form-based, 270-271
    headers, 260
    interpreters, 267

on server, 261
parameters, 270
permissions, 267
running, 263-269
    batch files, 264
    Mac servers, 264-265
    Windows servers, 264-265
setup files, 266
Visual Basic, 274
cgi-bin
    features, 259, 264
    directories, 382
changing
    borders, table, 180
    colors
        active images, 150-151
        hotspot, 150-151
        table text, 172-173
    field sizes, 209
    spacing
        table columns, 181
        table rows, 181
    tables
        widths, 178
        borders, 180
        Cell attributes, 170
        sizes, 179
    see also editing
character formatting styles
    logical, 88-89
    physical, 89-90
character formatting tags, 249
character styles
    Citation, 172
    defined, 382
    Emphasis, 172
    Strong, 172

characters
    adding special, 238-240
    limiting number, fields, 209
    Style menu, 90
Checkbox screens, 217-218
checkboxes, 201
    No Wrap, 176
    options, 217-218
    procedures, 203-205
CineWeb (video player), 344
Circle hotspots, 149, 152
Citation logical styles, 88
.class (file extensions), 231
<CLASS> tags, 251
clickable
    images, *see* imagemaps
    maps, *see* active images
    regiions, creating, 152
client-pull
    animations, 279
    defined, 383
client-side
    images, defined, 383
    mapping, 139-146
client/server, defined, 383
clients, defined, 289, 382
cloning radio buttons, 203-204
Center alignment buttons, 172
cobweb sites, defined, 383
Code logical style, 89
collecting data, Web site design, 53
collection information, part of form,
    198
colors
    backgrounds
        default, 78
        editing, 78-82
    body text, editing, 76-78
    links, editing, 82-84
Color Palette icons, 150

color palettes, defined, 383
Color Panel, 173, 176
    backgrounds, changing, 78-82
    commands (Windows menu), 41
    link colors, 83
color schemes, download time,
    decreasing, 59
colors
    backgrounds, multiple, 76
    selecting, 41
    setting, Inspector Page Screen,
        33-35
columns
    cells, adjusting widths, 175
    spacing, tables, 181
com suffix, domain names, 125
command formatting, tables, 165
Command key shortcuts, menu bars, 30
Command-Enter, 353
Command-H, 244
commands
    Active Links menu, Custom, 83
    Background menu, Custom, 177
    Body text menu, Custom, 77
    Bulleted List menu, Numbered, 95
    Edit menu
        Copy, 30, 129
        Cut, 30
        HTML Source, 228, 244-245
        Insert Invisible, 271
        Insert Invisibles, 252
        Insert Placeholder, 248
        Paste, 30, 129
        Preference, 25
        Preferences, 66, 144
        Remove Link, 134
        Source, 239
    File menu
        New Page, 70, 74, 159
        Open, 135, 159

Save, 74, 118
Save Frame, 193
Save Frameset As, 191
Save Page As, 118
Upload the Page, 319
Find What menu, Page Content, 116
Font menu, Heading, 71
Format menu
Bulleted List, 92
Definition format, 96
Heading, 85
Indent Left, 88
Indent Right, 87-88
Largest Heading, 71
List, 92, 94-96
Paragraph, 71
Term, 96
formatting, Frames, 165
List menu
Bulleted List, 95
Definition, 96
Numbered, 94
Term, 96
Normal Links menu, Custom, 83
Place, 231
Place Object, 280
Scope menu, Object, 116
Search menu
Find, 116-117
Spelling Checker, 117
Site menu, Replace Links, 325
Style menu
Bold, 70
Emphasis, 70
Lists, 90
Visited Links menu, Custom, 83

Window menu
Show Color Panel, 78, 173
Show Inspector, 33
Show Pasteboard, 38, 103
Window menu (Netscape), History, 387
Windows menu, Color Panel, 41, 83
comment blocks, defined, 383
comments
adding to Web pages, 252-253
tags, 253, 256
Comments icons, 252
commercial online services, Internet access, 313-314
Common Gateway Interfaces (CGIs) see CGIs
Common Ground (portable document software), 383
component-based programming
ActiveX, 334-335
Java, 332-334
OpenDoc, 336-337
compressions
defined, 383
digital video, 343
GIF images, 58
JPEG images, 58
CompuServe
features, 313-314
history, 14
conditionals, see if...then statements
configuring CGI scripts, 266-269
constraining image proportions, 111
constructing Web sites
home pages, 60
images for navigation, 62-63
support pages, 61
content area
Edit window, 26, 29
sizing, 29

content design, Web sites
audience, 47-48
purpose of site, 45-47
structure, 48-51
content tags, 232
CONTENT_LENGTH variables, NCSA
server, 268
CONTENT_TYPE variables, NCSA
server, 268
continuous document streaming,
defined, 383
control panels (Apple Desktop
Patterns), 34
controls, ActiveX, 334-335
converting
bulleted lists to numbered, 95
images to GIF format, 80
numbered lists to bulleted, 95
cookies (HTML), defined, 388
CoolFusion (video player), 344
coordinates
active images, 154
hotspots, determining, 146
Copy commands (Edit menu), 30, 129
copying
cells, 171
links, 129
source codes, 245
copyrights, 46
corporate presence sites (Web), 48
corporate servers, 315
counters
Analog, 276
Count, 276
Count WWWebula, 276
Internet Audit, 276
Logger.cgi, 276
Market Focus, 276
NetCloak, 277
ServerStat, 276

.CPT file extensions, 384
Create Table dialog boxes, 169
creating
bulleted lists, 91
clickable regions, 152
definition lists, 95-96
directory lists, 93
forms, 198-199
frames, 188-191
hidden fields, 271
hypertext links, 230
links
anchors, 129-131
copy and paste, 132
dagging-and-dropping, 131
other Web sites, 133
Page icon, 127-129
tables, 185-186
typing URL, 132
lists, 90-96
menu lists, 93
nested lists, 95
new Web pages, 70
numbered lists, 94-95
placeholders, 108
pop-up menus, 211-213
rectangle regions, Rectangle
hotspot, 149
style sheets, cascading, 250-251
tables, 166-169
term lists, 95-96
Crescendo Plus (audio player), 341
Custom commands
Active Links menu, 83
Background menu, 177
Body text menu, 77
Normal Links menu, 83
Visited Links menu, 83
Cut command (Edit menu), 30

Cyberdog, 336
CyberPound Site, 336
cyberspace, defined, 384

D

data
    retrieving from forms, 222-223
    collection, Web site design, 53
    repository, 281
databases
    CGIs, 281-283
    processing, 281-283
    scripts, requirements
        data repository, 281
        display page, 281
        script taking from database,
            281
        script writing to database, 281
    multimedia, 338-340
DATE_GMT variables, NCSA server, 268
DATE_LOCAL variables, NCSA server,
    268
decreasing download time, 59
default
    alignment, paragraphs, 85
    colors, backgrounds, 78
    paragraph indentations, 88
defining
    image region, 147
    objects' purpose, 198
definition
    commands (List menu), 96
    formats (Format menu), 96
    lists, 91
        creating, 95-96
Delete Row buttons, toolbars, 182

deleting
    background images, 82
    borders, tables, 178, 180
    cells, tables, 182-183
    links, 134
design theory, Web pages, applications,
    299-307
design tools, Web sites, 57
designing Web sites
    appearance, 51-63
    construction, 60-63
    content, 44-51
    first generation, 292
    folder organization, 65-67
    scientific approach, 296-298
    second generation, 293-294
    third generation, 295
desktop publishing
    controls, PageMill 2.0, 4
    history, 14-15
destination documents, defined, 121
dialog boxes
    Alternate Label, 108
    Apple Color Wheel, 177
    Background Image, 75
    Create Table, 169
    Find and Replace, 116-117
    Message Composition, Quote
        buttons, 394
    Open, 35, 67, 159
    Open File, 71, 79
    Preferences, 102, 145, 153
        Server window, 66-67
    Replace Links, 325
    Save As, 118
    Save Frameset As, 191
    Spelling Checker, 117
    Uploading, 319

digital
audio, 341
signatures, 384
video, 343-344
Director (animations), 345-346
directories
features, 233
lists, creating, 91-93
paths, URLs, 125
Unix, 66
Web site design, 65
disk caches, defined, 384
dithering, defined, 384
division (HTML documents), 384
DNS (Domain Name System), 384
.doc (file extensions), 231
document information, defined, 384
Document Structure tags, 232
Document-Based Query, 263
DOCUMENT_NAME variables, NCSA server, 268
DOCUMENT_URI variables, NCSA server, 268
documents, parts
Body, 232-240
Head, 232-233
Domain Name Servers (DNS), defined, 384, 385
domain names
defined, 384
suffixes, 125
URL parts, defined, 125
dots per inch (dpi), defined, 385
downloading
defined, 385
speeding up, 59
dpi (dots per inch), 385

dragging-and-dropping
links, creating, 131
images
features, 99-102
GIF icons, 158-159
Pasteboard forms, 203

E

Easter eggs, defined, 385
Edit menu
commands
Copy, 30, 129
Cut, 30
HTML Source, 228, 239, 244-245
Insert Invisible, 271
Insert Invisibles, 252
Insert Placeholder, 248
Paste, 30, 129
Preference, 25
Preferences, 66, 144
Remove Link, 134
features, 30
Edit mode, 158, 206, 214, 216
buttons, 24, 72
Inspector palette, 76
windows, 72
Edit windows
content area, 29
link location bars, 29
sizing, 29
toolbars, 27-29
editing
backgrounds
colors, 78-82
images, 79-82
body text colors, 76-78
defined regions, 153

images
　　borders, 112-120
　　Inspector palette, 107
links
　　colors, 82-84
　　names, 133
placeholders, 248
unrecognized HTMLs, 251
edu suffix, domain names, 125
electronic publishing, 349-350
elements, forms
　　buttons, 199, 201-207
　　fields, 199-200
　　pop-up menus, 199-200
Email.acgi, AppleScript/Frontier scripts, 275
embedded images, *see* inline images
Emphasis
　　commands (Style menu), 70
　　logical styles, 88
Encapsulated PostScript, *see* EPS
encoding files, defined, 385
Enliven (animation player), 346
Enterprise Server (Netscape), 313
environment variables, NCSA servers, 267-268
EPS (encapsulated PostScript)
　　features, 349, 385
　　files, 80
Ethernet, defined, 385
EveryWare Development, 282
extensions
　　.bat, 264
　　.sty, 250
　　files, 231
external images, defined, 385

F

FAQs (Frequently Asked Questions), 385
Fastrack Server (Netscape), 313
features, new to PageMill 2.0, 3-5
Fetch, uploading pages, 316
field types
　　password fields, 200
　　text areas, 200
　　text fields, 200
fields
　　Action, 221
　　defined, 200
　　form elements, 199-200
　　hidden, creating, 271
　　inserting text, 202
　　naming, 207
　　Password, setting, 219
　　setting character limit, 209
　　sizing, 209
file extensions, 231
file formats
　　.AIFF, 380
　　.AU, defined, 381
　　.AVI
　　　　defined, 381
　　　　formats, 343
　　.CPT, 384
　　EPS, 80
　　.GZ, 387
　　MPEG, 343
　　PCX, 80
　　PDFs, 349-350
　　PICT, 80, 392
　　QuickTime, 343, 394
　　QuickTime VR, 347, 394
　　selecting, 57-59
　　.SIT, 396

TIFF, 397

.WAV file format, 341, 398

.ZIP, 398

File menu

commands

New Page, 70, 74, 159

Open, 135, 159

Save, 74, 118

Save Frame, 193

Save Frameset As, 191

Save Page As, 118

Upload the Page, 319

features, 30-31

File Transfer Protocol, *see* FTP

files

downloading, defined, 385

encoding, defined, 385

naming, 74-75

organizing, 65-67

root directories, 65-67

preparing, Web site design, 57-59

Find and Replace dialog boxes, 116-117

Find buttons, Find and Replace dialog boxes, 117

Find commands (Search menu), 116-117

Find Next buttons, Find and Replace dialog boxes, 117

Find Object/Deep, searching levels, 116

Find Page/not Deep, searching levels, 116

Find What menu commands, Page Content, 116

Finder list boxes, 159

firewalls, defined, 386

fixed-width fonts, defined, 386

flames, defined, 386

folders

icons, Resource folder window, 66

Local Resource, setting preferences, 145

organizing Web site files, 65-67

pathnames, 67

Font Color menu, 41

Font menu

commands, Heading, 71

toolbar, 177

Font tags, 235

fonts

defined, 386

fixed-width, 386

monospaced logical styles, 88-89

proportional

defined, 393

Plain physical styles, 89

ForeSight Technologies, 282

<FORM ACTION> tags, 263

form elements

aligning, 205

buttons, 199

modifying, 203

Form modes, 221-222

<Form> tags, 235

format items, applying tag pairs, 229

Format menu

commands

Bullet List, 92

Definition format, 96

Heading, 85

Indent Left, 88

Indent Right, 87, 88

List, 92, 94, 95, 96

Paragraph, 71

Term, 96

features, 172, 229

formatting
   cells
      Inspector, 174-177
      toolbars, 171-174
   characters, styles
      logical, 88-89
      physical, 89-90
   paragraphs
      alignment, 85-86
      entire text, 85
      heading styles, 85
      indentations, 86-88
   tables, Inspector, 177-181
   Web pages
      background colors, 78-82
      background images, 79-82
      body text colors, 76-78
      link colors, 82-83, 83-84
forms
   CGIs, running, 265
   creating, 198-199
   data, retrieving, 222-223
   defined, 197
   dragging-and-dropping,
      Pasteboard, 203
   elements
      buttons, 199, 201-207
      fields, 199-200
      pop-up menus, 199-200
   limited by PageMill, 199
   parts
      backend program, 198
      information collection, 198
   planning, 199
   setting up, 207-218
Forms screen, Inspector palettes, 33, 36
Forms.acgi
   C script, 274
   features, 283
Fourth Dimension, 282

frames
   adding targets, 192-194
   creating, 188-191
   defined, 188, 386
   formating
      commands, 165
      settings, 189-191
   framesets, creating, 191
   offset, defined, 386
   relay, defined, 386
   screen, Inspector palette, 33,
      36-37, 90
   target, defined, 188
   Target menu, 192
   targets, setting up, 192-193
   tags, 187
<FRAMESET> tags, 187
Framesets
   creating, 191
   defined, 188
freeware, defined, 386
Frequently Asked Questions (FAQs), 385
Frontier (scripting environments), 386
FTP (file-transfer protocol)
   anonymous FTP, 380
   defined, 386
functions, CGI scripts, 259-260
future of the Web
   3-D images, 346-347
   animations, 345-346
   audio broadcasting, 340-342
   bandwidth, 348-349
   component-based programming
   digital video, 343-344
   electronic publishing, 349-350
   multimedia databases, 338-340

G

Gamelan Web sites, 333

GATEWAY_INTERFACE variables, NCSA server, 267

Get/Post menu, 221

.gif (file extensions), 231

GIF89a extension, 387

GifBuilder, 280

GIFs (Graphics Interchange Formats)
    animations
        features, 345
        interframe delay, 389
    defined, 387
    file formats (Web), 58-59
    frame offset, defined, 386
    files, blocks, 381
    GIF89a extensions, defined, 387
    icons
        dragging and dropping, 158-159
        features, 159
    interlacing, defined, 389
    transparent, 397

Global History files, 387

Globe icons, copying links, 132

Gopher, 287
    defined, 387
    history, 12

Graphical User Interface (GUI), 387

graphics
    editing, Out-of-Place, 157-162
    Interchange Formats, *see* GIFs
    see also images

grouping, hypertext links, 303-304

Guestbooks, 273-275

GUIs (Graphical User Interfaces), 387

.GZ file extensions, 387

H

<h1> tags, 229, 235

halo effects, transparent images, 59

head of HTML documents, 232-233

<HEAD> tags, 232-233, 236, 256

headers, CGI scripts, 260

Heading commands (Font menu), 71

Heading commands (Format menu), 85

heading styles, paragraph formatting, 85

helper applications, 347-349, 387

hidden fields
    creating, 271
    icons, 271
    screens, 271

hiding HTML tags, 244

History commands (Netscape Window menu), 387

history of active images, 138-139

hit counters, defined, 388

home pages
    defined, 388
    sections, 60
    Web site design, 60

Horizontal Align radio buttons, 176

horizontal rules
    aligning, 86
    buttons, toolbar, 72
    inserting, 72, 97-99
    resizing, 72, 97

hosts, defined, 125

HotJava browser, 388

hotlinks *see* hypertext links

hotspots, 62
    colors, changing, 150-151
    coordinates, determining with mouse, 146
    creating, 148-153
    defined, 138

toolbars, 139, 150
tools, 146
server-side compared to client-side
    mapping, 139-141
<HR> tags, 236
HREF links, *see* anchors; links
.htm (file extensions), 231
.html (file extensions), 231
HTML (HyperText Markup Language)
    advanced coding support, 4
    cookies, defined, 388
    copying Web sites, 46
    creating Web pages, 17-18
    documents
        Body, 234-240
        Head, 233
    links, hypertext, 230
    misreading codes, 243
    objects, placing, 230-231
    PageMill relationship, 19-22
    placeholders, 247-249
    publishing without HTML, 22
    shells, defined, 228
    Source commands (Edit menu),
        228, 239, 244-245
    Source windows, 240, 263
    tags
        attributes, 381

, 93
        browser support, 241-243
        case sensitivity, 228
        hiding, 244
        <IMG>, 139, 140
        <MAP>, 139
        modifying, attributes, 229-230
        <P>, 93
        pairs, applying, 229
        single, 232
        Version 3.0, 234-238
    unrecognized, editing, 251

HTML 3.2, PageMill 2.0, comparing, 241
HTTP (HyperText Transfer Protocol),
    288, 388
HTTP-USER_AGENT variables, NCSA
    server, 268
HTTP_REFERRER variables, NCSA
    server, 268
HTTPd, 313
"Huh?" icons, 251
human interface
    defined, 286
    Web page design, 286-290
hybrid database systems, 339
hypertext links
    creating, 230
    defined, 388
    grouping, 303-304
    limiting, 302-303
    see also links
HyperText Markup Language, *see* HTML
HyperText Transfer Protocol, *see* HTTP

I

<I> tags, 236
icons
    anchor, 151, 230
    Color Palettes, 150, 151
    Comments, 252
    folder, Resource folder windows, 66
    GIF, dragging-and-dropping
        images, 158-159
    Globe, copying links, 132
    Hidden Field, 271
    "Huh?", 251
    Image, 157, 158
    Insert Text Area, 202
    Java Applet, 254
    landscape, 162
    Magic Wand, 160

Non-Understood HTML, 251
Page, 118, 150-151, 157, 230
  creating links, 127-129
  toolbars, 74
Placeholder, 248-, 249
Preview mode, 213, 216
Resources, Preferences dialog
  boxes, 66
see also buttons
identifying applets (Java), 255
IETF (Internet Engineering Task
  Force), 388
if...then statements, 155
ImageMap.acgi, 278
imagemaps
  features, 62, 113, 137, 388
  files
    assessing, 153-154
    workings, 154-156
  history, 138-139
  Out-of-Place Editor, 39
  Web sites
    designs, 62
    preparing, 144-146
  see also active images
images
  3-D, 346-347
  active
    coordinate, 154
    creating, 147-153
    defined, 137
    history, 138-139
    images, defined, 379
    mapping, 139-141
    pixels, 146-151
    preparing Web sites, 144-146
    regions, 147
    URLs, 141
    workings, 142-146

aligning
  procedures, 86
  text, 106-107
animated GIFs, 345
  defined, 380, 387
  frame offset, 386
  interframe delay, 389
backgrounds
  deleting, 82
  editing, 79-82
bitmaps, 147, 381
borders, editing, 112-120
bulleted lists, 91
client-side, defined, 383
converting to GIF formats, 80
designating types, 113-115
dithering, defined, 384
download times, decreasing, 59
dragging-and-dropping, GIF icons,
  158-159
editing, Inspector palettes, 107
external images, defined, 385
GIF89a extensions, 387
GIFs
  defined, 387
  file formats, 58-59
  interlacing, 389
icons, 157-158
inline, 113-114, 389
inserting, 71, 99-106
  drag-and-drop, 99-102
  Pasteboard, 103-104
  Place Object buttons, 104-105
interlacing, 160
JPEG, 57-59, 390
labels, 99, 108
as links, 114
navigating Web sites, 62-63
object-oriented, 147
Out-of-Place Editor, 39

PICT file formats, 392
pixel depths, 393
placeholders, creating, 108
plain text blocks, defined, 393
progressive JPEG images, defined, 393
proportions, 111
resizing, 109-111
screens, Inspector palettes, 142
selecting, file formats, 57-59
server-side images, defined, 395
tags, 231
TIFFs, 397
transparency, 397
transparent, 160-162
    halo effect, 59
    GIFs, 397
View editor, *see* Out-of-Place editor
window, *see* Object screen
<IMG> tags, 139-140, 231, 236
indent left
    buttons, toolbars, 86
    commands (Format menu), 88
indent right
    buttons, toolbar, 86
    command (Format menu), 87, 88
indentations, paragraphs, formatting, 86-88
index.htm, first Web site page (PC), 60
index.html, first Web site page (Mac), 60
indexes, defined, 389
InfoLawAlert Web sites, 47
information, sending to CGI, 221
informational sites (Web), 48
inline images, 113-114, 389
Insert Multi-line buttons, 352
Insert Check Box buttons, 205, 217, 352
Insert Column buttons, 183
Insert Horizontal buttons, 352
Insert Horizontal Rule buttons, 97

Insert Invisible commands (Edit menu), 252, 271
Insert Password Field buttons, 201, 210
Insert Placeholder commands (Edit menu), 248
Insert Popup buttons, toolbars, 206, 353
Insert Radio Button buttons, 203-204, 215, 352
Insert Reset buttons, 353
Insert Row buttons, 182
Insert Single-line buttons, 352
Insert Submit buttons, 353
Insert Table buttons, 166-168
Insert Text Area buttons, 210
Insert Text Area icons, 202
Insert Text Field buttons, 201-202, 209
inserting
    backgrounds, patterns, 75
    horizontal rules, 72, 97-99
    images, 71, 99-106
        drag-and-drop, 99-102
        Pasteboard, 103-104
        Place Object Buttons, 104-105
    placeholders, 248
    text, field, 202
Inspector palettes, 33-37
    Edit modes, 76
    editing images, 107
    formatting Web pages
        background colors, 78-82
        background images, 79-82
        body text colors, 76-78
        link color, 82-84
    Forms screen, 33, 36
    Frame screen, 33
    Frames screen, 36-37
    Object mode
        editing images, 107
        resizing images, 110
    Object screen, 33, 35-36

Page screen
    features, 33-35, 73
    link colors, editing, 83
Page tabs, 75
Preview modes, 76
Integrated Services Digital Network, *see* ISDN
Interaction/IP, AppleScript/Frontier scripts, 275
interactive sites (Web), 308-310
interfaces
    defined, 286
    human, 286-290
    WYSIWYG, 1
interframe delays, 389
interlacing
    images, 160
    GIF files, defined, 389
International Standards Organization, *see* ISO
Internet
    accessing
        corporate servers, 315
        ISPs, 315
        online services, 313-314
    Adobe SiteMill, 323-328
    defined, 287-288, 389
    history, 12-14
    managing sites, 322
    pages, uploading
        Pagemill, 319-322
        UNIX servers, 316-318
    protocols
        PPP, 312
        SLIP, 312
        TCP/IP, 312-313
    servers, 312-313
Internet Audit, counter, 276
Internet Engineering Task Force, *see* IETF

Internet Explorer
    defined, 389
    HTML tag support, 241-243
Internet Explorer, *see* Microsoft Internet Explorer
Internet Protocol (IP), 389
Internet Service Providers, *see* ISPs
Internet Shopping Network, Web sites, 48
interpreters, CGI scripts, 267
interrelationships of pages, Web site design, 53-54
InterVU (video player), 344
InterVU MPEG Player, 342
intranet, 12, 287
IP (Internet Protocol), 389
ISDN (Integrated Services Digital Network), 389
<ISINDEX> tags, 237, 241, 269
ISMAP
    attributes, 156
    <IMG> tags, 140
ISO (International Standards Organization), 390
ISPs (Internet Service Providers), 315
italic
    physical style, 90
    text
        emphasis logical style, 88
        italic physical style, 90

J

Java
    animations, 345
    applets
        icons, 254
        identifying, 255
        placing, 254-256

defined, 390
scripts, as placeholders, 256
JavaScript, 332-334
macros, 254-256
Web sites, 337
JavaScript 411
Web sites, 337
Join Cells buttons, toolbars, 183
joining cells, 183-184
Joint Photographic Experts Group, *see* JPEG
Jon Weiderspan's CGI Applications Directory, Web sites, 284
JPEG (Joint Photographic Expert Group)
files extensions, 231
file formats (Web), 57-59
progressive images, 393
.jpg (file extensions), 231

K

key combinations
Command-Enter, 353
Command-H, 244
key shortcuts, menu bars, 30
Keyboard logical styles, 89
keys
private, 393
public, 394
keywords, 233, 390
knowbots, 390
Koan (audio player), 342

L

labels, images, 99, 108
landscape icons, 162
languages, defined, 288

LANs (Local Area Networks), 390
Largest Heading commands, (Format menu), 71
LAST_MODIFIED variables, NCSA server, 268
Latin-1 ASCII character sets, 239-240
Latin-1 Extended Character Set, 238
launching applications, 390
Left Align Text buttons (toolbar), 352
left alignment
buttons, 172
paragraphs, 85
Left Text Aligment buttons, 71
<Li> tags, 237
library sites (Web), 48
limits, placed on forms, 199
lines, spacing, 232
link locations
bars, 129, 150, 152
defined, 390
Edit window, 26, 29
<Link> tags, 237
links
anchors, defined, 380
colors
editing, 82-84
setting, Inspector Page Screen, 33-35
copying, 129
creating, 127, 131-132
anchors, 129-131
copy and paste, 132
dagging-and-dropping, 131
mailto:, 307
other Web sites, 133
Out-of-Place editor, 157-158
Page icon, 127-129
tables, 185-186
typing URL, 132

defined, 122-124

deleting, 134

destination documents, 121

dragging in Netscape Navigator, 133

editing names, 133

grouping, 303-304

hypertext, creating, 230

imagemaps, 62

images, 114

limiting, 302-303

pasting, 129

pathnames, 126-127

repairing, Adobe SiteMill, 324

replacing, Adobe SiteMill, 325-326

source documents, 121

testing, 134-135

types, 131

URL, 124-126

Web site design, 54-56

list boxes, Finder, 159

List commands (Format menu), 92, 94-96

List menu commands

Bullet, 92

Bulleted List, 95

Numbered, 94

Term, 96

lists

bulleted

converting to numbered, 95

creating, 91-93

defined, 91

creating, 90-96

directory, 91

menu, 91

nested, creating, 95

numbered

converting to bulleted, 95

creating, 94-95

options, multiple, 211-213

terms, 91

Lists commands (Style menu), 90

live objects, defined, 390

LiveObjects, 336

Local Area Networks, *see* LANs

Local Resource folder, setting preferences, 145

Logger.cgi, counter, 276

logical styles

character formatting, 88-89

types, 88- 89

logical tags, 306

lossless compressions, 58

Lynda Weinman's Browser-safe Palette, Web sites, 59

Lynn Weinmann's safe color palettes, 79

LZW compressions, 58

M

Mac servers, running CGI scripts, 264-265

MacADDICT Web sites, 55

MacBinary, 391

MacHTTP, 265

Macintosh helper applications, 347-348

Macromedia

Director (animations), 345-346

FreeHand, 226

Web sites, 346

macros, JavaScript, 254-256

MacTCP, 391

MacZilla (audio player), 342

Magic Wand icons, 160

mailto: links, creating, 307

managing sites, 322-328

manipulating, *see* editing

MAP NAME attributes, 156

Map radio buttons, Object mode screen, 114

<MAP> tags, 139
mapping
    client-side, 139-141
    overview, 142-146
    server-side, 139-141
MapServe, 278
Market Focus counter, 276
masking, *see* transparent images
Matt's Script Archive, Web sites, 283
memory, cache, 382, 391
Meng Weng Wong's Web sites,
    (server-push animations), 345
menu bars, 30-31
menu lists, 91-93
menus
    Active Links, 83
    Background, 177
    Edit, 30
    File, 30-31
    Font, 173, 177
    Font Color, 41
    Format
        features, 172, 229
        heading styles, 85
    Frame Targets, 192
    Get/Post, 221
    Normal Links, 83
    pop-up, 206
        creating, 211-213
        defined, 211
        selections, 213-214
    Style, 90, 172, 205, 229
    Visited Links, 83
    Window, 176
Message Composition dialog boxes,
    Quote buttons, 394
<META> tags, 237, 279

Microsoft
    Windows NT, 313
    Internet Explorer, 227
        HTML tag support, 241-243
        Web site testing, 64
    Site Builder Network Web site, 37,
        51, 60
.mid (file extensions), 231
Middle Align Object buttons, toolbars,
    106
MIDI (Musical Instrument Digital
    Interface), 341
MidPlug (audio player), 342
MIME (Multipurpose Internet Mail
    Extensions)
    audio broadcasting, 340
    defined, 391
modems, defined, 391
modes
    Edit, 206, 214, 216
    Form, 221-222
    Object, 204, 209-214, 217-218
    Preview, 214, 216, 218-219
    Raw HTML, 166
modifying
    form elements, 203
    tags
        attributes, 229-230
        values, 229-230
    see also editing
monospaced fonts, styles
    Code logical, 89
    Keyboard logical, 89
    Teletype logical, 88
.moov (file extensions), 231
Mosaic browser, 391
Motion Picture Expert's Group (MPEG),
    file formats, 341
.mov (file extensions), 231

movies
    QuickTime file formats, 394
    see also, video
MovieStar (video player), 344
moving cells, 170-171
Moving Pictures Experts Group, *see*
    MPEG
.mp2 (file extensions), 231
MPEG (Motion Picture Expert's Group)
    file extensions, 231
    file formats, 341, 343
    features, 391
.mpg (file extensions), 231
multimedia
    3-D images, 346-347
    animations, 345-346
    audio broadcasting, 340-342
    bandwidths, 348-349
    databases, 338-340
    digital videos, 343-344
    plug-in support, PageMill 2.0, 4
multiple
    colors, backgrounds, 76
    options lists, 211-213
Multipurpose Internet Mail Extensions,
    see MIME
    audio broadcasting, 340
    defined, 391
Musical Instrument Digital Interface, *see*
    MIDI

N

naming
    anchors, 130
    fields, 207
    Web pages, 74-75
Nancy McNelly's Rabbit In the Moon
    site, 141

Narrative Communications Web sites,
    346
National Center for Supercomputing
    Applications, see NCSA
National Science Foundation, 287
National Science Foundation Network,
    see NSFNet
navigating Web sites
    design, 54-56
    images, 62-63
NCSA (National Center for
    Supercomputing Applications)
    features, 391
    servers, environment variables,
        267-268
nested lists, creating, 95
net suffix, domain names, 125
NetAlly, 278
NetCloak, counter, 277
NetForms, 223, 274
netiquette
    defined, 391
    flames, 386
NetLink 4D, 282
Netscape
    extensions, 234-238
    Enterprise Server, 313
    Fastrack Server, 313
    History command, 387
    Navigator, 227, 392
        dragging links, 133
        HTML tag support, 241-243
        Web site testing, 64
    Official JavaScript Reference
        Guide, Web sites, 337
    plugins, 331-332
        audio broadcasting, 341-342
        digital videos, 343-344
    specifications support, PageMill
        2.0, 4

What's Cool page (Netscape Web site), 398

What's New page (Netscape Web site), 398

Network publishing, *see* desktop publishing

new features, PageMill 2.0, 3-5

New Page commands (File menu), 70, 74, 159

newbies, 47, 392

news servers, 392

newsgroups, Usenet, 397

Nielsen, Jakob, "Top Ten Mistakes in Web Design", 296

NNTP servers, *see* news servers

No Wrap checkboxes, 176

NOEDIT tags, 251, 256

Non-Understood HTML icons, 251

normal links, 82

Normal Links menu
commands, Custom, 83
features, 83

NSFNet (National Science Foundation Network), 392

Numbered commands
Bulleted List menu, 95
List menu, 94

numbered lists, 91
converting to bulleted, 95
creating, 94-95

O

Object buttons, toolbars, 159

Object commands (Scope menu), 116

Object mode
Inspector palettes, 204, 209-218
images
editing, 107
resizing, 110

screens
features, 198
radio buttons, 114

Object screens, Inspector palettes, 33, 35-36

object-oriented
databases, 339
images, 147

Object/not Deep, searching levels, 116

objects
Align, 172
placing in a page, 230-231
tables, within, 185

<OL> tags, 237

OLE
ActiveX, 334
OpenDoc, 336

online
publishing, 290
services, Internet access, 313-314
stores, 280

Open commands (File menu), 135, 159

Open dialog boxes, 35, 67, 159

Open File dialog boxes, 71, 79

OpenDoc, 336-337

Option-drag features, Pasteboard, 131

options
Checkboxes, 217-218
radio buttons, 215-216

org suffix, domain names, 125

organizing
root directories, 65-67
Web site files, 65-67

Out-of-Place editor, 140-141
creating links with, 157-158
graphic editing with, 157-162

P

\<P\> tags, 93, 232, 237

packet-switching, 312

Page Content commands (Find What menu), 116

Page icons, 118, 150-151, 157, 230
 creating links, 127-129
 toolbars, 74

Page screens
 Inspector palettes, 33-35, 73
 link colors, editing, 83

Page tabs
 features, 194
 Inspector palette, 75

Page/Deep searching levels, 116

PageMill 2.0
 Edit windows, 240
 Excel, and, 169
 history, 15
 HTML
  3.2 and, 241
   misreading, 243
 new features, 3-5
 practice session, 70-73
 tags, 241
 unsupported features, 241-244
 Version 1.0 vs. 2.0, 5

pages
 objects, placing, 230-231
 see also home pages; Web pages

Paragraph commands (Format menu), 71

paragraphs
 defined, 84
 formatting, 84-88
  alignment, 85-86
  entire text, 85
  heading styles, 85
  indentations, 86-88
 spacing, 232

parameters, CGI scripts, 270

parsers, defined, 392

password fields
 screens, 219
 settings, 219
 types, 200

Paste commands (Edit menu), 30, 129

Pasteboad
 images, inserting, 103-104
 features, Option-drag, 131
 forms, dragging-and-dropping, 203

pasting links, 129

PATH variables, NCSA server, 268

pathnames
 absolute, defined, 379
 defined, 67
 links, 126-127

patterns, backgrounds, inserting, 75

PCX file formats, 80

PDF (Portable Document Format)
 features, 392
 files, aligning, 86, 349-350

Perl (Practical Extraction and Report Language), 270, 274, 392

permissions, CGI scripts, 267

Personal Internet Launcher Web sites, 55

ph servers, 392

Photoshop
 Lynn Weinmann's safe color palettes, 79
 image editing software, 392

physical styles
 bold, 89
 characters, 89-90
 italic, 90
 plain, 89

physical tags, 306
PICT file formats, 80, 392
Picture radio buttons, Object mode
    screens, 114
pixels
    active images, 146-151
    defined, 112, 147
    depth, 393
Place commands, 231
Place Object buttons
    inserting images, 104-105
    toolbars, 71, 185, 254
Place Object buttons (toolbar), 230, 352
Place Object commands, 280
placeholders
    creating, 108
    editing, 248
    HTML, 247-249
    icons, 248, 249
    inserting, 248
    Object screen, 248
    running scripts with, 263
    screen, 247
placing
    applets (Java), 254-256
    objects in a page, 230-231
plain
    physical styles, 89
    text blocks, 393
planning forms, 199
plug-ins
    audio, 341-342
    defined, 393
    digital video, 343-344
pointer tools, 149
polygon hotspots, 149, 152
pop-up menus
    creating, 211-213
    defined, 211, 393
    form element, 199-200
    selections, offering, 213-214

Portable Document Format, *see* PDF, 392
PostScript, 349, 393
pound sign (#), numbered lists, 94
PPP (point-to-point protocol), 312
Practical Extraction and Report
    Language (Perl), 392
practicing PageMill, 70-73
preferences
    Local Resource folders, 145
    Remote Server Locations, 146
    commands (Edit menu), 25, 66,
        144
    dialog boxes, 66-67, 102, 145, 153
    Server window, 67
preparing files, Web site designs, 57-59
Preview
    buttons, 24, 72
    icons, 216
    modes
        Inspector palettes, 76
        testing hotspots, 139
        testing links, 134
    mode icons, 213
    windows, 24-25
Preview/Edit mode buttons (toolbar),
    353
private keys, 393
Prodigy
    features, 313-314
    history, 14
progressive JPEG images, 393
proportional fonts
    defined, 393
    plain physical styles, 89
proportions, resizing images, 111
protocols
    defined, 393
    PPP, 312
    SLIP, 312
    TCP/IP, 312-313
    URL parts, 124

prototyping Web sites, 51-52
proxies, defined, 394
public keys, 394
publishing
    desktop
        history, 14-15
        without HTML, 22
    online, 290

Q

.qt (file extensions), 231
queries
    document-based, 269-270
    form-based, 269-284
QUERY_STRING variables, NCSA server, 268
QuickTime
    file formats
        types, 343, 394
        VR, 347, 394
    Netscape (video player), 344
Quote buttons, Message Composition dialog boxes, 394
quoted text, Citation logical styles, 88

R

Rabbit in the Moon Web sites, 62, 141
radio buttons
    cloning, 203-204
    Horizontal Align, 176
    Map, 114
    Object mode screen, 114
    options, 215-216
    Picture, 114
    Vertical Align, 176
    working, 203-205
Raw HTML modes, 166

RealAudio (audio player), 342
Rectangle hotspots, 149, 152
rectangle regions, creating, Rectangle hotspot, 149
regions, defined, editing, 153
relational databases, 338-339
relative
    Font Size boxes, 173
    pathnames, links, 126-127
relevance feedback, defined, 394
Remote Server Locations, preferences, 146
remote terminal emulation, telnet, 312
REMOTE-ADDR variables, NCSA server, 268
REMOTE_HOST variables, NCSA server, 268
REMOTE_USER variables, NCSA server, 268
Remove Column buttons, 183
Remove Link commands (Edit menu), 134
renaming buttons, 220
Replace All buttons, Find and Replace dialog boxes, 117
Replace and Find button, Find and Replace dialog boxes, 117
Replace button, Find and Replace dialog boxes, 117
Replace Links commands (Site menu), 325
Replace Links dialog boxes, 325
replacing
    Placeholder icons, 249
    Web page items, 116-117
Request for Comments, see RFC
REQUEST_METHOD variables, NCSA server, 268
Reset buttons, 201, 220-223

resizing
  dragging, 109
  horizontal rules, 72, 97
  images, 109-111
Resource folder, windows, 66
Resources icons, Preferences dialog
  boxes, 66
retrieving data from forms, 222-223
RFC (Request for Comments), 394
Right alignment buttons, 85, 172
robots, defined, 394
ROFM CGI
  AppleScript/Frontier script, 275
  features, 223
root directories
  defined, 65
  pathnames, 67
  setting up, 65-67
root folder, *see* root directories
Row buttons, toolbars, 182
rows, spacing, tables, 181
rules
  CGIs, 154
  see also horizontal rules
running CGI scripts, 263-269
  placeholders, 263
  on server, 261

S

S-HTTP (Secure HyperText Transfer
  Protocol), 395
Sample logical styles, 89
Save As dialog boxes, 118
Save commands (File menu), 74, 118
Save Frame commands (File menu), 193
Save Frameset As commands (File
  menu), 191
Save Frameset As dialog boxes, 191
Save Page As commands (File menu),
  118
saving Web pages, 118-119
schematics, Web site design, 53-54
Scope menu commands, Object, 116
screens
  Applet Objects, 255
  Checkboxes, 217, 218
  Frames, 190
  Hidden Fields, 271
  Images, Inspector palette, 142
  Object modes, 198
  Password Fields, 219
  Placeholders, 247
  Placeholder Objects, 248
  Selection Fields, 212, 214
  Tables
    Cell, 175, Inspector palettes,
      170-171
    features, 238
  Unrecognized HTML Objects, 251
Script Editors (AppleScript), 395
<SCRIPT> tags, 241, 256
SCRIPT_NAME variables, NCSA server,
  268
scripts
  AppleScript/Frontier
    Email.acgi, 275
    Interaction/IP, 275
    ROFM CGI, 275
    Simple Mail Transfer Protocol
      (SMTP), 275
  C language
    Forms.acgi, 274
    NetForms, 274
  CGIs
    features, 259-260
    servers, 261
    see also CGIs; scripts
  defined, 258
  placeholders, 256

search engines, 46
    defined, 395
    Gopher, history, 12
Search menu commands
    Find, 116-117
    Spelling Checker, 117
searching
    levels, 116
    Web page items, 116-117
sections, home pages, 60
Secure HyperText Transfer Protocol, *see* S-HTTP
security
    firewalls, 386
    private keys, 393
    proxies, 394
    public keys, 394
    symmetrical cryptography, 396
Seidman, James
    mapping, 138
    Spyglass, Inc., active images, 138
selecting
    cells, 170-171
    colors, 41
    file formats, 57-59
    tables, 170
Selection Field screens, 212, 214
selections, pop-up menus, 213-214
Selena Sol's Pubic Domain CGI Script Archives, Web sites, 262, 283
sending information to CGI, 221
sensitive maps, *see* active images
Serial Line Internet Protocol, *see* SLIP
Server windows, Preferences dialog boxes, 67
server-push
    features, 395
    animations, 279, 345
server-side
    images, 395

includes, *see* SSI
mapping, 139-141
overview, 142-146
SERVER_NAME variables, NCSA server, 267
SERVER_PORT variables, NCSA server, 267
SERVER_PROTOCOL variables, NCSA server, 267
SERVER_SOFTWARE variables, NCSA server, 267
servers
    Apache Unix, 156
    corporate, 315
    defined, 398
    news, 392
    ph, 392
    relational databases, 340
    uploading pages, UNIX, 316-318
    Web, 288
ServerStat counter, 276
setting
    forms, 207-218
    frames
        format, 189-191
        targets, 192-193
    Inspector, 190-191
    Password fields, 219
setup files, CGI scripts, 266
SGI (Silicon Graphics, Inc.), 395
SGML (Standard Generalized Markup Language), 289, 395
shareware, 395
shells, 228
Shockwave (animation plug-ins), 345-346
shortcut keys, menu bars, 30
Show Color commands (Window menu), 78
Show Color Panel commands (Window menu), 173

Show Inspector commands (Window menu), 33
Show Pasteboard commands (Window menu), 38, 103
show-room sites (Web), 48
signature files, 395
signing names to Web site, 305-307
Silicon Graphics, Inc., *see* SGI
Simple Mail Transfer Protocol, *see* SMTP
single tags, 232
.SIT file extensions, 396
site design evolution, 292-295
Site menu commands, Replace Links, 325
SiteMill
   links
      repairing, 324
      replacing, 325-326
     managing, 323-328
sites, *see* Web sites
sizing
   content area, 29
   fields, 209
   images, 109-111
SLIP (serial line Internet protocol), 312, 396
<Small> tags, 249
SMTP (Simple Mail Transfer Protocol)
   AppleScript/Frontier scripts, 275
   defined, 396
soft returns, bulleted lists, 93
software component-based programming
   ActiveX, 334-335
   Java, 332-334
   OpenDoc, 336-337
source codes
   copying, 245
   viewing, 244-247
source documents, 121
Space Made For Moms, Web sites, 48

spacing
   tables
      columns, 181
      rows, 181
   lines, 232
   paragraphs, 232
special characters, adding, 238-240
specialty databases, 339-340
speeding up download times, 59
spell checkers
   features, 117-118
   commands (Search menu), 117
   dialog boxes, 117
spiders, *see* search engines
Split Cells buttons, 184
splitting, cells, 183-184
Spyglass, Inc., active images, 138
SQL (Structured Query Language)
   databases, 338-339
   features, 281
SSI (Server-Side Includes), 267
Standard Generalized Markup Language, *see* SGML
StarNine's WebStar servers, 313
statements, if...then, 155
stores, online, 280
StreamWorks (audio player), 342
<Strike> tags, 249
<STRONG> tags, 229
Strong logical styles, 88
structure of Web sites, content design, 48-51
Structured Query Language, *see* SQL
StuffIt Expander (compression software), 396
.sty (file extensions), 231, 250
style buttons, 171

Style menus
    characters, 90
    commands
        Bold, 70
        Emphasis, 70
        Lists, 90
style sheets
    cascading, 250-251
    creating, 250-251
    defined, 250, 396
<STYLE> tags, 241, 251
styles, Teletype, 205
<Sub> tags, 249
subdirectories
    Unix, 66
    Web site design, 65
Submit button, 201, 220-223, 271
Sun Microsystems, 254, 396
    Web sites, 296
<Sup> tags, 249
support pages, Web site design, 61
symmetrical cryptography, 396

T

Table buttons, toolbars, 169, 182
Table Cell
    attributes, changing, 170, 174
    Inspector palettes, 170, 171
    manipulation tools, 166
    screens, 175
Table screens, 238
<TABLE> tags, 166, 238
Table toolbars, 182-184
tables
    adding objects, 185
    attributes, 170, 177
    borders
        adding, 178, 180
        changing, 180
        deleting, 178, 180
    cells, 382
    creating, 166-169
    formatting
        commands, 165
        Inspector, 177-181
    selecting, 170
    sizes, changing, 179
    text
        adding, 171
        color, changing, 172-173
    widths, changing, 178
Tagged Image File Format, *see* TIFF
tags (HTML)
    <!–/NOEDIT–>, 249
    <!–NOEDIT–>, 249
    <–/>, 253
    <–>, 253
    </FRAME>, 187
    </FRAMESET>, 187
    </H1>, 229
    </HEAD>, 256
    </Script>, 256
    </STRONG>, 229
    </STYLE>, 251
    <APPLET>, 231
    <BODY>, 234

, 93, 232
    <CLASS>, 251
    cookies, 388
    <FORM ACTION>, 263
    <FRAME>, 187
    <FRAMESET>, 187
    <H1>, 229
    <HEAD>, 232, 233, 256
    <HTML>, 232
    <IMG>, 231
    <ISINDEX>, 269

<META>, 279
<P>, 232
<SCRIPT Language>, 256
<STRONG>, 229
<STYLE>, 251
<TABLE>, 166
<TITLE>, 232
Blink, 241
character formatting, 249
Comment, 253, 256
defined, 225
HTML
    3.0, 234-238
    features, 225-226, 232-244
    sensitivity, 228
images, 231
<IMG>, 139, 140
IsIndex, 241
logical, 306
<MAP>, 139
modifying
    attributes, 229-230
    values, 229-230
NOEDIT, 251, 256
<P>, 93
physical, 306
Script, 241
single, 232
Style, 241
see also HTML tags
Tango, 281-282
Target buttons, 192
targets, adding to frames, 192-194
TCP/IP (Transmission Control Protocol/Internet Protocol), 312-313, 396
Teaching a New Dog Old Tricks, Web sites, 263
Tecfa's JavaScript Manual, Web sites, 337

teletype
    logical styles, 88
    style, 205
telnet
    defined, 396
    remote terminal emulation, 312
Term commands (List menu), 96
Term format commands (Format menu), 96
term lists, creating, 95-96
testing
    links, 134-135
    Web sites, 64
text
    aligning to images, 106-107
    areas, type of field, 200
    boxes
        Cell Padding, 178, 181
        Cell Spacing, 181
        Width, 175, 178
    character formatting, 88-90
        logical, 88-89
        physical, 89-90
    enhancing with browsers, 20-22
    fields, types, 200
    heading styles, 85
    indentations, 86-88
    inserting, fields, 202
    paragraph alignment, 85-86
    plain blocks, 393
    spell checkers, 117-118
text-level, Body elements, 232
themes, adding to Web sites, 304
TIFF (Tagged Image File Format), 397
tiled patterns, download time, decreasing, 59
title bars, 397
<TITLE> tags, 232
titles, Web pages, 233

toolbar buttons
    Align Center, 230
    Center Align, 183
    Circle hotspot, 149
    Delete Row, 182
    form element, 199
    Insert Check Box, 217
    Insert Checkbox, 205
    Insert Column, 183
    Insert Password Field, 201, 210
    Insert Popup, 206
    Insert Radio Button, 203-204, 215
    Insert Row, 182
    Insert Table, 166, 168
    Insert Text Area, 210
    Insert Text Field, 201-202, 209
    Join Cells, 183
    Object, 159
    Place Object, 185, 230, 254
    Pointer tool, 149
    Polygon hotspot, 149
    Rectangle hotspot, 149
    Remove Column, 183
    Row, 182
    Split Cells, 184
    Table, 169, 182
toolbar icons, Insert Text Area, 202
toolbars
    Bold buttons, 70
    buttons, 352-353
    Center Align Text buttons, 86
    Center Text alignment buttons, 70
    Edit windows, 26-29
    Format menu commands
        Largest Heading, 71
        Paragraph, 71
    Horizontal Rule buttons, 72
    Indent Left buttons, 86
    Indent Right buttons, 86
    Insert Horizontal Rule buttons, 97
    Left Text alignment buttons, 71

    Middle Align Object buttons, 106
    Page icons, 74
    Place Object buttons, 71
    styles, 171
    tables, 182-184
    Top Align Object buttons, 106
tools
    Hotspot, 139, 146
    Pointer, 149
    table cell manipulation, 166
    Zoom, 162
Top Align Object buttons, 106
TR-WWW, 283
traditional relational databases, 338-339
Transmission Control Protocol/Internet
    Protocol, *see* TCP/IP, 396
transparency, 397
transparent
    GIFs, 59, 397
    images, 160-162
    halo effects, 59

U

<U> tags, 249
<UL> tags, 238
Uniform Resource Locators, *see* URLs
University of Illinois, Web sites, 295
Unix
    CGIs Web site, 268
    defined, 397
    history, 12
    organizing Web resources, 65
    servers, uploading pages, 316-322
Unrecognized HTML Object screens,
    251
Upload the Page commands (File
    menu), 319

uploading
    dialog boxes, 319
    Web pages
        Pagemill, 319-322
        UNIX servers, 316-318
URLs (Universal Resource Locators)
    active images, 141
    CGI parts, 260
    defined, 397
    directory paths, 125
    domain names, 125
    protocols, 124
    restrictions, 125
USEMAP attributes, <IMG> tags, 139
Usenet newsgroups, 397

V

values, modifying, tags, 229-230
Variable logical styles, 89
variables
    assigning values, 207-209
    declaring, 207-209
    defined, 208
    environment, NCSA servers, 267-268
versions, PageMill 1.0 vs. 2.0, 5
Vertical Align radio buttons, 176
videos, 343-344
viewing source codes, 244-247
ViewMovie (video player), 344
virtual reality, QuickTime VR file formats, 394
Virtual Reality Modeling Language, *see* VRML
Visited Links menu, 83

Visited Links menu commands, Custom, 83
Visual Basic, CGI scripts, 274
VRML (Virtual Reality Modeling Language), 346-347, 397

W-X-Y-Z

WAIS (Wide Area Information Server), 397
WANs (Wide Area Networks), 398
.WAV files
    extensions, 231
    formats, 341, 398
Web, defined, 398
Web browsers, 288-289
    customizing text, 20-22
    history, 13-14
Web crawlers, *see* search engines
Web page designs
    animated GIFs, 280
    animations, 278-280
        Client-Pull, 279
        Server-Push, 279
    comments, adding, 252-253
    download times, 298
    home page links, 297
    HTML
        PageMill relationships, 19-22
        publishing without, 22
    human interfaces, 286-290
    images (non-interrupting), 296
    link colors, 297
    navigational support, 297
    readable URLs, 297
    single screens, 297
    structures, 296
    technology, 296
    theory applications, 299-307

titles, 233
update sites, 298
WYSIWYG, 212-213
Web pages
creating, 70
defined, 73
download times, decreasing, 59
formatting
background colors, 78-82
background images, 79-82
body text colors, 76-78
link colors, 82-83, 83-84
interrelationships, Web site design, 53-54
naming, 74-75
navigating, Web site design, 54-56
saving, 118-119
testing, 64
Web projects, defined, 398
Web publishers
compared to Webmasters, 15-16
defined, 398
Web publishing, 290-291
Web servers
CGI part, 260
defined, 398
Web site design
audience, 307-308
consistency, 307-308
evolution, 292-295
first generation, 292
optimizing, 309
scientific approaches, 296-298
second generation, 293-294
signing names, 305-307
themes, 304
third generations, 295
Web sites
active image preparations, 144-146
ActiveX information, 337
Adobe Acrobat, 350
Apple Computer, Inc., 48
Browser-safe Palettes, 59
catalogs, 50
CGI Programmer's References, 262
cobweb, 383
copying HTML, 46
corporate presence, 48
creating links, 133
CyberPound Sites, 336
defined, 43, 60, 398
designing
appearance, 51-63
construction, 60-63
content, 44-51
folder organization, 65-67
Fetch, 316
Gamelan, 333
history, 14
InfoLawAlert, 47
informational, 48
interaction, 308-310
Internet Shopping Network, 48
JavaScript 411
features, 337
Snippet Page, 337
Jon Weiderspan's CGI Applications Directory, 284
library, 48
Lynda Weinman's Browser-safe Palettes, 59
MacADDICT, 55
Macromedia, 346
managing, 322-328
Matt's Script Archives, 283
Meng Weng Wong's, 345
Microsoft Site Builder Network, 37, 51, 60
Narrative Communications, 346
Netscape's Official JavaScript Reference Guide, 337
OpenDoc information, 337

Personal Internet Launcher, 55
prototyping, 51-52
Rabbit in the Moon, 62, 141
Selena Sol's Pubic Domain CGI
    Script Archives, 283
show rooms, 48
A Space Made For Moms, 48
Sun on the Net, 296
Teaching a New Dog Old Tricks,
    263
Tecfa's JavaScript Manual, 337
testing, 64
The CGI Collection, 284
Unix CGIs, 268
VRML information, 347
Webmasters
    compared to Web publishers, 15-16
    defined, 398
WebStar, 265
What's Cool page (Netscape Web site),
    398
Wide Area Information Server, *see* WAIS
Wide Area Networks, see WANs, 398
Width text boxes, 175, 178
Window menu commands
    history, 387
    Show Color Panel, 78, 173
    Show Inspector, 33
    Show Pasteboard, 38, 103
windows
    Apple Color Wheel, 77
    edit
        content areas, 26, 29
        link locations, 26
        link location bars, 29
        modes, 72
        PageMill, 240
        toolbars, 26, 27-29
    helper applications, 347-348
    HTML Sources, 240, 263
    Preview, 24-25

Resource folder, 66
servers
    CGI scripts, 264-265
    Preferences dialog boxes, 67
Windows menu commands
    Color Panel, 41
    Link Colors, 83
Windows NT, 313
word processing improvements,
    PageMill 2.0, 4
World Wide Web, *see* WWW
worms, *see* search engines
writing CGIs, 261-263
WWW (World Wide Web)
    accessing
        corporate servers, 315
        ISPs, 315
        online services, 313-314
    history, 12-14
    managing sites, 322-328
    uploading pages
        Pagemill, 319-322
        UNIX servers, 316-318
WYSIWYG
    creating, Web pages, 212-213
    frames, PageMill 2.0, 4
    interfaces, 1
    tables, PageMill 2.0, 3

Yahoo, 261
.ZIP file extensions, 398
Zoom tools, 162

Name _____ Title _____

Company _____Type of business _____

Address _____

City/State/ZIP _____

Have you used these types of books before? ☐ yes   ☐ no

If yes, which ones? _____

_____

How many computer books do you purchase each year? ☐ 1–5   ☐ 6 or more

How did you learn about this book? _____

      ☐ recommended by a friend   ☐ received ad in mail
      ☐ recommended by store personnel   ☐ read book review
      ☐ saw in catalog   ☐ saw on bookshelf

Where did you purchase this book? _____

Which applications do you currently use? _____

Which computer magazines do you subscribe to? _____

What trade shows do you attend? _____

Please number the top three factors which most influenced your decision for this book purchase.

      ☐ cover   ☐ price
      ☐ approach to content   ☐ author's reputation
      ☐ logo   ☐ publisher's reputation
      ☐ layout/design   ☐ other _____

Would you like to be placed on our preferred mailing list? ☐ yes   ☐ no   e-mail address _____

☐ **I would like to see my name in print!** You may use my name and quote me in future Hayden products and promotions. My daytime phone number is: _____

Comments _____

_____

_____

Hayden Books   Attn: Product Marketing ◆ 201 West 103rd Street ◆ Indianapolis, Indiana 46290 USA

Fax to **317-581-3576**   Visit out Web Page   **http://WWW.MCP.com/hayden/**

Fold Here

- -

NO POSTAG
NECESSAR
IF MAILED
IN THE
UNITED STAT

BUSINESS REPLY MAIL

FIRST-CLASS MAIL PERMIT NO. 9918 INDIANAPOLIS IN

POSTAGE WILL BE PAID BY THE ADDRESSEE

HAYDEN BOOKS
Attn: Product Marketing
201 W 103RD ST
INDIANAPOLIS IN 46290-9058

WANT MORE INFORMATION?

CHECK OUT THESE RELATED TOPICS OR SEE YOUR LOCAL BOOKSTORE

Adobe Press

Published by Hayden Books, the Adobe Press Library reveals the art and technology of communication. Designed and written by designers for designers, best-selling titles include the Classroom in a Book (CIAB) series for both *Macintosh* and *Windows* (*Adobe Photoshop CIAB, Advanced Adobe Photoshop CIAB, Adobe PageMaker CIAB, Advanced Adobe PageMaker CIAB, Adobe Illustrator CIAB, and Adobe Premiere CIAB*), the Professional Studio Techniques series (*Production Essentials, Imaging Essentials, and Design Essentials, 2E*), and *Interactivity by Design*.

Design and Desktop Publishing

Hayden Books is expanding its reach to the design market by publishing its own mix of cutting-edge titles for designers, artists, and desktop publishers. With many more to come, these must-have books include *Designer's Guide to the Internet, Photoshop Type Magic, Adobe Illustrator Creative Techniques, Digital Type Design Guide*, and *The Complete Guide to Trapping, 2E*.

Internet and Communications

By answering the questions of what the Internet is, how you get connected, and how you can use it, *Internet Starter Kit for Macintosh* (now in 3rd ed.) and *Internet Starter Kit for Windows* (now in 2nd ed.) have proven to be Hayden's most successful titles ever, with over 500,000 Starter Kits in print. Hayden continues to be in the forefront by meeting your ever- popular demand for more Internet information with additional titles, including *Simply Amazing Internet for Macintosh, Create Your Own Home Page for Macintosh, Publishing on the World Wide Web, World Wide Web Design Guide, World Wide Web Starter Kit, net.speak: The Internet Dictionary*, and *Get on the Internet in 5 Minutes for Windows and Macintosh*.

Multimedia

As you embrace the new technologies shaping of multimedia, Hayden Books will be publishing titles that help you understand and create your own multimedia projects. Books written for a wide range of audience levels include *Multimedia Starter Kit for Macintosh, 3-D Starter Kit for Macintosh, QuickTime: The Official Guide for Macintosh Users, Virtual Playhouse, Macromedia Director Design Guide*, and *Macromedia Director Lingo Workshop*.

High-Tech

Hayden Books addresses your need for advanced technology tutorials and references by publishing the most comprehensive and dynamic titles possible, including *Programming Starter Kit for Macintosh, Tricks of the Mac Game Programming Gurus, Power Macintosh Programming Starter Kit, FoxPro Machete: Hacking FoxPro for Macintosh, 2E*, and *The Tao of AppleScript: BMUG's Guide to Macintosh Scripting, 2E*.

Orders/Customer Service | **800-763-7438** | **Source Code** | **HAYB**

Hayden Books   201 West 103rd Street   ◆   Indianapolis, Indiana 46290 USA

Visit our **Web page** at `http://www.mcp.com/hayden/`

What's on the CD-ROM

This CD-ROM contains the following items. Some are Mac only or Windows only.

- Adobe Acrobat 3.0 Reader: Opens and prints PDFs either on the Web (using the PDF plugin for Netscape) or on your computer via the program.
- Anarchie, an FTP utility program used to upload and download files at FTP sites.
- GIFConverter 2.3.7. Converts files between GIF, TIFF, PICT, RIFF, and JPEG formats.
- Screen Ruler. A virtual ruler that can be dragged around the desktop.
- Shockwave files.
- Java Applets.
- MPEG/CD Player 2.0.5. Enables you to play MPEG audio files on the Mac.
- PhotoGIF. Photoshop plug-in that lets you save images previously converted to indexed color, bit-map, and gray-scale modes as GIF89 animated GIF files.
- SoundApp. A program for converting AU or WAV files to AIFF format.
- SoundEffects. A program for mixing and editing AIFF sound files.
- SoundMachine. A Netscape helper program for playing AIFF or AU sound files.
- Sparkle 2.4.5. Converts MPEG movies to QuickTime format.
- Lview Pro.
- Programs from EveryWare Software, including Bolero 1.0.1, Butler SQL 2.1, and Tango 1.5.2. Database management CGIs.
- WebFM. CGIs for processing Form information, such as guestbooks.
- Earth&Ware tutorial folder.
- Wham.
- Web usage 4.12.
- Map edit 2.25.
- Arachnophilia.
- Ragsoft Notepad+ 1.11.
- GIF Translator.
- vmpeg viewer lite.

 Note

Some Programs on this CD are shareware, which means if you keep them and use them for more than a few weeks you must pay for them. Please read the documentation with the shareware to determine the exact guidelines.